" 'The Art of Changing the Brain' *is* teaching. Zull argues that educators can use knowledge about the brain to enhance pedagogical techniques. He does an excellent job of demonstrating his thesis by describing good approaches: e.g., increasing reception of information by enhancing the sensory aspects of teaching materials; taking advantage of integrative mechanisms by allowing time for reflection; maximizing the adaptive functions of the brain by challenging students to be creative; using action areas of the brain by providing activities to confirm and extend learning. Teachers need to recognize that motivational-emotional systems of the brain modulate cognitive functions and that pedagogies [that] attempt to force students to learn in ways that violate brain mechanisms are likely to be counterproductive. Zull's years of experience as both professor of biology and director of a university teaching institute are apparent; the book is well written and appropriately technical for the audience interested in applying current knowledge about the brain to learning and instructing. Highly recommended."

—Choice

"Writing for all educators, [Zull's] theme is that a better understanding of brain function will promote a more flexible and varied approach to learning. The results offer a refreshing clarity. [In] his fine book . . . Zull has done a remarkable job of simplifying both brain function and learning processes. It is a synthesis of what we know about the brain and about learning, a synthesis that simplifies both fields to draw a usable map of the terrain of learning. I encourage educators at all levels to grapple with Zull's model . . . and integrate his insights with their own experience and understanding of the learning process. A work like *The Art of Changing the Brain* has long been needed."

—Pierce J. Howard,
Cerebellum

"This is the best book I have read about the brain and learning. Zull takes us on a fascinating and vivid tour of the brain, revealing the intricate structure of the organ designed by evolution to learn from experience. Using wonderful stories from his own experience, filled with insight, humor, and occasional twinges of pain, this wise and humane educator and scientist describes his concept that teaching is the art of changing the brain. His perspective forms the foundation for a teaching approach that can dramatically improve human learning."

—David A. Kolb,
Department of Organizational Behavior, Case Western Reserve University

"I found *The Art of Changing the Brain* to be deeply thought provoking. It is not only grounded in emerging brain research but relates such research directly to the experiences of students and the challenges of classroom teaching. As a middle school administrator, I believe that this book will become an excellent and unique resource for the ongoing professional growth of educators. The book can be profitably read by any teacher at any level, and I intend to use it in my own courses for students in education classes."

—Robert Brownlee,
Curriculum Specialist at Kirk Middle School, East Cleveland

"I have just discovered your amazing book. I find I reread, and make so many connections as I go, and I do not wish to rush!"

—Martha M. Decker,
Assistant Professor of Education, Morehead State University, Kentucky

"I read (devoured) this book three times, and I am overwhelmed by it. It is just perfectly and brilliantly thought through! The reader receives important information in small and easily digestible portions. The illustrations from the author's own teaching experience underscore the points he makes in a profound way."

—Margaret Arnold,
Education Graduate Student, Harvard Graduate School of Education, and Augsburg University

THE ART OF CHANGING THE BRAIN

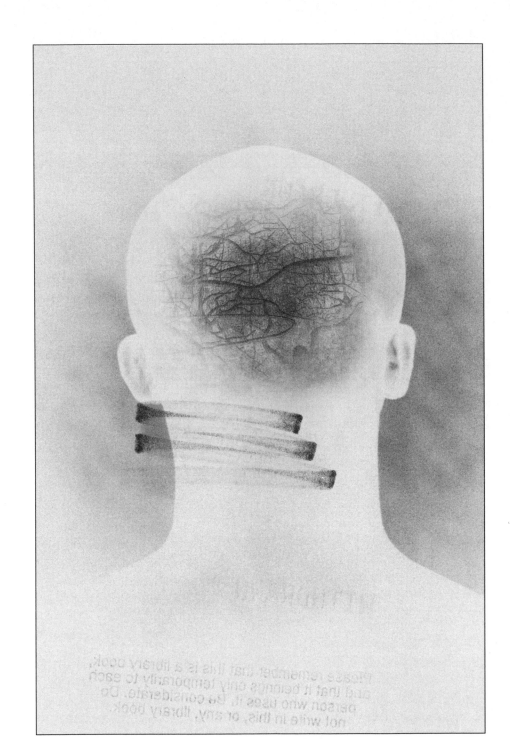

THE ART OF
CHANGING
THE BRAIN

Enriching Teaching by Exploring
the Biology of Learning

James E. Zull

STERLING, VIRGINIA

To my mother, Eileen Gates, who showed me the joy
of learning—and living—throughout my life

Published in 2002 by

Stylus Publishing, LLC
22883 Quicksilver Drive
Sterling, Virginia 20166

Library of Congress
Cataloging-in-Publication Data
Zull, James E. (James Elwood), 1939–
    The art of changing the brain : enriching
    teaching by exploring the biology of
    learning / James E. Zull—1st ed.
        p. cm.
    Includes bibliographical references.
    ISBN 1-57922-053-3 (hardcover : alk.
    paper)—ISBN 1-57922-054-1
    (pbk. : alk paper)
    1. Learning, Psychology of. 2. Learning—
    Physiological aspects.   3. Brain.
    4. Teaching—Psychological aspects. I. Title.
LB1057.Z85 2002
370.15'23—dc21
                              2002006443

First edition, 2002

Printed in the United States of America
All first editions printed on acid free paper

Who Should Read This Book?

My hope is that all educators will find value in this book. Whether you teach children, teens, or adults, you can only gain by reading and thinking about the brain. I have written for an audience at all levels of education.

But do not set this book aside just because you don't make your living by teaching. You are still a teacher!

Our daily lives require us all to teach. We must be understood by other people: our students, our children, our employees, our parents, our friends, and our enemies. Whether learning to read, doing a job, or just conversing with others, we want and need to help people learn. Life is learning; life is teaching. And the more you understand the brain, the more artful you can be when you must teach!

CONTENTS

ACKNOWLEDGMENTS

Some critics warned me that this book could not be written, or should not. And it didn't take long for me to discover good reasons for these warnings. The opportunities to make mistakes are unending. And I am sure I have taken advantage of a large number of them, despite striving to avoid doing so.

I apologize for these inevitable, but presently undetected, errors of content and interpretation. However, there would be many more were it not for the support of many dear and honest friends and critics.

Beginning with my colleagues at Case Western Reserve, I must first thank David and Alice Kolb. It was David's work and profound insights on human learning that triggered the very conception of the book. Once Alice showed up on the scene, she gave me such encouragement that my periodic instincts to abort were forgotten. I also thank Mano Singham, who is wiser about teaching than anyone I know and who cheerfully and analytically helped me keep my message on target for teachers. Lyn Turkstra read every chapter and covered the pages with comments as she gently but firmly guided me around the territory of the brain. In addition, Hillel Chiel, Alison Hall, David Katz, and Peter Whitehouse all added to my knowledge of the brain.

I am also indebted to my friends and colleagues in the Mind, Brain, and Education Program at the Harvard Graduate School of Education. Their support, insightful criticism, and personal engagement extended far beyond what I had any right to expect. I especially thank Kurt Fischer and Howard Gardner who both encouraged me at crucial times during my brief sabbatical at Harvard. I also got valuable insights from Marc Schwartz through his work on science education for middle school children. First among the students at Harvard is Juliana Paré-Bagolev, who read most chapters and gave many hours of her time, all the while continuing her own teaching and brain-imaging research on dyslexia and bringing a new child into the world. Other students who gave me valuable feedback are Mary Helen Immordino-Yang, whose comments prompted me to completely rewrite chapter 1, and Mike Connell, whose observations on certain chapters led to important changes and additions.

Kathy Schuh at the University of Iowa also critiqued parts of the book, and her comments deepened my understanding. I also am grateful to Neil Fleming, my New Zealand partner in thinking about teaching. His decades of accumulated wisdom proved invaluable in helping me clarify confusing places in the book, and the extensive and detailed critiques he produced represented an expenditure of time and effort that both surprised and humbled me.

My publisher, John von Knorring, first encouraged me to write a book on education and the brain and then stuck with me through several abortive efforts, in which I did not respect the task enough. When I finally began to make progress, he was first in line encouraging me and urging me on to publication. For all this and for his ability to distinguish good from bad, I am grateful. I also thank Larry Goldberg, my editor, and his team at Shepherd Incorporated, for their personal interest and careful work. It always seemed that this project was more than just a job to them.

I find myself groping for the right words to thank my family. I am amazed at their patience when I forgot important engagements and other responsibilities, while totally engrossed in writing or, worse, dreaming. I especially thank my wife, Susan, for the weekends sacrificed and the innumerable blank stares tolerated as I, lost in my theories, failed to hold up my end of the conversation. I never felt more support, and sometimes never more selfish, as she allowed me, indeed encouraged me, to pursue my ideas. This generosity and love continually reminded me that, no matter how it may have seemed at critical moments, in the end she is the best idea I ever pursued.

INTRODUCTION

A NEW PERSPECTIVE,
SOME STRUGGLES, AND A HOPE

Learning is about biology.

This obvious fact has been lurking just beneath our consciousness for a long time. It is why teachers felt excited as neuroscience blossomed in the past few decades. And it is why some predicted a revolution in education, once we found out how the brain works.

But as science gave us more information, teachers began to realize that this did not automatically produce better education. Neuroscientists could not tell us how to teach. In fact, biologists still pay little attention to our concerns. They are excited about science, not about education.

This means that, to a great extent, educators have been left to interpret neuroscience on their own. There is virtually nothing on this topic written by scientists, which is one reason I decided to write this book. There was a gap waiting to be filled.

But revolution is not my goal. There is no reason to abandon the good practices that cognitive science and education research have given us. Rather, I hope to deepen and enrich our understanding of these practices. Biology can enrich what we already do.

This enrichment comes, to a great extent, from the perspective that biology provides for the teacher. Often, our perspective of teaching is from above. We view the learner as needing our help, which we hand down to him. From this perspective we can forget that the actual learning takes place down there in the brain and body of the learner. When we turn this around and begin to ask about the learning itself, we may see things differently. We may see both ourselves and our students as the biological creatures we are, and this more grounded perspective is what ultimately enriches us.

* * *

Let me briefly explain some challenges the book presented, and how I tried to deal with them.

When my friends first heard the title of my book, some of them reacted strongly. One remarked that her first thought was of "mind control." Another said, "It sounds aggressive! Are we really going after their brains?"

Although these comments seemed a little extreme, they did give me pause. I even considered changing the title. But I couldn't bear the thought that you might look at my book, there on the shelf, read the title, and completely miss the main message.

This main message is that *learning is change*. It is change in ourselves, because it is change in the brain. Thus the art of teaching must be the art of changing the brain. At least this much should be up front.

Another struggle was the question of defining learning. I was advised that I must tell the reader what I mean by learning. Someplace in the book I must give my definition. But I have not done so. Or, at least, you will not find a particular place in the book where I focus on a definition.

I had two reasons for this decision. First, I came to feel that inventing a definition would make more trouble than it was worth. Such definitions, in themselves, can need explaining, and the last thing I needed was to sow further confusion or add to the explaining.

Second, one of my goals is for you to find your own definition of learning. Learning is about change, and it is change. It is a living, growing thing that comes through different routes and leads to different ends as our lives evolve and grow. I cannot even say that I have yet defined it, but I am *developing* a definition. And I am content for you to feel the same. If you find your own definition changing as you read, you will understand the life in learning, and you may want to put off constructing your own definition, at least for a while.

When they looked at my manuscript, my friends in the learning and education field sometimes wanted to define me. This became another struggle. Am I a constructivist, an associationist, or a traditionalist? Where do my allies lie in the learning debates, if I have any?

If you are inclined to ask that question, let me suggest that you read more than one or two chapters before you decide. I am not sure where

I fit, and it could be that I am simply a misfit. I say this because my starting point is always biology. I just go where biology leads me. Sometimes what I see is rather traditional, and sometimes it is far out on the wings of constructivism. Or it might be something quite different from either. But I don't care, as long as I believe I have been faithful to the biology. In the end, I am a biologist.

This question of defining things also is apparent in the way I speak of "brain science" or "brain research." You will find that I jump around a lot between cognitive science, cognitive neuroscience, and neuroscience without paying much attention to the terms at all. I have just been sloppy about this.

There is a reason for this sloppiness. I have come to distrust the definitions of disciplines that we invent as our knowledge grows. These definitions are useful for the experts but can be confusing to others. And they may imply divisions and differences that don't really exist. Even experts get caught up in this, sometimes arguing fiercely that something is really "cognitive" rather than "neuronal."

The teachers who read my manuscript sometimes wanted more specifics. Exactly what should teachers *do* in order to "change the brain"? My instinct was to shy away from making suggestions, but I didn't always follow that instinct. So you will find some specific ideas, especially in chapters 6 and 7, and I frequently mention things that I have tried or would like to try. But I still don't have a lot of faith in giving directions to teachers. In fact, I have often noticed that when teachers start telling other teachers how to solve their problems, things can quickly get tense. For the most part, we seem to want to solve our own problems, and I am happy to leave it that way.

I also struggled to keep the book at a reasonable length. This sometimes meant that I could only mention a topic or idea that really deserved much more attention. I often felt frustrated with what I wasn't saying! I tried to rectify this with endnotes, which occasionally became quite lengthy, or by referencing a specific article where the science details can be found. So if you find yourself frustrated or impatient with something, it is possible that you may find what you need, or part of what you need, in these notes.

Finally, I am particularly sensitive to the reactions of my biology and neuroscience colleagues. You may feel that my biological generalizations are inadequate or even misleading. I only touch the surface of our knowledge about nervous systems. This is necessary, and I have worked hard to be accurate, but if you still cannot forgive me, at least you should know that I am fully aware of this shortcoming.

*   *   *

Let me end this introduction by telling you about a hope. When I first started, I wanted the book to be brilliant. I was sure that my ideas were unique and important. But along the way, I have been rightly humbled. This subject is majestic and my brain isn't.

But it wasn't humility that led me to change my hopes: it was my recognition of a bigger goal. It came to me when, after one of my workshops, a teacher came up to me and said, "I am going to change how I teach. This was so useful!"

What a rush! Someone found my ideas useful. And I realized that, in the end, this is what matters the most. The greatest testament is to have my ideas applied: to have been *useful*.

I

THE SWEET EDGE

LEARNING IS PHYSICAL—
WE CAN UNDERSTAND!

> If you stand right fronting and face to
> face with a fact, you will see the sun
> glimmer on both its surfaces, as if it
> were a scimitar, and you will feel its
> sweet edge dividing you through your
> heart and marrow. Be it life or death,
> we crave only reality.
> —*Henry David Thoreau*

Our students were demanding better teaching. Tuition was growing every year and they wanted their money's worth.

But most of us were just scholars and researchers. No one had ever explained teaching and learning to us, so we just mimicked the way we had been taught. This wasn't good enough any more.

Our solution was to create a "teaching center." This center would organize seminars and discussions about teaching and help individual teachers who wanted to improve. Our center needed a director and, for reasons that are forgotten now, that task fell to me. Explaining teaching became my job.

It wasn't long before I began to feel frustrated. Teaching how to teach was trickier than I had imagined. I was beginning to wonder if it could be done at all.

Then came my brilliant idea. We would videotape our best teachers and find out what they do. Then we could extract their secrets and explain them to all the faculty.

Some teachers were flattered to be taped and put on a performance. Others were self-conscious and tightened up. But most interesting of all, some teachers refused to be taped.

My friend John was typical of these. He was not camera-shy. In fact he was a bit of a ham and liked the attention. But, like the aborigines, John feared that the machine would take away his soul. Well, not his soul but the soul of his teaching. Whatever was out there producing that magic in the classroom would just refuse to show up. The teaching gods were real, and they were stubborn. No video cameras!

* * *

Teaching is a mysterious process. Whether it is John in his class or our third grader with her homework, we are not sure how it works. We explain things, but even our best explanations may not help. Then, out of the blue and for no apparent reason, learning just happens.

So it is easy to understand why John felt as he did. Good teaching is fragile. It might not be a good idea to immobilize it on a piece of magnetic videotape, trapped like a firefly in a bottle. The light might fade for lack of air.

You may feel the same about this book. Won't the crude facts of science contaminate the magic in teaching and learning? Rather than helping, won't they just drain away its life and light?

But even if you tend to agree with John and are worried about losing the magic, I suspect you also understand what Thoreau is saying in his lucid and poetic claim for the power of simple facts. Part of our nature wants to understand, wants to put the mysterious on a firmer, factual footing. And we know that, far from destroying the light, facts give us light. That is why we crave them, why their edge is sweet.

On Facts

It might sound quaint to begin with Thoreau and talk about facts. It is the twenty-first century, and we have learned to distrust absolutes. Rather than speak of facts, or reality, we talk about our *metaphors*. We explain what "happened," but we don't blame anyone.

Some call this more relative view of things postmodernism. As the name suggests, it implies that we have moved beyond the day of "modern" science, with its beliefs in absolute facts, and have come to a more sophisticated time where we recognize how relative our facts can be and how their meaning depends on our individual experience.

There is no doubt that this perspective has value. For example, it helps us recognize our differences. We each see the world through our own metaphors, and we all have our unique reference points for learning.

But in our common speech, we still talk about facts and reality. Science keeps moving ahead, discovering new facts. Facts and realities haven't disappeared. We still need them to understand each other. For example, we aren't talking about ultimate reality when we say "there is an oak tree in my yard." All we mean is every time we look out our window we see the tree, and if we accidentally run into that tree, we will be knocked flat on our backs. These things never change, and that is enough for us to call them facts. No matter how deeply we understand postmodernism, we still try not to run into trees.

This is what I mean when I talk about facts. I am going to build on things that come from repeated experiments and have been shown to be dependable. It is this reliability that make our facts so sweet and that makes us crave them.

A Bridge Too Far?

As I proceeded with this project, I became more and more aware of its difficulties. It is one thing to point out facts about the brain and another to translate them into facts about learning. An even greater challenge is to move from any facts that we may agree on about learning and convert those into facts about teaching. As John Bruer has argued, this may not be possible with our present knowledge. It may be "a bridge too far."[1]

But no one wants teachers to ignore biology. Ultimately, we will still have to reconcile everything with nature. If we find our theories about teaching to be in disagreement with biology, we must reconsider them. So, if it is too early to build bridges between biology and pedagogy, someone should still watch over our growing understanding of the brain. It is never the wrong time to look for ideas about how to help people learn—even if those ideas come from biology.

Getting, and Keeping, the Courage

We all have our beliefs about learning, and most of us will express them at any opportunity. The same can be said for teaching. We have all been to school, and so we all have our opinions about teaching. The difficulty is that these beliefs and opinions are both strong and different! So it was inevitable that if I took on this project, I would step on some toes, no matter what I said.

I also knew that not everyone would appreciate my point of view. But, along the way I drew courage from people like Edelman and Lakoff, who have argued powerfully for a biological understanding of cognition and learning.[2] I heard them affirm what I believe, which is that all the products of the mind come from the brain and its interactions with the body and the world. As a biologist, I think I understand Edelman better, and I was especially compelled by his insistence that we must recognize the biological origins of the brain in evolution and in development, if we are to understand the human mind and heart. As he says, "there must be ways to put the mind back into nature that are concordant with how it got there in the first place."

So, trusting these greater minds than mine and clinging tightly to my faith that better understanding always opens up new paths for action, I managed to persist. Facts about how the brain works were bound to have applications in teaching. Eventually, teaching would become the *applied science of the brain.*

How I Worked

How did I go about this risky project?

I was not trained as a neuroscientist, but for many years my work was directly related to one of the important questions neuroscientists ask: How do cells send signals to each other? As a result I knew something about cells and how they communicate, which is an important part in understanding the brain.

Beginning with this part of neuroscience, I began to pry open the other doors. And I do mean *pry.* Bit by bit I got myself through these doors, exploring what I found, learning about the anatomy of the brain, about brain imaging, about behavior, about the emotional brain, about sensory and motor systems, and so on to this day. Indeed, as I write I am still prying away!

But through all my prying, I understood my limits well. What I was finding was not "real knowledge" but "book knowledge." I would never understand the brain the way practicing neuroscientists do. My contributions would not come from new understandings about the brain.

But teaching was a different matter. There were possibilities for a contribution there, and that is where I focused. I just kept asking about teaching. Whenever I pried open another door, I looked around and asked, "Is there anything here for the teacher?"

And it seemed that I kept getting answers. Over and over I stumbled onto ideas that I had not known before. True, these were still just ideas, but at least they came from what I believed to be facts. And, they were what kept me going.

The Art of Changing the Brain

I had always believed that the brain operates by physical and chemical laws, and thus, that learning is physical. But I had never been challenged to put that belief into any practical use. Now, I was trying to use the concept, and that forced me to be much more concrete. Whatever it meant to say "learning is physical," I had to apply to teaching as well. Inevitably I realized that if a teacher has any success at all, she has produced physical change in her student's brain. Teaching is the art of changing the brain.

I don't mean controlling the brain, or rearranging it according to some "brain manual." I mean, *creating conditions that lead to change in a learner's brain.* We can't get inside and rewire a brain, but we can arrange things so that it gets rewired. If we are skilled, we can set up conditions that favor this rewiring, and we can create an environment that nurtures it.

An art, indeed!

The Power of the Physical

When we don't understand, we are tempted to invoke some mystical authority, a teaching god or a wicked witch of the west. But ultimately true power lies in the mundane physical nature of the real world. Ultimately, even the spiritual is physical.

I came to understand this in a deeper way as I pursued my quest for the teaching secrets I hoped were buried in the physical structure and function of the brain. In fact, I came to think that physical experiences and images are required in order to understand anything at all.

Again, I am being quite literal. It seemed that I could only understand things when they were described in physical terms. My digging up facts about the brain began to help me see why. This seems to be an innate characteristic of the brain itself. All that the brain knows comes from the physical world, the things in its environment, the physical body that holds the brain inside itself, or the womb that holds that body as it develops.[3] A physical brain means a physical mind; *meaning* itself is physical. This is why we need metaphors. Without reference to physical objects and events, there is no meaning.

Education and Physical Models

As I followed this path, I realized that we also have physical models for teaching and learning. For example, some teachers believe that the student is a physical recipient of knowledge. She is a "blank slate" or a "vessel." Others believe that learners construct their understandings like a carpenter builds a house or an artist paints a picture.

So I began thinking about metaphors for the future of teaching. I imagined that we would begin to invent tools to create learning and to help us repair mistakes—tools for changing the brain. We will use that wonderful tool-building instinct that was an essential part of our survival throughout evolution. Just as we invented the hammer to drive a nail, we would invent tools to facilitate learning.

Again, let me remind you that I am not talking about inventing a "learning hammer" for driving knowledge into the brain. And I don't mean some new chemical that we can inject to improve learning. What I mean is that we will understand what conditions, what environments, and what practices make learning work better.

Biology, Philosophy, and Education

The last step along this path came as I thought more broadly about what these ideas mean for the way we help people learn. Ultimately, how we teach depends on how we believe the mind works, and how we understand behavior. It depends on our philosophies. I recognized that my physical view of things is really a philosophy.

This may surprise you, because we don't often think of biology as related to philosophy. It seems too technical for that. We think that science is about inventing new medicines, new machines, or new enjoyments for ourselves. But in some ways those are just side products. Ultimately the most important goal of biological science is to understand the physical basis for life, thought, love, and meaning.

So, biology is not really separate from philosophy. It is a search for meaning, and now, in the twenty-first century, it turns out that our search is leading somewhere. In fact, biology has created a revolution in philosophy. This has come about through application of new understandings about the structure of the brain and the mechanisms at work inside it, what we call cognitive science and cognitive neuroscience.

This impact of biology on philosophy is stated most directly by Lakoff and Johnson in their book *Philosophy in the Flesh,* which begins as follows:[4]

> The mind is inherently embodied.
> Thought is mostly unconscious.
> Abstract concepts are largely metaphorical.
> These are three major findings of cognitive science. More than two millennia of a priori philosophical speculation about these aspects of reason are over. Because of these discoveries, philosophy can never be the same again.

My guess is that these claims have not pleased all the philosophers of the world, but the arguments are strong and their connection with biology undeniable. Further, if philosophy will never be the same, neither will education!

Overview

Now you have seen why I believe that understanding the brain will enrich teaching. It will give us new ideas for educational tools, and it will change our ideas of how the mind works. It will change our practice and our philosophy.

I try to make this case in more detail in the remainder of the book. It is divided into four parts:

Part I (chapters 2–5) is about *foundations* for learning. The metaphor here is that there are things that underlie and thus can support our effort to help people learn. One of these things is the overall arrangement of the brain, a structure that produces learning naturally. Another part of this foundation is a requirement for a balanced use of the capabilities of different parts of the brain. And a third is the interaction of emotion structures with cognition structures in the brain, which helps us understand motivation, reasoning, and memory. In our foundation metaphor, emotion seems to be the mortar that holds things together.

Part II (chapters 6 and 7) focuses on neuronal networks, their relationship to knowledge and learning, and the practical impact of this information for the teacher. These chapters contain more specific suggestions about what teachers should actually *do*. One of the most fundamental ideas is that a teacher must start with the existing networks of neurons in a learner's brain, because they are the physical form of her prior knowledge. This emphasis on prior knowledge is well accepted in educational theory, but the biological meaning enriches our appreciation of it. The teacher's task is to produce physical change in those networks, and we learn how to do that by seeing how nature does it.

In Part III (chapters 8–12), I revisit the five major parts of the cerebral cortex: the sensory cortex, the post-sensory integrative cortex, the frontal integrative cortex, the motor cortex, and the major structures associated with emotion. Each of these chapters gives us ideas about different aspects of learning, such as the value of experience, why we need to reflect, how learners come to own their knowledge, how learning is confirmed and extended through action, and how the effective teacher can make use of knowledge about emotion.

Finally, you will find a short epilogue entitled "Enrichments." Here I summarize different ways that understanding the brain can enrich the teacher. Remembering that enrichment means adding to what we already have, I briefly argue that our *insights*, our *realities*, our *separateness* (or boundaries), our *ideas*, and our *values*, our *values* are all enriched when we think of teaching as the art of changing the brain.

Revisiting the Teaching Gods

You can see that I am now far beyond videotaping classes in my search for better ways to help people learn. But I haven't forgotten about John and his concerns. In fact, I still think about those teaching gods. A good class can be almost a religious experience. Things happen that we didn't predict, sometimes wonderful things and often mysterious!

As you can see, I don't deny the mystery. I only want to solve it. And the solutions must be buried in that physical structure we call the brain. It is physical. That means we can understand!

Notes

1. See J. T. Bruer, "Education and the Brain: A Bridge Too Far," *Educational Researcher* (November, 1997); also see Chapter 3 in H. Gardner, *The Disciplined Mind* (New York: Basic Books, 1998).
2. G. Lakoff, and M. Johnson, *Philosophy in the Flesh—The Embodied Mind and its Challenge to Western Thought* (New York: Basic Books, 1999); G. M. Edelman, *Bright Air, Brilliant Fire; On the Matter of the Mind* (New York: Basic Books, 1992).
3. We could say that our brain also comes from the programs that are coded in our genes. That might sound less physical, somehow. But, of course, those programs are just the result of the physical structure of DNA.
4. Lakoff and Johnson, p. 3.

PART I
FOUNDATIONS

How does learning come from the structure of the brain? How does information become understanding? What is the origin of motivation? How do feelings affect reason and memory?

2

WHERE WE OUGHT TO BE

THE NATURAL RELATIONSHIP BETWEEN BRAIN STRUCTURE AND LEARNING

'tis a gift to come down where we
ought to be.
                    —*Amish hymn*

It was so pretty, it had to be true.
    —*James Watson on discovering
                the double helix*

Being director of a teaching center had some terrific perks. One of the best was that I was expected to learn about learning. You might not consider this a perk, but I did. It was a luxury for me to read and study about how people learn. I never had time before.

So I looked for new reading. What I wanted wasn't in biology or psychology books I had seen. I needed to get beyond synapses, stimulus/response, habituation, and Pavlov's dogs. My hope was to understand understanding. What must a brain do to comprehend?

It was then that I discovered David Kolb's book, *Experiential Learning*.[1] It wasn't particularly about biology, but still it came closer to what interested me, so in I plunged.

Kolb began by talking about people I had heard of, but never read before, people like Dewey, Piaget, and Lewin. Combining their ideas about development and learning, he described a new "learning cycle." He said deep learning, learning for real comprehension, comes through a sequence of experience, reflection, abstraction, and active testing. These four cycle 'round and 'round as we learn.

I was skeptical of this idea at first. Surely there were many other ways to explain learning. It seemed too simple, too arbitrary.

But I gave it a chance. And, without warning, as I sat in my office on one warm spring afternoon, it all came together. I still remember taking that slow, deep breath, holding it for a second, and then releasing it with a sound somewhere between a laugh and a sigh.

I stood up and began to pace and talk to myself. "It is biological! Of course, it has to be. Everything is in the right place! It's too pretty not to be true!"

I surprised myself. I turned from skeptic to believer on that day. Things just came down where they ought to be.

*   *   *

In biology, the way things work depends on their structure—their physical structure. Genetic inheritance depends on the structure of DNA. Digestion depends on the structure of the gut. Any function found in any living organism must depend on some structure of some part of that organism.

This was my habit of thinking, and so it seemed that if the function we are interested in is learning, we should look for the structure that produces it, and the place we should look is in the brain. Ultimately, the structure of the brain should explain learning. It's only natural.

That is what I saw on that warm spring afternoon. What I knew about the brain told me that the learning cycle should work, and it told me why. For the first time I saw a structure designed for human learning, for understanding and comprehension.

First Look

In this chapter I will give you my proposal for this natural connection between brain structure and learning. We don't need to know much about the brain to do this. Neurons and synapses can wait until later, as can the complicated structures that lie deep in the brain. For now we can simply look at the outside of the brain and talk a little bit about what different parts do.

In the illustration shown below you can see a view of the left side of what is called the *cerebral cortex*. The *cerebrum* is the large part of the human brain that is thought to be responsible for much of the thinking and learning we do, and the *cortex* is the layer of tissue that coats the cerebrum, like the bark of a tree; hence the name *cerebral cortex.*

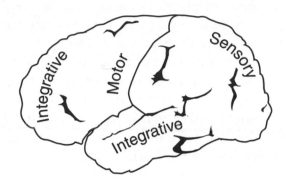

This illustration shows three functions of the cerebral cortex, and roughly which parts of the cortex are engaged in each. The functions are *sensing, integrating,* and *motor* (which means moving). Notice that there are two integrating regions of cortex; we will discuss the difference between them later in this chapter.

These three functions of the cortex are not an accident. They do the key things that are essential for all nervous systems. They sense the environment, add up (or integrate) what they sense, and generate appropriate movements (actions):

$$\text{Sense} \Rightarrow \text{Integrate} \Rightarrow \text{Act}$$

These three functions are seen in nervous systems ranging from those in simple animals to the human brain. In the paragraphs that follow I expand on this somewhat and describe more about these three brain functions.

The sensing function refers to the receipt of signals from the outside world. In people, these signals are picked up by the sense organs; eyes, ears, skin, mouth, and nose.[2] They are then sent on to special regions of the brain for each of the senses. These signals come in small bits and have no meaning in their raw form. They are just little individual pulses of electrical energy coming in from the sense organs.

Integration means that these individual signals get added up so that whatever is being sensed is recognized in the sum of all these signals.

The small bits merge into bigger patterns that become meaningful things like images or language. In the human brain these meanings are then integrated in new ways that become ideas, thoughts, and plans. At their most basic, these integrated meanings become plans for actions. For example, they get added up in ways that generate a plan for *what* action is needed and *where* the action is needed.

Finally, the motor function is the execution of those plans and ideas by the body. Ultimately, motor signals are sent to the muscles that contract and relax in coordinated ways to create sophisticated movements. Importantly, we should realize that even *speaking* and *writing* fit in here because they involve some of the most sophisticated patterns of muscle contractions that the body carries out.

Brain Connections: An Overview

This transfer of signals from sensory input through the brain to motor output is a general pattern for all nervous systems, including the human brain. The most direct and simplest route for signaling in the brain, then, would be as shown in the illustration below. Sensory input could come from the outside world or from our own body, but once those signals have entered the sensory part of the cortex, they flow first through the integrative part of the brain nearest the sensory part, then through the integrative part nearest the motor brain, and then to the motor brain itself. Once action has been initiated, that action is detected by the sensory brain, so the output of the brain becomes new sensory input.

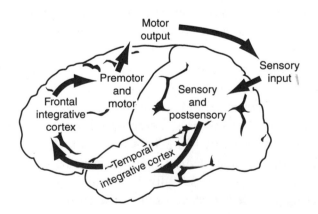

I want to stress that this picture is highly oversimplified. Later we will see that there are many other links, including parallel links and connections where signals go in both directions. What I have shown you is probably the simplest way to look at what the brain does.

Looking for Learning

Our objective is to get ideas about learning from the structure of the brain. We are looking for a structure that generates comprehension and understanding in people, something more than pure memory of facts or physical skills. It isn't necessarily obvious how this type of learning can come from the structure we have been talking about. Somehow deep learning should emerge from sensing, integrating, and acting.

But this is where biology takes us, so we have to keep looking.

The Learning Cycle

The learning cycle explained in Kolb's book is a key part of this search for learning, and this is the point where we can bring it into the story.

The cycle is shown below, in a simplified form.[3] It relies heavily on the ideas of Dewey and Piaget, among others, and you may recognize some of the terminology as originating from these giants in the study of human learning.

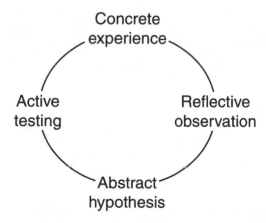

The cycle is based on the proposal that learning originates in concrete experience; hence the term *experiential learning*. But experience is *not*

the whole thing.[4] In fact, it is just the beginning. Learning depends on experience, but it also *requires* reflection, developing abstractions, and active testing of our abstractions.

As you reflect on the learning cycle, remember that this is just the basic idea and that its implications are important and complex. I can't do it justice at this point, but I will expand on it in later chapters.

Natural Learning

Let me remind you that when I first saw the learning cycle, I was skeptical. It seemed arbitrary. Why does the cycle stress these particular four things? Why are they placed in this sequence? Why is there any sequence at all? And what about other things like memory, feedback, or trial and error?

I might still be struggling with these and other questions if I had not seen the natural link with biology. You may have seen it already, but if not, the idea is illustrated below.

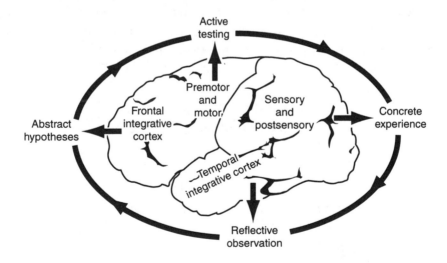

Put into words, the figure illustrates that concrete experience comes through the sensory cortex, reflective observation involves the integrative cortex at the back, creating new abstract concepts occurs in the frontal integrative cortex, and active testing involves the motor brain.[5] In other words, the learning cycle arises naturally from the structure of the brain. This *is* a pretty idea!

Is This about Teaching?

I will explain more about this connection between the learning cycle and the way brains are put together shortly. But I am worried that you may be wondering how this connects with teaching. Maybe you think that I am so enamored by my pretty idea that I have forgotten what the book is supposed to be about.

So I want to take a short break and talk about a teaching connection that comes up immediately if we accept the brain cycle that I propose in my model. Let's start with a story.

*   *   *

Lilly Conferences on college teaching were a discovery I had made when I became director of our teaching center. They were always interesting and energizing, and I was looking forward to the session on this particular morning. The title was something like "Improving Teaching in Large Classes."

I was surprised when the presenters began by discussing the record-keeping problems with large classes. How can you avoid making mistakes when you have a class of 1,000?

I agreed that this is important, but I began to get bored as the session went on. My real interest was in learning.

Finally, my frustration got the best of me, and I blurted out my question. "This is useful, but before we finish could you talk a little about learning? What is your experience with improving learning in large classes?"

She looked blank for a moment and then replied, "Well, this session isn't really about learning; it is more about teaching!"

This startled me, but I persisted, "But how can you separate teaching from learning?"

In all sincerity, she replied, "You can teach well, do all the right things, without any learning. Learning is up to the student. If I am teaching right, I am doing my part!"

The Teaching Trap

Is this right? Can we teach without anyone learning?

It does seem true in some ways. You may have experienced something similar yourself. You may have tried your best to help someone learn, but discovered that it just didn't work. You were there, you taught, but learning just didn't happen.

Or did it? Just because your learner didn't understand what you hoped he would, does that mean he learned nothing?

This is where our model comes in. If indeed learning begins through sensory experience, then the teacher is in a trap. *Anything* she does can produce learning, because it is sensory experience.

It happens in school all the time. A student may not learn history in our history class, but he may learn that his teacher thinks history is interesting. Or he may learn that his teacher dislikes students, or that he is just overwhelmed. The student has an experience of some sort. His brain processes that experience, and ultimately he acts on it in some way. His action may be to close the book and look out the window, but that is because his experience has taught him that he doesn't need to listen, or that he doesn't care to listen.

You can plug in your own examples. You may remember when your "teaching" was wasted on an employee, a child, or a parent. It was wasted because your "student" didn't learn what you hoped he would. But he did have an experience; he did have sensory input. And his brain did something with that experience.

The more we understand learning, the more we will realize this. We can't separate teaching from learning. The brain won't let us off the hook that easily.

Rationale for Natural Learning

The brain cycle, then, provokes us to think about the sensory input that students get in our classes. But it doesn't end there. It also suggests that we should look at its implications for other parts of learning.

However, Before we can do that, we need more details about what happens in the four parts of the cerebral cortex we have identified and how these functions match up with the learning cycle.

I have tried to summarize this match by lining things up in the two lists below. On the left side, I have listed a few things that our four parts of the cortex are known to do, and on the right side I have tried to show how a particular stage of the learning cycle seems to fit the capabilities of it's matched region of cortex.[5]

Important functions of each part of cortex	*Match with each stage of the learning cycle*
The sensory cortex receives first input from the outside world in form of vision, hearing, touch, position, smells, and taste.	This matches with the common definition of concrete experience, with its reliance on direct physical information from the world.
The back integrative cortex is engaged in memory formation and reassembly, language comprehension, developing spatial relationship, and identifying objects, faces, and motion. In short, it integrates sensory information to create images and meaning.	These functions match well with what happens during reflection, for example, remembering relevant information, daydreaming and free association, developing insights and associations, mentally rerunning experiences, and analyzing experiences.
The frontal integrative cortex is responsible for short-term memory, problem solving, making decisions, assembling plans for action, assembly of language, making judgments and evaluations, directing the action of the rest of the brain (including memory recall), and organizing actions and activities of the entire body.	This matches well with the generation of abstractions, which requires manipulation of images and language to create new (mental) arrangements, developing plans for future action, comparing and choosing options, directing recall of past experience, creating symbolic representations, and replacing and manipulating items held in short-term memory.

(Continued)

Important functions of each part of cortex	*Match with each stage of the learning cycle*
The motor cortex directly triggers all coordinated and voluntary muscle contractions by the body, producing movement. It carries out the plans and ideas originating from the front integrative cortex, including the actual production of language through speech and writing.	This matches with the necessity for action in completion of the learning cycle. Active testing of abstractions requires conversion of ideas into physical action, or movements of parts of the body. This includes intellectual activities such as writing, deriving relationships, doing experiments, and talking in debate or conversation.

The point of the list above is to point out that the four parts of the cortex do things that are qualitatively different from each other. When we look at those things, we see the many ways they fit the four parts of the learning cycle.[6]

Example: Learning a New Word Through the Learning Cycle

Let's go through a specific example of how the learning cycle meshes with the functions of these different parts of the brain. Then we will examine actual brain imaging studies that seem to support this proposal directly.

Suppose my task is to learn a new word from another person who knows its definition. Let's say the word is *flabmonk*. When I see or hear *flabmonk,* I have concrete experience. This is a visual and/or auditory sensory event for my brain. When I reflect on the word *flabmonk,* I remember other words and images that seem related or similar. I may recall that flab suggests fat, monk could be a religious person, or it could be an animal. This is the reflective brain at work; it primarily involves memory. As various possibilities come to me, I begin to develop an abstract idea for the meaning of *flabmonk*. I may think, for example, that a *flabmonk* is a new species of animal, or it may be a fat religious person, or a pompous fundamentalist. This is my abstracting brain at work. It is converting past images into new images, and then into new words—new symbols for the real thing. Finally, I test my hypothesis. To do this I must act; I must speak or write. So I ask, "A pompous fundamentalist?" This requires activity by my motor brain. Instantly, my teacher responds. "Yes!" she says and laughs out loud! I have tested my idea.

Or he says, "Sorry, good guess! Try again." I have tested and my test failed, but now my sensory brain has new input and the cycle can start again.

Here is a summary of this example:

1. Hear words or see words = concrete experience

2. Remember related words, images, or ideas = reflection

3. Generate new words or ideas = abstraction

4. Speak or write new words or ideas = active testing

5. Hear or see new words and teacher's response = new concrete experience

Our hypothesis about the brain would say that number 1 involves the sensory cortex, number 2 involves the back integrative cortex, number 3 involves the frontal integrative cortex, number 4 involves the motor cortex, and number 5 reengages the sensory cortex.

Brain Imaging Studies

One of the most important developments in neuroscience over the past few decades is the creation of methods for examining what parts of the brain are most active when we are doing different things. These brain imaging tools have opened the way to much deeper understanding of how brains think and what parts are most strongly engaged for specific tasks. A brief description of two of these methods is included in the notes for this chapter.[7]

Many brain imaging studies support the suggestions I made for learning a new word. Let's look at one of them.

The experiments illustrated in this chapter are related to brain processing of words. Each image shows the areas of the brain that are most active when we are seeing and hearing words, mentally creating a verb, and speaking words.

We can clearly see the activation of specific parts of the cortex in the sensory events of seeing and hearing. (And, by the way, it also is our first demonstration of the actual location of the visual cortex and auditory cortex.) Experiments like this have been done for many visual and auditory processes, and these regions are well established.

The mental generation of verbs, which involves comprehending meaning (activating the back integrative region of the brain) and preparing to speak the verb (which activates the lower region of the frontal lobe), is shown in the lower right panel of this illustration.[8]

Actually speaking the words activates the motor cortex region responsible for driving the muscle contractions needed in speech, which is shown in the lower left panel.

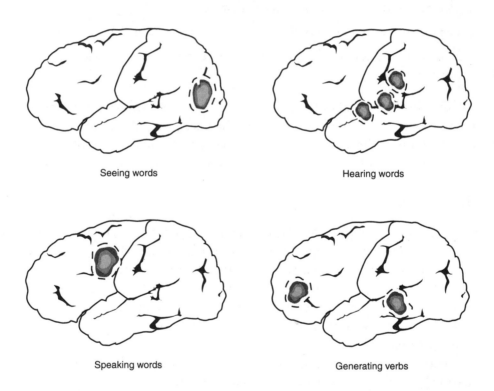

Seeing words

Hearing words

Speaking words

Generating verbs

Together, then, these results demonstrate the separation of the experience, reflecting, abstracting, and active testing parts of the learning cycle in different parts of the brain.[9]

How Long Does a Learning Cycle Take?

You may be bothered by this example because it happens rather quickly. You might have gone through the whole cycle in a few seconds. But it wasn't instantaneous. You did need a second or two to reflect on *flabmonk* and make a guess about its meaning. It could have taken much longer, of course. If the word were a French word and you had taken French in high school, without a dictionary you might have thought for days, developing and testing several different ideas about a definition in that time. Only if you already knew the word could the process be instantaneous.

You also might have tried to speed things up by using a dictionary. But you would still be using the learning cycle. After reflection you would develop the hypothesis that you won't be able to recall the word, or at least not in a reasonable time, so you act on that hypothesis by turning to a dictionary.

This may seem like cheating, somehow, but my point is that we always seem to go through the four steps in one form or another. It could even be that we reflect on an experience for years, eventually arrive at an abstract understanding, and finally we confirm our understanding through some action. For example, we change our behavior as a test of our new hypotheses about how to live. Eventually we attain wisdom and regulate our lives by use of the learning cycle.

Our brain has the capacity to reflect, develop ideas, and take actions continually. We are always in the middle of a multitude of learning cycles, getting new sensory information, thinking about different experiences, getting new ideas about their meaning, and testing those ideas. This is the story of our day-to-day lives.

Potential Confusions

Drawing the learning cycle the way we have is a little misleading. We can get the idea that the cycle goes just in one direction all the time. That is true in the sense that a cycle can't be completed until all steps have occurred, but the structure of the brain tells us that the communication between the different regions of the brain can go both ways. Signals can bounce back and forth between different parts.

In fact, the reverberation of signals between meaning and hypothesis reminds us of what seems to happen anytime we think hard about something. We conceive meanings that have implications, and when we put those implications into a hypothesis, we are reminded of other, possibly conflicting, meanings that imply something else or add complexity to the implications. As a result we create a new hypothesis or modify our old one. So it goes until we decide to act on our hypothesis, and then we find out how well we have done our thinking!

There are also shortcuts that make it possible to skip over one part or another. We will see this more clearly in chapter 3 and in chapter 12, but it is important that you realize here that we are not talking about a simple merry-go-round.

Of course, the same is true of learning. We bounce back and forth between reflection and ideas all the time as we think about our experiences and try to make sense of them. Often we will almost skip reflection completely and try a shortcut directly to an idea or even an action. Trial-and-error learning in its least complex forms can be considered simply use of the sensory and motor brain, omitting the integrating brain completely. We try (act) and we fail (sense).

As we would expect, the way the brain is put together and the way learning goes overlap each other in these more complex ways as well as in the simple linear path suggested by our drawings.

Questions for Teachers

The idea that the learning cycle is the natural result of the structure of the brain should encourage us to think about how we might use it to help people learn. We will examine that approach more extensively later in the book, but in the mean time here are some questions that may lead to a few interesting ideas.

- What if we view our "teaching" simply as sensory input? Could we use knowledge of the sensory brain to guide us in our practice? Would this change how we plan our teaching and how we present information?

- What if the assignments we give were intentionally designed to integrate experience and memory through reflection? Could we use our knowledge of the integrative brain to guide us? Would assignments be different? Assessments?

- Could we insist that students develop their *own* abstract ideas and explanations—that is, use their integrative frontal cortex?

- How would we bring the motor brain into our teaching? How can we insist that students actively demonstrate their ideas—not our ideas, but theirs?

- How can we challenge students to use their sensory brains to *observe their own active testing of ideas.* How can we make them aware of their own learning?

- When we try to help people learn, can we find ways to encourage them to use all parts of the learning cycle?

- Why not say that all learning is experiential, school learning included? The structure of the brain does not change when we enter a school, so why should we think school learning is different? Aren't classes experiences? Won't students reflect on that experience? Won't they generate their own ideas about what the experience means? Won't their actions come from these ideas? In fact, isn't that the way it has always been?

As I have indicated, we will address some of these questions later in the book, but that doesn't mean you can't begin to think of your own answers now!

Starting a Foundation for Learning

This chapter is the first step in creating a foundation for learning. The building blocks for our foundation are the sensory, reflective, abstracting, and acting brain. We use those parts of our brain through experience, reflection, hypothesizing, and active testing. Everything I say from here on can be supported by these ideas.

Without biology, the learning cycle is theoretical. But with biology, it seems that we are closer to fact. The brain is actually constructed this way. We can build our ideas about teaching on a solid and secure foundation.

In the next chapter we may find ourselves feeling even more secure. As we look deeper into the structure of the brain, we will get a strong sense of the need for proportion in our foundation. And of greatest interest, we will begin to see that if we get the proportions right, our foundation becomes something more than a support. It becomes an agent of change in the learner.

Notes

1. D. A. Kolb, *Experiential Learning:* Experience as the source of learning and development, Prentice Hall, Eaglewood Cliffs, NJ (1984).
2. The chemical senses, taste and smell, are located in regions of the cortex that are not visible in this illustration.
3. This brief description does not show the deep conceptual foundation on which the cycle rests. This cycle combines experience, perception, cognition, and behavior into one learning theory. Each of these represents a major field of psychology/biology.
4. *Experiential learning* is often thought of as simply giving people experience. But I stress that little true learning takes place from experience alone. There must be a conscious effort to build understanding from the experience, which requires reflection, abstraction, and testing of abstractions.
5. It is important not to overinterpret these illustrations. They are not meant to be precise or anatomically accurate, but to help convey these general the ideas. Here are a few potential misunderstandings: (1) The connections do not directly follow the pathway shown by the lines or arrows. For example, the connections sometimes follow the folds of the cortex and sometimes pass through other, deeper brain structures on the way. (2) The connections simply mean that the process *can* occur. There are no physical, lock-step mechanisms implied. Also, there is no implication that these are the only connections one could draw. (3) The brain illustrations are not exact. For example, in the sensory brain we have not really labeled the exact cortical sections for visual, audio, or touch. I will be more precise about this in later chapters. (4) The drawings showing sensory input and motor output do not imply direct entry or exit of information and actions to or from the cortex. This requires connections with the sensory organs such as the eye or the skin and connections with the muscles of the body through the spinal cord.
6. The reader should not take these lists of function as rigid or absolute. Different functions dominate different anatomical parts of the brain, but some of these functions also involve multiple areas. This is true in general about cognitive activities, which are complex and undoubtedly involve interactions between different brain regions.

7. The two imaging methods that I will mention are called PET and fMRI. In PET a small amount of radioactivity is injected into the subject, and when parts of the brain become active, they take up more of that radioactivity. Uptake is measured by sensitive detectors that send the information to a computer to produce the image. PET images are quite diffuse and tend to exaggerate size of the brain area that is affected. In fMRI no radioactivity is needed. Instead, a large magnet detects changes in the amount of oxygenated hemoglobin in the bloodstream that supplies specific areas of the brain. When such areas of the brain are more active than others, their oxygen requirements increase, which is detected and imaged by a computer. fMRI images show changes in smaller areas of the brain than those seen in PET images; they sometimes appear confusing because of the scattered appearance of these small areas. All PET and fMRI studies are averages of several subjects and require careful controls so that the background signals can be subtracted.

8. The area of the brain engaged in comprehension of language was identified by Wernike long before imaging techniques had been developed. Likewise, the frontal region required for assembly of language has been known for over half a century (Broca's area). In fact, all four of the imaging results shown in this illustration are merely confirmatory of the functions of these regions of cortex, whose functions have been previously known.

9. With permission; illustration modeled after M. I. Posner and M. E. Raichle, *Images of Mind* (New York: Scientific American Library, 1997), p. 115.

3

HOLDING A JUST BALANCE

BRAIN CONNECTIONS THAT CHANGE
DATA INTO KNOWLEDGE

Fortunate is the man who takes the
right measure of himself and holds a
just balance between what he can
acquire and what he can use.
                    —Peter Mere Latham

Hamilton was a sincere young man from the Midwest. He struggled in my class, so I asked him to come in for help. I learned his story as we worked together that semester.

A "latchkey" child, Ham had spent a lot of time watching television. His parents were both teachers and they valued learning. They encouraged Ham to watch educational TV, and he grew up on *Sesame Street*, PBS, Nature, and The Discovery Channel. Ham remembered a great deal of what he saw on TV, and his knowledge helped him in school. Compared to other students, Hamilton learned and remembered a lot from his school subjects.

He continued his affair with TV in college. "Did you see Discovery last night?" he would ask his classmates, but they would just laugh and talk about the soap operas.

It may or may not surprise you to learn that things did not go well for Ham in college. I learned later that his troubles began immediately in English composition, which all freshmen take. He struggled to produce logical arguments in his writing or even to assemble coherent paragraphs. He seldom rephrased things or asked questions. In my class, Ham was virtually inactive. He listened intently, but he didn't take notes and he didn't ask any questions. It was as if he were watching a movie.

I felt that I helped Ham some, and he did pass my course. But I didn't see him at the beginning of the next semester, and eventually I found out he had withdrawn from college. I never heard anything more about him.

*   *   *

I have touted the learning cycle as a way to deep understanding. What this means is that the bits and pieces of information, or data, that enter the brain through experience ultimately get converted into what we call *knowledge*.

So how does this work? What is the origin of this transforming power?

One of the keys lies in what I call *balance*. As we realize more about how the brain divides its work and how the parts are connected to each other, it will become apparent that balanced use of all parts is essential for the kind of learning we are discussing. We will also begin to realize what we should balance and the fulcrum on which this balance turns. We see another aspect of our foundation for learning.

Hamilton's Problem

I have had many suggestions about Hamilton's problem, the most common one being that he had some sort of learning disability. In a generic sense, it is hard to disagree with that diagnosis. He was disabled in some way.

But my thought is that his disability was not necessarily of a clinical nature. It is just speculation, of course, but it seemed to me he had simply formed the habit of acquiring more than he could use. Or, put another way, he never understood that what he was acquiring should be used. His learning was out of balance. He soaked up information and enjoyed it greatly, but that was the end. He didn't do anything with his information. He didn't use it to create ideas or actions.

If I am right, it is an extreme case, I admit, but students who remind me of Ham are not uncommon. In fact, I often hear complaints about such students from my colleagues: "They are too passive." "They don't ask questions." "They don't put things in their own words." And, the most common of all, "They just memorize!"

My amateur diagnosis of such passive students is that they do not use the idea and action parts of the brain effectively and rely almost totally on their sensory and memory brain. They have information, but it does not produce useful knowledge.

Transforming

To get a deeper appreciation for my idea of balance, it will help to look more carefully at some of the things that happen when information in the brain is changed into understanding.

The process of changing data into knowing is what Kolb calls "transformation of experience."[1] It becomes evident in different ways, and here I divide it into three parts. First is a transformation from past to future. Our experience is in the past, by definition, but the ideas we create are for actions we will do in the future. They are plans. Without this transformation we rely totally on the past and our reflections about it. Ultimately we rely on memory. But if we use our experience to produce new thoughts and actions, we create a future. The potential of knowledge gained in this way is unlimited, and it can change how and what we do indefinitely into the future.

Second is a transformation of the source of knowledge from outside ourselves to inside ourselves. Our experience comes from outside the brain, but the brain has the ability to turn that outside experience into knowledge and understanding. The new knowledge comes from within. We no longer need to repeat, or even remember, exactly what we experienced from the outside. I suggest that this is the essence of what we mean when we speak of taking ownership of knowledge. It is a *change in the learner* from a receiver to a producer. Since we do not rely on the outside for understanding, we do not have to wait for new information to arrive to deepen our comprehension. We can move from passive to active and become creators of knowledge.

The third part is a transformation of power. If we bring our entire brain into learning, we will find control passing from others to ourselves. We will know what we need for further learning and we will take charge of getting it rather than remaining dependent on others.

Our own brain will begin to give the orders. We will move from a position of weakness and dependence to one of strength and independence.

You can see that this transformation is important. It represents at least part of what we can legitimately call "deep learning." It is learning that changes a life.

I will argue that all these changes happen at the same juncture in the learning process, a juncture defined by the structure of the brain itself. I believe that this juncture is the fulcrum on which information is leveraged into understanding.

Back to Balance

Ham was missing all these elements of transformation. His mind was in the past, it depended on sources outside himself, and thus he had no power. He had no control over his own learning.

I am not saying that he didn't need information or that he should abandon his television programs. Experience and information are necessary parts of learning. They are the raw materials for it. But by themselves they are not enough; they are about half of what it actually needed.

The structure of the brain tells us this. There is a part for receiving, remembering, and integrating information that comes from outside. And there is a second part for acting, modifying, creating, and controlling. If we are to learn in the way that transforms, we must use both of these parts of the brain.

Brain Structure

Generally, the receiving and remembering part of the brain is located toward the back of the cerebrum, and that which generates ideas and actions is in the front. Metaphorically, we might say that the brain turns its back on the past and points forward to its future.

The division between back and front of the cerebrum is illustrated below. You should not confuse this division with the terms *forebrain* and *hindbrain,* which have precise meanings used by biologists to describe different parts of the brain as they develop in the womb. The division I am talking about is really a separation between the front and back parts of the cortex. I will use the terms *back cortex* and *front cortex* to refer to them.

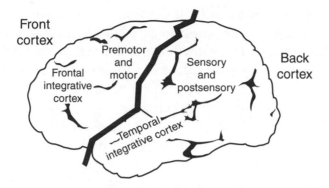

The way I have illustrated this division may seem obvious, but in fact it is somewhat deceiving. In all our illustrations, it appears that the "back" of the cortex is at the far right of the drawing. But that is just the back of the head, not the back of the cortex.

We can understand this apparent contradiction by looking at how the cerebral cortex develops in the womb. The illustration below shows this process, starting with a small bulblike structure at the end of some complex structures that make up older parts of the brain we are ignoring for the moment. Pay attention to the arrows and the *B* and *F* (back and front) locations as the brain grows during embryonic and fetal development of the cortex, through stages A to B to C to D.

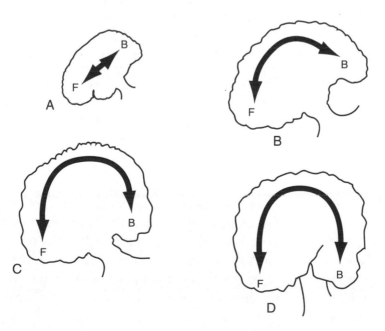

As shown, the front and back segments of the original small knob remain in the same relative positions, while the tissue between them expands dramatically. This growth is up and out, so the final structure is shaped like letter *C* turned face-down. Technically, then, the ends of the *C* represent the parts of the cerebrum that are farthest from one another structurally and developmentally.[2]

This developmental picture shows how the front cortex and back cortex come from the development of the brain as well as from the function. It tells us that if we want to compare the functions of the front and back of the cortex, those most distant from one another, then we should look at the ends of the *C* structure, the so-called *prefrontal* and *temporal* cortex, respectively. I stress this not only to be accurate, but because we will shortly see that it is the connections between these two regions of cerebral cortex that are key to the transformations we are examining.

Review of Functions

In chapter 2 we outlined some specific functions for the sensory, integrative, and motor cortex. Now we are talking about the two types of integrative cortex, that in the front and that at the back.

What happens in these two "ends" of the cortex? Consider these functions that are associated with each.

Back integrative cortex	Front integrative cortex
Memory of stories, memory of place, understanding language, flashbacks, emotions related to experiences, long-term memory (facts, people, faces, experiences)	Choice, decisions to act, inhibition, emotions associated with action, responsibility, mental energy, consequences, predicting, creating

This comparison shows the functional difference between the back and front integrative cortex. Sensory input to the brain, input from the outside world, goes predominantly to the back half. This part of the cortex is heavily involved in long-term memory—the past. It is the part where our knowledge of both the inanimate and living world is mapped. It is where we remember people and their personalities. And it is the part where connections are made between different past experiences. Much of what is there came from the outside world.

The front integrative cortex is about the future. It is where we develop ideas and abstract hypotheses. New things appear, and plans are developed here. It is where we organize our thoughts into bigger pictures that seem to make sense. Things are weighed here; it is where we decide to do or not to do something. It is where we take charge.

Reversing the Scales

If we look at Ham and other passive students, we can see they are using predominantly the back half of their cortex. Very few of the prefrontal functions show up in these students.

Could it be the other way? Is it possible that some students underuse their sensory and reflective cortex, while overusing their idea and acting cortex? Is it possible to find imbalance on the other side of the scales?

I think so. Let me tell you about another student of mine who seems to illustrate that type of imbalance.

*   *   *

Michelle took my biochemistry course for nurses. The students were all pretty nervous about this course. Many of them thought they already hated chemistry, and biochemistry sounded even harder.

In contrast to Ham, it was difficult to keep Michelle quiet. Her hand would shoot up all the time. At first I was happy about this, but soon I began to sense something strange. I was confused by her questions. Although they sounded logical, they began to seem empty.

It took me some time to realize that they were empty! She was fishing without bait, drawing a hook back and forth through the water hoping to latch onto something.

This continued after class and in my office hours. Her vocabulary began to change, and she would use words from biochemistry, but underneath it was the same. Her sentences were fine, even her paragraphs, but in the end they had no content.

On her exams, Michelle would write long answers in good English, but still they were vacuous. She would fill pages with prose that seemed intelligent and meaningful at first but which evaporated when read carefully.

At that time, I was not able to help Michelle much. I might do better now, but I'm not sure. Like Ham, she was disabled in her learning, and during the time in my class she never seemed to understand the value of using her back cortex—the value of gathering information.

*   *   *

Michelle is another extreme example, but I suspect that you have seen parts of this behavior in many students. Our gut response to them is that they need discipline. These students just need to go home and study! They need to get their information and think about it instead of speculating, going off the track in an irrelevant direction, or guessing.

My proposal is that, for a variety of reasons, these students underuse their sensory brain and their reflective brain. Some of my colleagues call these students "experience poor." The scales are tipped heavily toward generation of ideas and actions, but there is not enough experiential data to work with and no time spent in reflection.

Connecting Back and Front

Both Michelle and Ham need better communication between the back and the front of their cortex, between temporal cortex and prefrontal cortex.

But since the prefrontal and temporal cortex are so distant from each other, you might wonder if the connections between them are strong. Maybe it isn't so easy to keep balance. Maybe the front and back parts of our brains don't talk to each other much.

But, again, the actual physical structure of the brain gives us new insight. In fact, some of the most obvious wiring in the brain is designed exactly for this front/back connection.

You could confirm this yourself with the simplest of dissections of one of the cerebral hemispheres. If you were to gently slice open the top of one hemisphere from front to back and a few centimeters from the midline, you would see large tracks of fibers running along from back to front. And if you dissected carefully, you would find four major bundles of nerves that carry signals between front and back.

These nerve bundles are called *fasiculi*. They are shown diagrammatically in the picture below. Each one has a specific name, but for our purposes I have labeled them with numbers. As you can see, numbers two, three, and four directly connect temporal integrative cortex with prefrontal cortex.[3] And as I mentioned in chapter 2, the signals on these fasiculi travel in both directions. They allow the receiving brain to communicate back and forth with the idea brain.

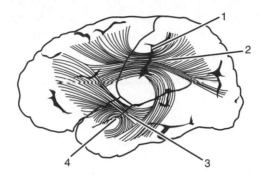

It is clear that the brain is wired so that the front and back talk to each other and that evolution placed great value on these connections. Other than the major connection between the two hemispheres, this back-front connection is the most obvious wiring in the brain.

What might this mean for educators?

You probably see my point and wonder why I make so much of it. After all, it's not that educators ignore passivity in some students or superficiality in other students. We don't need brain anatomy to tell us that these are serious problems. But once we see the fact in this physical form, it becomes more compelling. At least for me, this is true. It is the basis for my speculations about Ham and Michelle. I just can't ignore this signal from biology. We are meant to use both front and back of our cortex!

The Transformation Line

Earlier in this chapter we talked about the transformation of the learner from a receiver to a producer of knowledge. Specifically, we pinpointed a physical place in the brain that defines this transformation. By now, it should be clear that I am speaking of this bridge between front cortex and back cortex.

We can also see this bridge in the learning cycle, as shown in the illustration below. It carries us over the line that separates the experience and reflection part of the cycle from the abstraction and active testing part. Data enters learners through concrete experience where it is organized and rearranged through reflection. But it is still just data until learners begin to work with it. When learners convert this data into ideas, plans, and actions, they experience the transformation I have described. Things are now under their control, and they are free of the tyranny of information. They have created and are free to continually test their own knowledge.

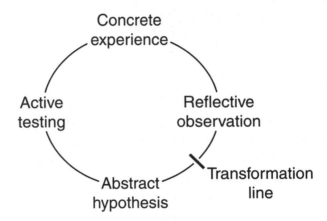

A Practical Example

I have proposed that the balanced use of the back cortex and front cortex will produce better learning. Often, however, we tend toward pedagogical approaches that stress one over the other. The traditional, didactic approach (delivering information) tends to focus on back cortex functions, and the discovery approach (proposing and testing ideas) on the front cortex functions.

You can imagine my enthusiasm when I discovered that this idea of balance has been developed into a specific middle school science curriculum by Marc Schwarz and Phillip Sadler, who are educators and researchers associated with the Mind, Brain, and Education program at the Harvard Graduate School of Education.[4]

Their project focused on the value of asking students to improve various physical devices, such as an electromagnet, based *both* on information that they were given didactically and on their own experimentation. In the example I saw, the teacher showed students an electromagnet, talked about what they do and how they are used, and prompted the students to think along lines that the teacher felt were important by using a questionnaire. This was followed by a hands-on experience in which students were asked to design their own electromagnet and to make improvements in it. They were also asked to develop their own hypotheses about electromagnets and test them.

This work was strongly based on theories of skill development advanced by Fischer,[5] and the importance of "scaffolding" to help students perform at their maximal level. But, what drew my attention was the way it uses the learning cycle and how it engages all the parts of the brain that we have discussed here. It combines concrete experience with reflection, both arranged and supported by the teacher, with freedom (and requirement) for student abstraction and active testing of those abstractions. It is exquisitely balanced.

And it works!

Schwartz and Sadler showed that students taught solely by the traditional method gained understanding slowly and at a low level, while students using the discovery approach alone seemed to learn quickly at first, but their comprehension did not grow over time. In contrast to both of these methods alone, students using the balanced approach increased their understanding steadily and reached levels significantly higher than the other two groups in the end.

Balance and Justice

Up to now we have developed this idea of balance as a practical matter. The structure of the brain teaches us that we should challenge our learners to use both the front and back cortex.

Now I want to turn our attention to the idea of a "just" balance, the phrase used by Latham in the quote at the beginning of this chapter. Balance is also a matter of justice. If we do not teach to both the back and the front cortex, it is unjust for students. Keeping a just balance is our duty.

I hope this is apparent to you, but let me explain what I mean if it is not.

We provide an unjust education if we do not give every student the maximum opportunity for learning. Depending on their natural abilities, imbalance in education deprives some students of learning more than others. Those who are naturally more creative, or have better memories, or are more reflective, or are more active have different opportunities if we do not provide balance. That is unjust.

Pressures Toward Imbalance

I believe teachers are under pressure to deliver an imbalanced, hence an unjust, education for our students. The greater risk is that there will be more Hams than Michelles in our classrooms, but it goes both ways. Let's look first at some pressures that drive teachers toward teaching for the back cortex.

The "information age" is itself a major factor in this pressure toward acquiring. Notice that we do not call it the "understanding age." In this era it often seems that information itself is the highest value; the more we have, the better.

That idea, however, can be challenged. We could argue that it is possible to have too much information. Information comes too fast for us to integrate and comprehend. Despite this danger, there is constant pressure to increase the amount of information in our classes. The number of things we feel we should tell our students continually increases.

A second component of this pressure comes from within. Our image of what it means to be a teacher is distorted in favor of the back cortex. We feel it is more important to have subject knowledge that it is to be creative as a teacher. Our greatest fear is that we will be found wanting in our subject knowledge. If we do not have enough facts, we are not qualified to be teachers.

A possible unexpected result of this pressure is that we may actually overwhelm our students with facts. I speak from personal experience. Early in my career I occasionally found myself intentionally cramming extra material into my plans for a lecture. I did this because I was slightly nervous that my students might ask too many questions and find out that my understanding of the material was not as deep as I would like them to think.

There is also pressure in the other direction. Here we find the newer ideas of active learning and learning through play. These are the result of the strong reactions—some might say overreactions—to the old-fashioned methods such as lecturing or structured lessons. The short-comings in these traditional methods are apparent, so we try something new. One new thing is an emphasis on social interaction and talking in learning. We are reminded of the effortless learning of children at play, and so we try to make the classroom more playful.

But this can also produce imbalance. It can swing too far. We can find ourselves stressing action and creativity at the expense of scholar-ship and information. We may make the classroom into a playroom but lose track of the intense concentration needed for true accomplishment. We find our learners drifting far off track and even devising ways to reduce serious grappling with challenges. We risk trivializing learning.

Toward a Just Balance

There will be a great deal more on pedagogy and how one might teach for understanding in later chapters, but as we close this discussion, I would like to direct our thinking toward ourselves and our practices. I would like to ask if they have the elements needed for a just balance.

First, we should recognize that a basic element of justice is the ques-tion of who it is about. One could argue that in a court, it is about the defendant, and in a class it is about the learner.

For most of my thirty-five years in teaching, I did not think of that. And I am not alone. Recently one of my more honest colleagues blurted out as much. "It is all fine to talk about different students and how we can help them learn," he said. "But the fact is that I hardly ever think of that. I mostly worry that I might make a mistake, or that I might give out wrong information. I don't worry about learning."

Beyond this fundamental point, we can critique ourselves by look-ing at the transformations we spoke of early in this chapter. We can ask if our teaching is designed to support those transformations or not.

What about the transformation from past to future? If we stress balance, then we must include both past and future in our thinking.

The teacher can enrich students' minds by telling them things that are already known. That is the past. She can even tell her students what she believes will happen in the future, but for the students that is also the past. Information that enters the brain from outside is, by definition, in the past for that brain. The question really becomes, "Do teachers create opportunities, even make demands, for students to transform the information which came from their past into their future?" Do we even think about this? Or do we emphasize what is known, rather than what students think or do? Balance would require both.

What about the "outside-to-inside" transformation? Again, the outside is necessary and important for balance. As teachers, we are on the outside, but we have great influence by the way we manipulate, mold, and enrich the information our students need. For balance, we must give equal thought to how students take ownership of that information. How it is transformed from "ours" to "theirs"? How does the learner move from receiver to producer? It is possible that he must first be a receiver, that he must first get something with which to work. We know how to do this part. But how often do we challenge our learners to become producers of knowledge?

Finally, and most interesting, is the transformation of power. At the beginning, through sensory input, learners are dependent on some outside authority to inform them. This can be the teacher, or it can be a book, or today it often is the Internet. The source is not important, but for learning to happen, learners must continually take in new sensory input from outside themselves. The question is, when do they take over power themselves? How do teachers facilitate that? Or might they even resist it?

I believe this is an issue and a challenge for all teachers. I have changed immensely in the past decade, but occasionally I still resist when student questions begin to take up too much time. I have my plan and I have to get on with it. My old instincts still show up once in a while when I resist yielding power to learners. Balance is not easy.

Looking for the Enemy

We are unhappy with our Hams and Michelles. How did they get that way? Why are there so many of them? Whose fault is it?

Unless we believe that genetics has played a nasty trick on us and the "smart gene" has mutated, we tend to blame society for problems like these. With Ham we might blame television, and with Michelle, weak discipline at home or elsewhere. Or we can blame computers, calculators, videogames, liberals, or conservatives. Whatever.

This is unproductive and probably ultimately irrelevant, but it is our nature. So while we are looking for the enemy, we might glance briefly in the mirror. Again, speaking for myself, I can see some clear problems close to home.

What does school teach children? What do teachers actually teach? Arithmetic, reading, and writing, we all hope. But what do we model for them day after day?

On the one hand, school is about authority and control. It is about waiting for someone else to give assignments. It is about knowledge being located somewhere outside us: in books, in the teacher's brain, on educational television, or on the Internet. It is about facts and information. In short, it is about the back cortex.

At the other extreme, school can ignore the back cortex. We may stress creativity without requiring facts. We may encourage talk without substance. We may promote students who have little knowledge. We may deny students quiet time. We may model what our Michelles become.

Adding to Our Foundation

The message in this chapter is that our structure for learning should have a well-proportioned foundation. There should be balance between receiving knowledge and using knowledge. If this is achieved, then our foundation can do more than just support. It can be an integrated part of the larger structure.

But we still are missing one key element, perhaps the most important part. We still need the mortar that holds everything together, and that mortar is emotion.

Notes

1. See David Kolb, *Experiential Learning* (New York: Simon & Schuster, 1983). Transformation of experience into knowledge is a process, not a single step, and not even four steps. Kolb stresses the four stages of the

learning cycle and points out that each one is "transforming" in its own way. My point is that the structure of the brain suggests a major division of function between the reflection and the abstraction step in the learning cycle, and that crossing this division transforms the learner.

2. It is of interest that the structure of the cortex at the ends of this C-like structure, the hippocampus at the "back" end and the olfactory sensory cortex at the "front" end, are also both of an evolutionarily older type of tissue than the remainder of the cortex. Smelling and memory may be the oldest parts of our modern brain.

3. Number one makes a more direct connection between the sensory cortex and the motor cortex. It bypasses major areas of integration.

4. M. Schwartz and P. Sadler, *Goals and Technology Education: The Example of Design Challenges.* Proceedings of the Second AAAS Research in Technology Education Conference. (Washington, D.C.: Am. Assn. for Advancement of Science, 2001).

5. Fischer reviews two decades of his work on skill theory and child development in the *Handbook of Child Psychology,* 5th ed., vol. 1, W. Damon and N. Eisenberg, eds. (New York: Wiley, 1997), pp. 467–561.

4

OUR TRADE AND OUR ART

EVOLUTION OF THE BRAIN
AND MOTIVATION OF THE LEARNER

My trade and my art is living
—*Michel Eyquem de Montaigne*

Dave and Eddie were friends of mine in college. They were dear friends, as college friends usually are. But they both puzzled me.

I met Eddie first, because he lived in my dorm. He was one of the brightest people I knew. He liked to talk about IQ, because his was so high, and that annoyed me slightly, but Eddie had redeeming features. He was sensitive and a good listener. And he always understood what I was talking about. I loved him for that.

Surprisingly (to me, anyway), Eddie did not get top grades in college. The reasons never seemed clear. He cared a lot about grades, and he studied hard. But somehow he was always disappointed. He would blame himself for not coming up to his potential, but as far as I know he never found the answer.

Dave was very different. We became friends when I began to help him with chemistry. We had some great times when after a struggle the light would break through, and we would laugh in genuine pleasure. Dave was earnest, good natured, and honest. He didn't care who knew how he struggled; he just wanted to understand. I found myself pulling for Dave. I came to love him, too.

Dave had a plan for his life. He wanted to serve. Specifically, he intended to become a physician and help people in the third world. But I was skeptical. I didn't think he would get into medical school. He truly surprised me as semester after semester he came up with a 4.00 GPA. And, sure enough, eventually Dave became a doctor in what was then the Belgian Congo.

I thought about these college friends for a long time. How could Dave do so much better than Eddie? Something about the way they used their brain was different in an important way. But it was only recently that I found my answer—the answer I will try to explain in this chapter.

*   *   *

Sometimes we assume that learning only happens in certain places or at certain times. For example, we may think that we only learn in school, or on the job, or when we study our assignments.

However, you may have questioned that idea when we looked at experiential learning and the learning cycle in chapter 2. There isn't any particular time or place especially suitable for the learning cycle. We are always having experience, reflecting, getting ideas, and taking actions. We could say that the learning cycle is about life itself. DeMontaigne's claim that his trade and his art was living can just as well apply to learning. When asked what we do for a living, instead of saying "I teach" or "I trade stocks," we could say, "I learn."

This idea is a biological one. It becomes glaringly obvious when we look at brains evolved, and their biological role. It will help us understand the difference between my college friends Eddie and Dave. And it will help when we encounter someone who says, "I don't want to learn." It is all a matter of how things fit into our lives.

What the Brain Wants

One way to begin thinking about emotion is to ask ourselves what we want or what we don't want. If we try to answer these questions, we will find out what we care about. We will find our fears and hopes, the things that are the source of our emotions. So we might say that our best chance to help another person learn is to find out what they want, what they care about.

This sounds like an important idea for teachers, but at the same time it seems impractical. How can we find out what is important for every student? Even the student herself is often not so sure about what she wants.

It is useful to go back to biology here. Our common origin through evolution means that we all share some basic wants. Above all, the brain wants *survival*. The sensory, integrative, and motor brains combine to make a survival machine. We sense the facts of our environment, integrate those facts to see if they mean danger or opportunity, and initiate action to avoid the danger or grasp the opportunity.

Even a worm does this. If we pick up a night crawler to bait our hook, the worm senses that it has been picked up, knows this is not good, and twists and wiggles violently to escape.

This survival machine is self-regulated. Each brain controls its own body. Even the worm is in control. Maybe there is no lurking fisherman with his hook, but the worm responds as it will, right or wrong. It must be so because the stakes are so high. To survive we must be in control, or believe that we are. Wanting survival means wanting control.

Tools for Survival (Old Tools)

The most fundamental things required for survival appeared first in evolution. These basic survival tools are ancient, and they are powerful. They have worked for a long time.

There are two fundamental things that brains want; to be safe and happy. We use two parts of our survival machine to achieve these goals: our fear system and our pleasure system. The original versions of these two systems seem to have evolved at least 250 million years ago, and their modern-day forms control the behaviors of simple animals like snakes or lizards. Underneath, even we remain a little bit reptile.

Of course we are much more complex than a snake, or at least we believe we are. We don't think snakes feel jealousy, smugness, or pride. But to a great extent we are still ruled by those two powerful emotion systems of fear and pleasure. They are the "I want this" and "I don't want that" systems. Our fear system makes us want to run, fight, hide, or even "play possum," so we get defensive, short tempered, sullen, or lazy. Our pleasure system makes us want to come closer, get more, make ourselves more visible, or keep doing more, so we smile, make jokes, hug a friend, and go to work.

The value of the fear system for survival is obvious, but it may not be so apparent why we need a pleasure system to survive. But we do. For example, sweets and fats are the main foods that give us energy, and our pleasure system makes us want to eat them. Sex is another example. In fact, sex behaviors and eating behaviors seem to come from the same part of the brain pleasure system. We *must* want these things.

Tools for Survival (Newer Tools)

As far as we know, a worm doesn't think about how it can avoid the hook or how it can stay out of the path of the fisherman. But the human brain would. We survive by thinking, planning, and deciding. Our cognitive brain is a powerful tool for survival.

We are constantly evaluating what is going on around us for danger and for opportunity. Our brain looks to the future, makes generalizations about our environment, and develops strategies to enhance our opportunities and minimize dangers so we can survive. Even our highest mental achievements, our calculus, poetry, or philosophy, come from a brain that evolved these types of skills just to survive.[1]

The thinking, analyzing, and planning part of the brain is the cerebral cortex, which we discussed in chapter 2. It is called the *neocortex (new cortex),* because it is thought to have become a major part of the brain just recently, in evolutionary terms. It may be as young as 5 million to 10 million years![2]

The illustration below demonstrates the evolution of the neocortex. It shows the brain from a different perspective than we have used so far. This perspective is gained by exposing the inside surface of one hemisphere by "splitting" the left side from the right. On the newly exposed surface of either hemisphere we see an inner C-shaped ring of cortex (darkened areas), lying beneath an outer ring of neocortex (light areas.) The inner ring is the *limbic cortex,* and it contains some areas that are apparently evolutionarily much older than the neocortex. We will discuss the limbic cortex later; the point of the picture is to demonstrate the increase in neocortex that took place as smarter animals appeared on the scene in evolution.

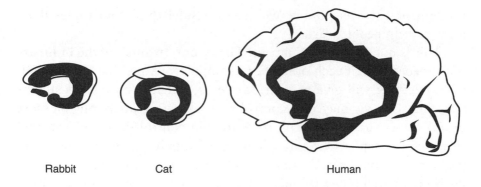

Rabbit   Cat   Human

Emotion and Learning

We are born with the capacity for fear and pleasure, but not necessarily with knowledge of *what* to fear or *what* gives pleasure.[3] We learn most of those things. Looking at learning emotions helps us see the connection between emotion and cognition.

Think of sensory experience. We feel something that hurts, and that triggers the fear system. Or we feel something good, and that triggers the pleasure system. We only need to be burned once to fear heat, and we only need to taste sugar once to want it again. These tools for survival are also powerful learning tools. Learning what we should fear and what we should love is essential for survival.

As with the fear and pleasure systems, our cognitive brain also learns what gets results. Success in thought generates understanding, and understanding allows survival. If we could not understand our world and plan for our future in it, we could not survive. It is not surprising, then, that cognition also triggers our internal reward system. We enjoy real learning, and we want to learn. In order to survive we had to *want* to learn.

Helping People Learn

I have said all brains want to survive, and they have survived so far by understanding their environment, controlling their own actions, avoiding danger, and searching for pleasure. Cognition, control, fear, and pleasure are four things brains use to survive, and they are fundamental to every brain. We must consider these four things if we hope to help people learn.

This is not an easy assignment. These four "wants" of the brain are not independent of each other. For example, we hope that understanding something will give us control over it, but fear may block understanding. Our we may lose control by seeking to satisfy our pleasure brain. Or we may give up pleasure to gain control or accept fear and suffering to keep it. The entanglements of cognition, control, fear, and pleasure are obvious and endless. And, to complicate matters, our stubborn insistence on control means that we just keep on deciding things, right or wrong!

This may sound slightly ridiculous, and indeed when closely examined, all our lives have their ridiculous elements as we muddle along in response to our thoughts and emotions. But actually, this is serious business. Our brain takes itself very seriously. No matter how we behave, whatever our attitudes, whatever we believe, it all comes from a brain that got that way in the desperate struggle to survive.

Because it is so serious, no outside influence or force can cause a brain to learn. It will decide on its own. Thus, one important rule for helping people learn is *to help the learner feel she is in control*. This is probably the best trick that good teachers have, and we will examine it more in chapter 12.

Our evolutionary view also helps us understand why learning is a natural process when it has to do directly with the life of the learner. If people believe it is important to their lives, they will learn. It just happens. A second rule then is that if we want to help people learn *we must help them see how it matters in their lives*. I stress, we must help *them* see. The learner herself must see it and believe it. That does not happen just because *we* say, "It matters!" Our job is not that easy.

Finally, we should remember that the fear and pleasure machinery in our brains are at work all the time. In basic ways, they run our lives, as they have for millions of years. We may not still consciously worry about survival, but we still respond directly to the fear and pleasure systems. Our emotions still seem very important and if we want to help people learn, *we must expect to encounter emotion, and we must take it seriously*. We cannot dismiss the learner's emotions, even when they seem trivial or unjustified to us.

Motivation

We have been skipping around the edges of a question of great importance for learning and teaching: What motivates the learner?

Our worries about this make us think a lot about rewards for learning. In schools it has led to a complex system of bribes and extrinsic rewards, which sometimes are based on mistaken ideas about motivation. These include grades, gold stars, scholarships, and even praise. If it is really learning that we want, these are all off the mark. We may get people to do things with extrinsic rewards, but we can't get them to learn.

Actually, it is not so much that they off the mark, but rather that extrinsic rewards are aimed at the wrong target. They are aimed at things outside learning. They have no natural relationship to the internal life of learning.

What the teacher needs is an understanding of intrinsic motivation, rewards that are automatically connected with learning and that we have evolved to want. If we want to help people learn, we should not worry about how we can motivate them but try to identify what already is motivating them.

Alfie Kohn addresses this subject in his book, *Punished by Rewards*.[4] He concludes that when we try to help someone learn by offering an extrinsic reward, the chances are that learning will actually be reduced.

It is not hard to see why Kohn says this. The first thing our controlling brain sees in a reward or punishment is *loss* of control. It may not be a conscious recognition, but the brain evolved to detect and resist exactly this type of thing for over five million years. It is not going to give in now. In fact, one of the things our brain does best is decipher deceptions like extrinsic rewards. This is one of the main things we practice from our earliest childhood!

The brain sees through the extrinsic reward. It sees the extrincity. The reward is tempting, true enough, so we devise all sorts of ways to get the reward without carrying out the learning, the job, or the assignments. Students seem to do this quite effectively in our colleges. Sometimes they even get As (the reward) in courses they hardly remember taking a few months later.

The Use of Extrinsic Rewards

Despite everything I just said, I do not think extrinsic rewards are useless. I have too much life experience to throw them out completely. And
there is not much hope that we will suddenly drop all our extrinsic
reward systems. What I suggest is that we should recognize a couple of
positive effects that extrinsic rewards can achieve and try to use them
in a more sophisticated way.

One of the values of extrinsic rewards is that they can get a learner
started on something. Often people do not actually know what they are
going to enjoy, and they may not even start to look into many possibilities unless there is some motivation other than an intense life interest.

We may take those important first steps if we are offered an extrinsic reward. This is quite common in college. Students take particular
courses because they believe they can easily get a good grade to "pad"
their GPA. But sometimes, once they have started, they realize they
actually enjoy the subject and it becomes an important part in their life.
This is one reason engineering students sometimes become history
majors, or premed students end up as poets. Initially they were enticed
by some extrinsic factor, but then they do well because they find they
actually care!

Extrinsic rewards can also sustain a learner at times of pressure and
difficulty. For example, a premed student may truly enjoy studying cat
anatomy, but at times it is exhausting and depressing. Too much to
learn! But this student may get over the hump by remembering the
extrinsic reward. That 4.0 GPA is still possible, and so our student will
get a little burst of energy for her studies. She still must have intrinsic
motivation to keep her going in the long run, and to actually *learn*, but
she may dig back in better if she has a little extrinsic reward on the side.

The main value of extrinsic rewards is that they may be the first
step in moving toward intrinsic rewards.

Eddie and Dave

I'm sure you see my idea about Eddie and Dave by now. Dave was
intrinsically motivated. Dave believed that learning chemistry was part
of being a doctor. In his mind he was already a doctor, just a develop-

ing one. This was his life. He had his plans for control of his life, and learning chemistry was just part of the plan. He was focused on the process, not the goals. Dave viewed learning chemistry as part of the action rather than the fruits. He was a learning doctor.

On the other hand, I think Eddie let extrinsic rewards become his focus. He lost sight of the intrinsic ones. The grades, the end point, became the objective. It is possible that, in fact, school itself was extrinsic for him. He was there because that was what young people did when they finished high school, but he hadn't found out how it fit into his real life. He couldn't really see his life as a professional "grade getter." So Eddie couldn't fit his classes and his studies into his life story. My guess is that Eddie's brain rebelled. It just wouldn't work for those extrinsic rewards any more.

Why Talk about Brain Structures for Emotions?

Our instincts about what we want and what we don't want are produced by physical structures in the brain that have evolved over hundreds of millions of years. With all that history we can't blame emotion on the learner. We might create conditions where her emotions begin to change, but direct control is not possible. There is little use in saying, "Don't feel that way!"

What can we do about emotion and the student? Think for a moment about a car. Specific physical structures make the car work as it does. For example, the gas pedal is directly connected to the engine in a way that lets in more or less gas when we push or release the pedal. If we sense our car sputtering and we notice that the gas gauge indicates the tank is empty, it does no good to curse the car or to encourage it. Instead, we must understand the physical facts and use them to our advantage. We nurse the car along at slow speed, allowing it to coast wherever possible, and guide it gently in the shortest line toward the nearest gas station.

In the same way if we know the structures in the brain that produce emotion and if we know a little bit about how they work, we may see ways to nudge our student toward learning. Then we can be grateful when our students sputter, because that is valuable information. It helps us see what we should do.

The Fifth Cortical Function (But Was It the First?)

Let's define some parts of the brain that seem to be central in emotion. We will start with the limbic cortex. Remember that the cortex is the surface layer of tissue—the bark—that covers the brain. We discussed the limbic cortex earlier when we talked about the evolution of cognition and survival. It is not visible if we look at an intact brain, as the sensory and motor cortex are. But as I explained at the beginning of this chapter the limbic cortex can be seen if we split the brain into its right and left hemispheres and look at the inside surfaces that become exposed.

There has been some debate about the functions of the limbic cortex. For many years it was believed to be the main part of the cortex involved in emotion. But in the last decade, LeDoux[5] has urged abandon that view and recognizing that emotion engages many parts of the cortex. This is certainly correct, but new research continues to point to a strong connection between the limbic cortex and emotion.

In the illustration below I show you two major areas of the limbic cortex that become more active under emotional conditions: the *anterior cingulate* and the *posterior cingulate,* particularly an area called the *retrosplenial cortex.*[6] This will interest us again in chapter 12, but for now we can just note that the evidence continues to point toward the limbic cortex in humans as a essential player in emotion.

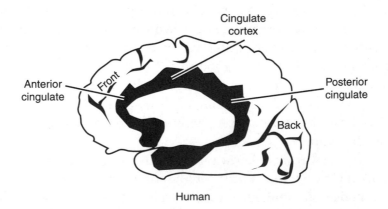

The connection with emotion and the observation that parts of the limbic cortex are evolutionarily older than the neocortex allows us to make a suggestion that I hinted at earlier. Emotional functions may have preceded the appearance of higher cognitive functions in human brain evolution. Emotion may be more fundamental than cognition, even in humans.

The Hidden "Lumps"

Emotions are greatly influenced by parts of the brain buried deep inside the lobes of each hemisphere. These buried parts are lumps, or clusters of cells, rather than the bark-like tissue that forms the cortex. To see these lumps we would need to dig carefully beneath the cortex.

We will not look at pictures of these structures, some of which are immensely complex and convoluted, but in the illustration below I show you the names and approximate locations for two of the major ones; a fear center and important pleasure centers. This illustration cuts away the cortex in the general regions we would have to remove to reach them.

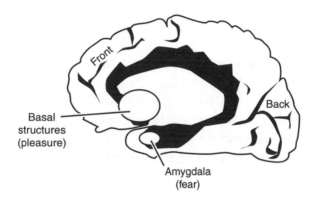

The fear region is called the *amygdala*. This is a little bit of an over-simplification, since the amygdala also plays a role in other emotions, but fear and its related emotions such as anger and rage seem to originate primarily in the amygdala, which is a distinct structure with the shape and approximate size of an almond.

Pleasure regions in the brain are less well defined than fear regions and have not been localized to a single lump of tissue. But they do seem to be in the same general region of the brain. This region, as shown in the illustration above, is deep below the front cortex. Let's call the structures in this area the *basal structures*.[7] You should recognize that this is my own term, and you will generally not find it used this way in neuroscience books.

My Student Tony and Me

Before we look at what the amygdala, basal structures, and cingulate cortex do, let me tell you a story that will help illustrate some of the points I will try to make here. Then we can return to the story at the end of the chapter to see if our brain biology has done us any good.

*   *   *

Tony was one of those tall, good-looking, dark-haired, young men who usually get the benefit of the doubt when doubts arise. He was cocky, not at all self-conscious, and charming. A freshman, Tony was mostly interested in improving his chances with the girls in the class, and I could see he expected success in that arena.

Now I am a serious person and I take learning seriously. I expect my students to show that they are trying, and I found myself irritated with Tony. His whispered smart remarks from the back row, and the giggles they elicited got to me, I admit.

I reacted to Tony by encouraging him to get into the class discussion. He resisted this, and we settled into battle mode. As he realized I was serious, Tony's body language began to change. The jokes and giggles subsided, but, still in the back row, his posture was slouched, his legs spread and extended straight in front of him, his arms up and hands clasped behind his head. He looked away from me, but not far away—just over my left shoulder, if I recall. Every part of his body said, "I don't care! And I want you to know it!"

Tony didn't know he was doing this. He was surprised when one day one of his classmates said, "You must be really mad at Zull!" Tony looked up, startled, and replied, "What do you mean?" "I can tell by the way you sit" came the reply, and suddenly Tony saw it. His face turned pink and when I wasn't looking, he slowly straightened in his chair and began looking at his assignment.

It was striking. As Tony studied his assignment, his body began to relax. Almost for the first time, it seemed, he was cognitively involved in class. As we went on, he began to take notes, and he physically bent over his work. He began to relax, and so did I.

*   *   *

Tony's behavior (and mine) probably rings a bell with anyone who has tried to teach a class. The story illustrates the emotional brain at work in the intense dynamic of the teacher-student relationship. As we will see, the amygdala, the basal structures, and the anterior cingulate all played their part in this story.

The Amygdala and the Teacher

We have called the amygdala the fear center. Another, perhaps more useful, name would be the danger center or the negative emotion center. Our amygdala says, "This is bad for me!" It is taking care to be sure that we react to bad developments.

The amygdala is located at the end of that sidewise C under what we have called the back cortex. In chapter 2 we said this part of our cerebral cortex is mainly for analyzing our experience and making meaning of it. This certainly fits our idea of what the amygdala does. It helps decide meaning; it does not solve problems, create new ideas, or plan new actions.

Once again the structure of the brain supports an idea for teachers. Experience is always monitored for danger. We don't need to know all the details, but some physical facts about the amygdala seem relevant for teachers. Perhaps the most important one is that the amygdala gets its information rather directly from concrete experience. In his book *The Emotional Brain,* LeDoux describes how sensory signals go directly to the amygdala, bypassing the sensory cortex *before we are even aware of them.*[8] This so-called "lower" route begins to make meaning of our experience before we have begun to understand it cognitively and consciously. Our amygdala is constantly monitoring our experience to see how things are.

When we want to help someone learn, we should be aware that our learner will be quickly and subconsciously monitoring the situation through her amygdala. This isn't something she decides to do. It just happens.

Our learner may be wary already, since, after all, she is confronted with someone who may want to take control. What else would an "instructor" do? When the amygdala senses this danger, or some other possible danger, it sends signals directly out to the body, and these signals are also subconscious. They produce body language, and in an extreme case, they may directly trigger body movements such as jumping back, pulling someone out of danger, or running away. These ancient survival mechanisms are still at work in all our brains.

The dominance of these amygdalar processes may not be obvious to us at first. To help realize how strong they are, you might remember the 2000 presidential election in the USA. Even people who were known for keeping their cool were overcome by anger and negative emotion. The Sunday morning talking heads literally became the screaming heads! Amygdalar activity was apparent everywhere.

There is another side to the amygdala story. In some situations the amygdala becomes *less* active than normal, and negative emotions seem to diminish. An example of this is the response of the amygdala when we see happy faces. When that happens the amygdala seems to become less active than it is under normal conditions. It seems to drop its guard a bit.

Of great interest to teachers, the same thing seems to happen when the cortical brain becomes involved in cognitive tasks. For example, if someone puts her mind to solving a puzzle, the amygdala becomes less active.

This seems to be a good sign for the teacher! If we learn how to get our students more involved in their work, they will feel *less* nervous and afraid. If we focus on the work itself rather than the extrinsic reward, the intrinsic reward systems can begin to engage.

Brain Structures for Pleasure

Parts of the brain that contribute to feelings of pleasure, joy, satisfaction, fulfillment, or happiness may be even older than the amygdala.[9] If that is so, it seems uplifting. Maybe positive emotions are even more fundamental than negative ones. Maybe love is more important than fear.

As I mentioned previously, these structures in the brain are located deep and low beneath the front cortex. One such structure is called the *septum*. Stimulation of the clusters of cells in this region causes animals to enjoy themselves immensely. For example, cats begin to purr, groom, play, and rub their bodies against any object in their vicinity.[10] Also, the pleasure drug cocaine and the intrinsic opiate compounds, enkephalins and endorphins, bind strongly to another part of the basal structures, the *globus pallidus*.

These findings and others suggest that noncortical structures beneath the front cortex are involved in positive emotion. The connection between the front cortex and happiness goes further. The generation of feelings of well-being has also been linked strongly to the release of dopamine throughout the front cortex. Since dopamine is thought to be the primary chemical modulator of good feeling, the places it is found in the brain are also implicated in the positive emotion,[11] so the entire front cortex is also implicated. Dopamine also binds to one of the basal structures near the septum, the nucleus accumbens, and this binding is greatly enhanced in cocaine addicts.[12]

Pleasure and Movement

The anatomical location of brain systems associated with pleasure suggests something about the origin of pleasure and the role of these brain systems in learning.

Remember that the front cortex is about action. It is the place where goal-oriented activity is controlled and ideas about actions are generated. In fact, some neuroscientists suggest that the role of dopamine in reward is to produce a "go" signal.[13] That is, the dopamine may not be the reward itself, but rather it may produce action, which is the reward.

It might not surprise you to hear that some of the basal structures are associated with action. For one thing, they regulate the actions needed for us to satisfy our drives such as thirst, hunger, and reproduction. They also are the central structures for control of complex pathways of activation and inhibition that produce coordinated and useful voluntary muscle contractions. They produce actions of great value.

Is there, then, a connection between happiness and movement? Is it possible that activity in these movement centers of the brain also generates pleasure?

At a basic level, this seems to make sense. Play, sex, dance, music, games, eating, talking, and many other pleasures all involve physical movement.[14] But can we take it further than this direct connection with body movement? I suggest we can.

My argument is that we also get enjoyment and satisfaction through anticipation of movement and imagined movement. We see this in progress toward a goal, such as when we solve a puzzle, derive an equation, or construct a work of art or a piece of furniture. And we see it in stories that lead our minds toward a goal. In fact, this is probably the most important thing that keeps us reading a good book or watching a movie. We want something to happen, or we are curious about what will happen—anticipated movement!

Success is progress toward a goal, and nothing succeeds like success. This could be one of the most important aspects of intrinsic motivation. *Achievement* itself is rewarding, and that may simply be because it is recognized as movement.

It goes on and on. When we feel deeply affected by something, we say we are "moved" or "speak of a moving experience." On the flip side, restriction of movement is painful. Loss of our freedom to move is used for punishments ranging from incarceration to making a child stand in the corner.

A rationale for such a connection between movement and pleasure can be found in the fact that movement lets us discover new things. Random reflex movements are the first step as a child learns to turn her eyes and then her head toward sounds. Exploring the results of random movements then leads to laughing, walking, running, and eventually speaking. Natural selection required that we move our bodies, and one way to achieve that, the most productive way, is to connect pleasure with movement. It is how we make discoveries, how we encounter the world, and how we learn.

Passive and Active Learning

The postulated connection between the basal structures and pleasure leads to an interesting prediction about passive versus active learning. Specifically, any learning that involves some sense of progress and control by the learner might be expected to engage the basal structures. This would be learning that is pleasurable. On the other hand, learning that involves recall of associations would be more connected with the back part of the cerebral cortex, the receiving part of the brain. This learning might be less pleasurable and require more effort.

These qualitative generalizations fit our general experience. We know that memorizing associations is hard work. The payoff is that we gain specifics and details because the associations are precise. There are right answers!

On the other hand, active learning that involves choice and actions by the learner is pleasurable and effective for developing concepts and applications. This type of learning gives an understanding of the big picture and the relationships in a topic.

A recent brain imaging study bears out these predictions about the brain and different types of learning. Poldrack and his colleagues[15] found that activation of the basal structures occurred when the learner was engaged in postulating answers and getting feedback on them, an active learning setting. But when the learner was simply asked to memorize associations, the basal structures were less active and the back areas of cortex near the memory systems were more active.

The authors of this paper stress the competition between these two types of learning, but our interest is that a learning protocol where the learner could sense movement by getting feedback on her own propositions triggered the basal structures, while direct memorization did not. It seems that the more pleasurable learning protocol engaged the basal structures.

A Center for Control?

When we eventually figure everything out, the anterior cingulate could turn out to be the most interesting part of the brain. Damasio suggests that this region is key for social reasoning, especially judging the outcome of behaviors. For example, it is the part of the brain responsible for our ability to recognize that we should not undress in public and to decide not to do so! Damasio ties this in with a broader picture of reasoning; in his research he has described how people make intelligent, and often useful, intuitive decisions that depend on their emotions and occur without conscious thought.[16] We will discuss this entanglement of emotion and reasoning in the next chapter.

Another fascinating emotion proposed for the anterior cingulate is the "urge to speak." Certainly part of the control we believe we have in our lives comes through our belief in the power of speech. We are quite convinced that if we can talk, if we can just explain, everyone will understand. We can gain, or regain, control.

What Happened to Tony

One of the best things about brain research is that it helps us realize what is going on as we live our normal lives. As I began to recognize that all these little bits of behavior come from a physical structure in the head, I thought differently about them. I found myself accepting student and teacher behaviors as natural results of the physical world, rather than tending to make judgments about them. And I felt that this made me more professional as a teacher.

My story about Tony may illustrate this. In the past I might have dismissed Tony as a "student from hell." For better or worse, I now view Tony in a totally different way. It goes something like this.

*   *   *

At first Tony acted for his own pleasure. I suspect that his front brain had the idea of sexual conquest. If so, this was a pleasant idea, and his pleasure centers generated action and anticipated some action! He flirted, joked, and used typical male ways of seeking attention. Whether he was aware or unaware of his courtship behavior, he just couldn't be still if he was to engage those pleasure centers.

But it seems that when I entered the picture, Tony sensed danger. His amygdala warned him that he might be in some trouble. His life was not threatened, but he may have sensed that he might lose some things he valued, not the least of which might have been his pride or his sense of control. He began to evaluate his situation and his options; his anterior cingulate was in high gear, trying to make judgments about what actions he would take.

In the meantime, Tony's amygdala was sending signals to his subconscious movement control system in his front brain and he completely changed his actions. The muscles he began to use and how he used them were driven by negative emotions, and he took on postures and behaviors characteristic of challenge.

Tony's brain was also fighting for control. I was trying to make him change, and his control center resisted that. We would call it stubbornness, but really it was just his control brain responding to the amygdala. He had pretty much decided that he *would not learn* from me!

Tony only decided to take a different tack when he got new information from his classmate. The way this new information came was of great importance. It wasn't in the form of reprimand or persuasion from me, which might well have been fruitless, but simply an observation from a third party, someone who was not engaged in the struggle. Tony's brain felt free to interpret this information on its own, and he began to feel back in control.

In the end, as he became engaged in his cognitive work, Tony's amygdala calmed down. He found new pleasure in regaining control of his own brain, he took on new body language, and he began to do good work.

Our Trade and Our Art

In this chapter I have focused on emotion and its influence on motivation, attitude, and behavior in the teacher-learner relationship. I have tried to show the natural fit between learning and living. Since living is about what we want, we are not surprised to find that learning will also be about what we want. We will always be motivated to learn things that fit into what we want and to resist those that don't, especially things that look like potential threats to our happiness or that seem as if they might take away our control of our lives. Specific structures in our brain deal with this type of thing, and they still function powerfully in our modern human brain. This is the way we evolved and the way we are, so part of the art of changing the brain must be built on these biological realities.

But there is more to this story of emotion and learning. In fact, I worry that I may have given the impression that emotion is driven *just* by certain parts of the brain. You might think that emotion and cognition are physically separated in the brain, and that would be too simple. In fact, we could argue that the entire brain is an organ of emotion, and that emotion, reason, and memory are all linked together. Learning is even more our trade and our art than we have realized!

We will see why in the next chapter.

Notes

1. Some argue that the abilities of the human brain go far beyond what we needed for survival. For example, see Steven Pinker, *How the Mind Works* (New York: W. W. Norton, 1998). Pinker asserts that music has no value for survival. But that is hard to judge. Maybe we can't think of its value for survival, but that does not prove there is none. We might discover it later.

2. To put this number in perspective, it may help to realize that cellular life is thought to have begun about 4 billion years ago. If the human cortex appeared sometime between 40 million and 4 million years ago, this would be about one one-thousandth to one one-hundredth of the evolutionary time up to then.

3. Some emotional responses may be instinctive rather than learned. One possible example is a fear of movements or shapes that resemble snakes. We may also react spontaneously with fear or pleasure to facial expressions.

4. A. Kohn, *Punished by Rewards: The Trouble with Gold Stars, Incentive Plans, A's, Praise, and Other Bribes* (New York: Houghton Mifflin, 1983), Chapter 8.

5. J. LeDoux, *The Emotional Brain* (New York: Putnam, 1997), pp. 85–103.

6. A. W. McDonald III and colleagues, *Science* (2000), 288 p. 1385; T. J. Maddock, *Trends in Neuroscience* (July 22, 1999), p. 310; and J. D. Greene and colleagues, *Science* 293 (2001), p. 2105.

7. Pleasure-related structures include the basal ganglia, basal nuclei, ventral striatum, and septum. All of these are noncortical and are found deep in the brain.

8. *The Emotional Brain*, 160–170.

9. P. D. MacClean, *The Triune Brain in Evolution* (New York: Plenum Press, 1990), Chapter 2.

10. Ibid., pp. 344–345.

11. The exact function of dopamine remains unclear. It may be a producer of pleasure, or it may draw our attention to things that look like pleasure. But it is clear that dopamine is somehow tied importantly into what the brain ends up wanting. Maybe a good way to define dopamine would be to call it the "wanting" molecule. See S. Wickelgren, *Science* 278 (1997), pp. 35–37.

12. C. Pert and S. Snyder, *Science* 179 (1973), p. 1011; M. Herkenham and C. Pert, *Proceedings of the National Acadamy of Sciences*, USA 77 (1980), p. 5532; J. K. Staley and D. C. Mash, *Journal of Neuroscience* 16 (1996), p. 6100.

13. E. T. Rolls, *The Brain and Emotion*, (New York: Oxford Press, 1999), p. 199.

14. MacClean *(The Triune Brain)* also discusses the connection between pleasure and movement, as does C. Hannaford in her clever and intriguing book, *Smart Moves: Why Learning is Not All in Your Head* (Arlington, Va.: Great Ocean, 1995).

15. R. A. Poldrack and colleagues, *Nature* 414 (2001), p. 546.

16. A. Damasio, *Descartes' Error: Emotion, Reason, and the Human Brain* (New York: Grosset/Putnam, 1994); A. Bechard and colleagues, "Deciding Advantageously Before Knowing the Advantageous Strategy," *Science* 275 (1997), p. 1293.

5

A FEELING
OF THIS BUSINESS

IN THE BUSINESS OF REASON
AND MEMORY, FEELINGS COUNT

Has this fellow no feeling of this business that he sings at grave-making?
—*William Shakespeare (Hamlet)*

I met Kerry many years ago when he first became an assistant professor. We both taught biology, but Kerry liked to use a lot of mathematics in his teaching. This upset his students, who believed that they
would escape math by studying biology!

As you might predict, Kerry began to have problems. True, many
students were unhappy, but the bigger problem seemed to be with
Kerry himself. He was disappointed. "These students can't do even simple math!" he would complain.

Over the years Kerry developed a short fuse for these frustrations.
It took little to trigger an outburst. I admit that on occasion I would
even avoid him if I could, just because I knew what was coming.

But I have to give him credit. Kerry didn't give in. He just worked
harder. He developed a course to improve the math skills of biology
students. He spent hours with students who struggled. And he wasn't
unappreciated. Some students were grateful that he cared, and he was
nominated for teaching awards more than once.

One day I couldn't avoid Kerry, and he confronted me with his lat-
est story. But right away I sensed this one was different. He was

bemused and provoked—not provoked in a negative way, but provoked into thinking.

"The other day I derived an equation for a student," he said, "and she seemed to understand it. But then, out of the blue, she floored me with her question."

"You know what she asked?" he went on. "She looked right at me and said, 'How did you know how to do that? How do you know how to derive equations?'"

"She had me!" Kerry exclaimed. "I couldn't answer. I just have a feeling for it!" Then, after a pause, he went on. "And I don't know how to teach that feeling."

Maybe I'm wrong, but it seemed that this made him sad.

* * *

A former president of our university, who worried that our undergraduates were not serious enough, coined the phrase, "Learning is suffering." His claim provided material for good-natured joking over the following years, but it also provoked our uncertainties. Could it be true? Must we suffer if we are to learn?

These days, we are more likely to hear another view: "Learning is fun." This has a good ring to it, but what happens if we focus on the fun too much? Can learning happen if education depends only on jokes, games, and entertainment? If it is fun, is it always learning?

The conflict in these different perspectives is similar to the difference between Hamlet and the grave digger implied in the quote that opens this chapter. Must the grave digger suffer, as Hamlet implies? Or should he find happiness in his work? It is tricky for a grave digger.

It is tricky for a teacher, too. We sense that suffering and singing are both part of learning. We know that feelings affect rationality and memory and that these effects can be both bad and good for learning. The permutations are extensive. We will have to be sophisticated about feelings if we are to help people learn!

Strange as it may seem, understanding the brain can help us in this task. When we examine more about how the brain is wired and how the brain interacts with the body, we can see why things are so complex, but we can also see what is realistic and what is not. We begin to recognize both our limits and our opportunities. We begin to get a feeling for this business.

Feelings

In chapter 4, we focused mostly on the subconscious role of emotion. When we become aware of our emotions, we call them *feelings*. So emotion and feelings are not the same. The difference is also obvious when we remember that feelings are in the body. To feel is to sense things, and we sense things with our bodies. Emotions in the brain produce feelings in the body.

This idea was proposed by William James in his oft-quoted example of a hypothetical encounter with a bear.[1] Imagine that you are taking a peaceful walk in the woods, when suddenly you see a large bear running straight toward you. Probably you would run away as fast as you can. Later, assuming that you still exist, you would tell your friends and family, "I never ran so fast in my life! I was so scared!"

But James claimed fear wasn't what made you run. You would be bear lunch if you waited until you felt fear. It just doesn't come that fast. He separated emotion and feeling in time. First you see the bear, then your brain reacts with emotion, then you run, and finally you feel fear.

The biologist of today might put it like this: your sensory brain sends signals to your amygdala when you see a bear. The amygdala then sends signals to the motor control systems in your front cortex, and you start running like mad! If you survive, you will feel the fear in your body, but that will come last.

The Body Talks to the Brain, and Vice Versa

Even though we tend to think of the mind, and even the brain, as somehow separate from our grubby body, the truth is that the brain is as much a part of the body as is our liver. Learning engages the brain and other parts of the body as well. As Carla Hannaford says, "Learning is not all in your head."[2]

The brain interacts with the other parts of the body in two different ways. First, millions of cellular wires (see chapter 6) carry signals back and forth. This is the way the brain senses what is happening moment by moment in and around the rest of the body and the way it sends out instructions for what the body should do.

Second, the brain produces chemicals that are dumped into the bloodstream, and these chemicals are specific messengers about what the brain is experiencing. Likewise, various parts of the rest of the body produce chemicals that are picked up by the brain and tell the brain what is happening in the body.

These chemical messages are slower than the wiring and can be less precise. But they are compelling. They are responsible for our feelings, our inclinations to do things, or our awareness of the qualitative nature of what we are sensing. Feelings give texture to events and implicit signals that we may not be able to label immediately. But they persist, and eventually they are expressed, sometimes in ways that we understand and sometimes in ways that surprise us.

One of the most ancient parts of the brain, the *hypothalamus,* is responsible for the release of chemical signals from the brain into the bloodstream. This structure is located just underneath the basal structures discussed in chapter 4, and it gets a lot of input both from these structures and from the amygdala. This allows the hypothalamus to send messages about the emotional state of our brain out into the body.

For example, if we are in danger, the amygdala starts sending signals to the hypothalamus, and this triggers a signal for danger that goes to the adrenal glands near our kidneys (and far from the brain), and these glands then release adrenaline into our bloodstream. Adrenaline, of course, makes our heart beat faster and generates a tension that ultimately is relieved by either running away or turning to fight. In addition, adrenaline has been shown to inhibit the front-cortex functions, such as judgment and reasoning. It is hard to think and make good decisions when we feel afraid.

More than a dozen of these "feeling" chemicals are known, and it seems certain that many others remain to be discovered. Another immensely interesting one is oxytocin, which triggers complex maternal behaviors and even the feeling of affection.[3]

The hypothalamus also gets chemical information that tells the brain what is going on systemically throughout the whole body. For example, it tells us if our sugar level is low and we should eat. It tells us this through a feeling: hunger. Of course, hunger does not automatically result in eating. It just makes us want to eat. This is how feelings work.

My Friend Kerry and the Role of Feelings in Reason

If we look at our language, we can find many metaphors that suggest a connection between the body, feelings, and thinking: "I feel that you are right." "My gut tells me." "Something bothers me about that."

"I'm not comfortable with that idea." "That proof isn't satisfying." It goes on and on.

We might even say that there is no such thing as cold reason. Reason seems to be always driven by emotion and need. It seems unlikely that reason could ever occur without emotion.

I tried to illustrate this in my story about Kerry at the beginning of the chapter. If anyone ever believed in reason, Kerry was that person. Yet, when his student asked that unanswerable question, "How did you know to do that?" he was brought up short. He recognized that underneath his cold reason was a complex mesh of feeling. He could not give instructions for reasoning because he could not describe either how this feeling worked or how his students could get it for themselves.

I have tried many times to think of cognitive tasks that do not involve feelings. So far, I have failed. Let me show you another example.

Try a math problem. Let's multiply 31 by 41. This seems like a case where we use our cognitive brain to make a cold calculation. But how do we know our answer is right? Ultimately, it is a decision based on a belief. We can check out the answer by dividing it back with 31 or 41, and that will increase our confidence, but still that confidence is a feeling. And we won't move on until we have that feeling. Knowing is a feeling.

Not only is knowing a feeling, *getting to knowing* is full of feeling. We feel progress as we do our first step in the multiplication. We feel confidence. But if our answer is challenged, we feel uncertainty—a tiny bit of fear. We feel motivated to prove our answer. And so it goes. Every part of this simple cognitive act seems to be driven or evaluated by a feeling.

I think this is what Damasio means by his term, *somatic marking*,[4] or "body marking," in which our body can develop certain feelings associated with specific cognitive tasks. Those feelings are part of cognition. Our emotional centers trigger our hypothalamus, and the wiring of the brain in our bodies, to produce characteristic body feelings as we struggle with problems and solve them. Specific feelings in our body go with the specific problem-solving tasks we undertake with our brain.

Wiring Emotion to Thinking

All this interaction between feelings and rationality suggests the existence of connections between the reasoning centers and the emotion centers in our brain. How else could it work?

Part of this wiring is illustrated in the picture below, which shows connections between the amygdala and the neocortex. Signals travel from the cortex to the amygdala, and vice versa. These reciprocal connections occur both with the back cortex and the front cortex.

The outgoing connections from the amygdala travel primarily to regions of the cortex that are involved in the memory part of reflection (temporal cortex) and the creative and judgment part of abstraction (frontal and anterior cingulate). This suggests that the amygdala is set up to influence memory, ideas, plans, and judgment.

You might also notice that more connections run *from* the amygdala to the cortex than those that run the other way. LeDoux suggests that this explains why emotions tend to overpower cognition, rather than the reverse. That is, our emotions influence our thinking more than our thinking influences our emotion.[5]

The connections of the basal structures (pleasure centers) and the limbic cortex with the neocortex are very extensive and are too complex to illustrate clearly here. Both of these "emotion" regions receive signals from the sensory and integrative cortex. Some of the basal structures then modulate output to the motor cortex, releasing some actions and inhibiting others. They play a major role in the control of our actions.

The anterior and posterior cingulate get information from the entire limbic cortex by way of an internal cable running completely around from back to front. In addition, some of the most direct connections made by the anterior cingulate, are with the basal structures, the amygdala, and the hypothalamus. These connections are strong and go in both directions.[6] In sum, all the structures known to influence emotion and feelings are connected with each other and with the entire neocortex.

Battle for Attention

Even though it may run contrary to common belief, there is good reason to think that feelings are essential for rationality. On the other hand, we all know that feelings can interfere with reason, even destroy it. Is this a contradiction? How can feeling be both good and bad for rationality?

One explanation is that we are capable of having many feelings at once. Even while we are making progress in some thought problems and feeling good about it, we may suddenly be distracted by new, and more compelling, feelings. Some feelings demand our attention. They take our mind off our thinking. Good thinking requires that we pay attention, but that is hard to do if someone threatens us. We may have trouble paying attention to an abstract problem when our amygdala is sending danger signals to our logical brain. And the same is true of our pleasure centers. Logic and its pleasures can suddenly seem inconsequential when we see an attractive person of the opposite sex.

The issue here is competition. And the brain function is *attention*. This is an important subject that will keep arising. We will not be able to discuss it adequately, but one fairly simple idea is suggested by recent brain research. Different sensory signals physically compete for attention in the brain, and those that are the strongest win out.[7] It is a physical battle.

If reason is to win out, it must produce stronger feelings than the competition!

A Specific Competition

Feelings become especially distracting when we really care about the answer to a problem. If the answer is important to us, our feelings become distracting. The feeling of wanting a particular result is powerful, and it can win out in its competition with rationality. It screams for attention.

There are countless examples of this. Scientists fight it all the time. For example, we may hope our experiments turn out in a particular way, and that hope can interfere with our ability to look at all the data and apply "cold reason." We want the true answer, but we also want *our* answer. These feelings compete.

This is an important negative effect of feelings on rationality. But it is not a moral issue. It isn't a sign of weak character when our reason is distorted by our feelings. It's just nature at work. We all pay the most attention to the things that matter the most in our life.

What about discipline? Can't we just discipline our brains to ignore distractions? Most of us tend to think we can. But we can miss a key point. If self-discipline is to work, we must care about discipline more than the other things that vie for our attention. We can achieve discipline when we *feel* that discipline is what we want the most.

Ultimately we are at the mercy of our feelings, and if we are ever to become artful teachers, we must attend to this battle for attention. We must find some way to encourage our learners to *want* to use their reason.

Anita's Memory

The rest of this chapter is about memory and feelings. I won't even try to discuss memory in any detail, but a few points will help us think about the complexity of the subject and the challenges for a teacher.

Let's start with another story. This one is about one of my premedical students. It is firmly fixed in my memory because it remains a mystery. It interests and puzzles me, so I remember it well.

*   *   *

Anita was a bit of a loner. She sat near the front of my class, but off to my left side. This meant I faced in her direction most often, since like most right-handed teachers, I tended to stand at the right side and naturally looked more often toward the left. (Bad teaching technique, by the way!)

Where she sat turned out to be important. She was trying to get the most "face time." She needed to see me and watch my lips and face as I talked.

Anita was memorizing my lecture! She did take notes, and she wrote down the chemical structures I put on the board, but Anita was memorizing my exact words.

I found this out when she began to come in to see me outside of class. She would ask me something, and sometimes when I would answer, she would look at me and say, "That's not what you said in class!" And she would repeat an exact sentence she remembered from class!

This was surprising, but I didn't really begin to worry about Anita until I noticed something else. It was the words themselves that she remembered, not the concepts. That was why she got so upset when I used different words.

So, I did worry about Anita. I expected that she would have trouble with exams, but I was in for another surprise. She consistently teetered on the brink of an A for most of the semester and eventually ended up with a high B.

Anita's story would probably be just a curiosity, except for what happened a few months later. I was walking through the halls on my way to my office, when I came face to face with her. She was with a friend, and after we exchanged greetings, she began to introduce me to her companion. "This is my ———," she began. Then she looked at me and said, "What subject do you teach again? I take so many courses I forget which is which!" and she laughed happily.

Maybe I am making too much of this, but I never got over it. Anita could remember my exact words in a lecture as long as she needed to, but once the need was over, she even forgot what courses she had taken!

Approaches to Memory

Again, I have given you a dramatic example of the points I want to make. Both Anita's ability to remember—and her ability to forget—seem extreme. But I am sure that you have had similar experiences. People often struggle to recall even a single major point about some subject they thought they had learned. This is one reason it is so hard to define learning. We only need ask, "How long does learning last?" to see the problem.

If we don't use or repeat things, our memory grows dim. And yet, if something made sense to us or engaged us emotionally, we also can recall amazing amounts of detail in the short term and sometimes in the long term, too.

Memory is a complicated business for the teacher. We want students to remember but not to memorize! And of course, this was exactly my concern about Anita. She memorized but did not remember.

Anita typifies one approach to memory. She memorized in order to learn. But there is a second approach—to learn so we can remember. These seem like polar opposites. In one we make a frontal attack on facts, charging directly into memorization. In the other, we wait for memory to emerge, almost as a side product from the process of learning.

Time and Memory

Of course, memory is about time.[8] Part of having a good memory is to recall things long after they happened. But there is also value in remembering things only for a short time. We may need information for just an instant to solve a problem, but then it is actually an advantage to *forget* that information and briefly replace it with something else that is important for solving the problem.

This is using memory to accomplish a task rather than as an information source, and this type of memory is called *working memory,* or *short-term memory.* In a way, it is more about forgetting than it is about remembering, since we need to empty the short-term memory space in order to put something else there.

Long-term memory is not just extended short-term memory. The two are qualitatively different. We won't go into details of these differences here, but the topic will come up in chapters 9 and 10.

What We Remember

Long-term memory is that mix of feeling and fact that allows us to recall, or more accurately, reassemble information that comes from our lifetime of learning.[9] We can divide the things in our long-term memory into two categories: those that we are conscious of (*explicit*) and those that we aren't (*implicit*). Our brain is full of large amounts of both, and our understanding of what we learn is powerfully influenced by both.

You may not have thought much about implicit memory. That would be natural, since it is, after all, implicit. But implicit memories exist, and they influence how we feel, how we respond, and what we can do. These are things that we do unconsciously like walking or reacting spontaneously in specific situations. We aren't aware of remembering them.

LeDoux gives us an example of implicit memory in a story that a French physician, Edouard Claparede, told about one of his patients who suffered from severe amnesia.[10] The amnesia was so bad that this patient could never recall meeting Claparede, even though they visited hundreds of times. Each time they met, the patient would introduce himself to Claparede and shake his hand. However, one day Claparede hid a pin in his hand, so when they shook hands and introduced themselves to each other for the hundredth time, the patient was pricked by the pin. And yes, the next time they met, this patient suddenly withdrew his hand when the ritual handshake was offered by his doctor. He didn't know why, but he was afraid to shake hands.

This distinction between explicit memory and implicit memory has many implications for a teacher. Behaviors, beliefs, and feelings can all be stored in implicit memory, so when we want to help someone learn we must watch for these as well as for what they remember explicitly. People may know more than they are able to tell us.

People may also learn more than we explicitly tell them. This takes us back to our discussion of experiential learning in chapter 2 and the idea that many implicit ideas in a teaching experience have nothing to do with what is said.

Our common experience, however, is with explicit memory. This is what we want to see when we are trying to help people learn. We often make decisions and judgments about our students based absolutely on their explicit memory. People's lives are changed by the effectiveness of their explicit memory system.

It is common to divide explicit memory into two types, *semantic* and *episodic*. Semantic memories are facts, labels, and names of things. They are the most concrete of our memories. Often they are the things that show up on multiple-choice tests or game shows like "Who Wants to Be a Millionaire." To a great extent, we run our lives on semantic memories: our address, our birthday (and hopefully that of our spouse), names of streets, towns, friends, faces, and so on, endlessly.

Episodic memories are stories. They are the memories we reweave as we recreate an event or an episode in our life. They may be the memories that we are most confident about, but they are probably the most likely to contain errors simply because it is the nature of the episode we remember, not the details.

When we want to help people learn, it helps to be aware that they may not be able to tell us all that they remember, and that when they do tell us their memories, some parts may be wrong. Teachers might be right not to trust memory when they assess learning!

Memory and the Brain

Memories don't seem to be located in any particular place in the brain. If anything, they are probably spread out in several different places. For example, a memory of a visual experience may be stored in several parts of the sensory brain, and memory for sequences, or the order of things, has been localized to the motor brain.[11]

But the processes of *recall* and *formation* of memories have been localized to specific parts of the cerebral cortex. Recall of semantic memories engages the left frontal cortex and parts of the back cortex on both sides, while recall of episodic memories seems to engage the right frontal cortex as well as the back cortex.[12] On the other hand, formation of explicit memories requires a special structure in the back cortex (temporal cortex) called the *hippocampus,* but formation of implicit memories probably does not. Thus, there is a biological basis for separation of the different kinds of memory in addition to a psychological one.

A Place for Making Memories

Long-term explicit memories are formed in the hippocampus. This is a strange name, and it may be hard for you to store it as a semantic memory, but maybe we can use episodic memory and put a story around it. The story is that when the hippocampus was first identified, it reminded people of a sea horse with its curled tail. Thus, it was named with the Greek term that means horse-shaped (hippo) sea monster (kampos.)

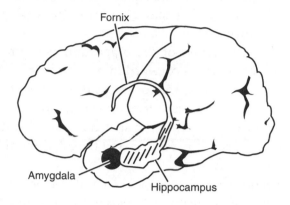

Fornix

Amygdala

Hippocampus

Like the amygdala, the hippocampus is buried beneath the integrative cortex of the temporal lobe. The picture above shows roughly where it is buried and what it looks like from the side. The curved tail-like structure attached to the body of the hippocampus (fornix), which inspired its sea horse name, can be seen in this figure.

A fairly early discovery about the hippocampus was that this part of the brain is involved in remembering location, or place. Since remembering where things are—things like food or enemies—is essential for survival, this type of memory is fundamental.

But the hippocampus is now known to have a broader function in long-term memory. In fact, it is now thought to be on the route taken by all the information in the surrounding integrative cortex of the back cortex. The current idea is that sensory input, which has been integrated into images, patterns, faces, sounds, and location, all finds its way there. It seems that when information of this sort associated with a particular event or "episode" arrives at the hippocampus, it becomes assembled into an even bigger picture of the episode itself. All the parts of the memory are associated with each other, and it becomes "a memory." The hippocampus is the master integrator.

But it does not store the memories itself. Rather the integrated information finds its way back to various parts of the cortex in a form that is susceptible to recall, or reassembly, any time later.

Memory and Feelings

The hippocampus, then, sends its signals back to the cortex that surrounds it. But there is another major pathway for signals to leave the hippocampus, the fornix.

If you look at the picture of the hippocampus again (above), you will see that the fornix circles forward in our familiar C structure. The interesting point for us is that the fornix sends its fibers forward to our old friends, the basal structures buried under the front cortex. A lot of signals from the fornix end up in the structures we identified earlier as potential pleasure centers, the septum and the adjacent nucleus accumbens, for example.

These connections are suggestive. They don't prove anything but are consistent with a connection between feelings and formation of explicit memories. It is worthwhile for teachers to think about how such connection might influence learning.

The hippocampus also sends some signals to the amygdala. Our amygdala may miss the potential danger in some of its raw sensory data, but once that data begins to be assembled into an episode, a threat may become apparent. This explanation for the connection between the hippocampus and the amygdala is speculative but interesting. If we are to avoid danger, we need to recognize things that lurk in our memory as well as in our immediate experiences.

Feelings Help, Feelings Hurt

Let's talk about the contrary effects of feelings on memory. This brings us back to our "learning is suffering" vs. "learning is fun" debate.

You may have experienced this contrariness of the brain in one way or another. You may remember times when you were a little anxious and tense and found it hard to pay attention. But later you realized your memory of the situation seemed clear. The feelings that were part of the experience seemed to help you remember it.

On the other hand, you may have been in real stress for a long time and found that your memory was faulty. The best-known examples of this are situations that soldiers experience in battle, producing "post-traumatic stress disorder (PTSD)," or childhood abuse, where memories sometimes seem to be obliterated.[13] These effects have been studied biologically. Let's look briefly at each one.

The damage that intense feelings can do to long-term memory is probably a direct effect of our body talking to our brain by way of the chemicals circulating in our blood. Earlier I described how this activates the "fight or flight" response through the release of adrenaline into the bloodstream.

However, the adrenal gland also releases another chemical into the blood, *cortisol*. This chemical is longer lasting and begins to change our metabolism in slower but more fundamental ways. Of great interest, cortisol seems to have a rather specific effect on cells in the hippocampus. High cortisol levels in the bloodstream can damage cells in the hippocampus and even kill them. Extreme stress can permanently damage our memory centers, and this effect has been implicated in cases of extreme depression and in PTSD.[14]

The good part of the story is the part about tension improving memory. Earlier we talked about adrenaline inhibiting the front cortex and its creative functions, but it has an opposite effect on the back cortex, actually improving the work of the hippocampus and increasing long-term semantic memory.

These positive effects of the short-term stress hormones on memory were studied for many years by James McGaugh,[15] and they are an interesting example of the role of parts of the body other than the brain in memory. McGaugh's first studies showed that injections of adrenaline into the bloodstream (i.e., outside the brain) enhanced memory in rats, and later he discovered a direct effect of the amygdala on adrenaline release in the back cortex. Both brain chemistry and body chemistry alter memory.

False Memories

My student Anita trusted her memory. But I have learned not to trust mine. Not only do I forget, I remember things that didn't happen. I suspect we all do.

Once I watched a Cleveland Cavaliers basketball game against the Chicago Bulls. Michael Jordan was the curse of Cleveland, but this time

the Cavs were winning. I was a rabid fan, and this game was as exciting as any I had seen. I distinctly remember our shortest player, Mark
Price, blocking one of Michael's shots near the end of the game. In fact,
this block was the deciding moment in the game.

Imaging my surprise when the news reports of the game made no
mention of this crucial play by Mark Price. I was so upset I called a
friend who had videotaped the game. And sure enough, nowhere on
that tape could we find my crucial play! It didn't happen. Not at the
end of the game, not earlier in the game, never!

Schacter has studied what happens in the brain during false memories. And, indeed, the brain behaves differently when we recall something that really happened and when we recall something that didn't
happen.[16] His studies showed that the part of the brain that is needed
for memory formation, the part around the hippocampus, was activated
for *both* false memories and true ones. But when a true memory was
recalled, a second part of the brain also became more active. This second part was the region of sensory cortex that was involved in the real
event when it was sensed by the brain. In these experiments, people were
asked to remember spoken words, so recall of words that had actually
been spoken activated the hearing part of the sensory cortex, the auditory cortex. This part of the brain was silent for the false memories.

False memories aren't usually irrelevant. They are memories that
could have happened. They fit into the experience, just like my memory of the ball game. It appears that our hippocampus will assemble
memories that fit the context, even when the sensory data is not there.
There is enough sensory data to build a context, but our brain may fill
in missing details. This seems to be particularly true of the left cortex.

As we will see in later chapters, this ability of the brain to interpo-
late and extrapolate is normally a good thing. It is part of what makes
us creative and intelligent. But with memory, it can be a different story!

Remembering Anita

Earlier in this chapter I told you about my student Anita. She remembered my lectures verbatim and got a good grade in my class, but
couldn't even remember what I taught a few months later. It might be
instructive to think about Anita in terms of some of the biology we
have been discussing. Let's look at the good things first.

It is clear that Anita's brain was effective at forming semantic memory. To do this she had to reduce competing input to a minimum, and she accomplished that by sitting alone and, possibly more importantly, by focusing not only on my words but on my face and body language as well. My guess is that the entire sensory experience of my lecture became part of her memory. A substantial element of implicit memory probably boosted Anita's explicit memory. She took in more than she knew. Other students who focused just on my words may have remembered less.

There are two negative points about Anita's story. First was her reliance on memory. Anita was not using her front cortex much, if at all, in my class. But that could be the result of stress, or challenge, in the class. This would fit the biology we described previously. Anita knew this was a hard class and she got up for it. So, if her adrenaline level was high, her front cortex would be turned down, but her memory centers in the back cortex would be turned up. That trade-off might be an important part of her story.

The other negative point is her loss of memory with regard to the class a few months later. Could this be stress related? Could it be cortisol at work? Like most premedical students, Anita was under at least mild stress all the time. We don't know if this stress is adequate to produce hippocampal damage or not. But it is possible. And one does wonder about an educational system that rewards memory for the moment, driven by stress, rather than memory for the long term. How does the brain deal with that?

However, we know that memories are rebuilt, not drawn out of a file. This rebuilding may take a little time, so maybe Anita's hippocampus was fine. Maybe she just needed more time to rebuild that particular semantic memory during the instant of our encounter in the hall.

A More Unified Picture

Often in science, we examine parts of those things as though they were actually separate from each other. But almost always, the parts we study are actually connected to other parts. This is certainly true for the brain. We study the different parts and talk about what they do, but ultimately we have to look for the more unified view.

Let me point out a few aspects of what we have discussed in this chapter where it seems especially important to discuss the connections and interactions.

I described a separation of the feelings that help us reason from those that damage reason. But in my mind these are not really separate from each other. They are both at work all the time, and it is especially important for teachers to realize this. If we can discern which feelings are helpful and which are damaging, we might even turn the damaging ones into helping ones.

Explicit memory and implicit memory may not be that separate either. Facts and figures of explicit memory are supported by elements of implicit memory. We remember our home address partly because it is associated with implicit feelings and images related to "home." But those implicit feelings and images can become explicit if we become aware of them. Maybe explicit memory and implicit memory require each other!

Episodic memory and semantic memory may also be strongly interconnected. Rote memory may actually not be rote at all. We may "memorize" by brute force, but the actual memory may depend on the context or the feelings we had as we began to succeed in our memorization. In other words, semantic memory may depend on episodic memory, the feelings and stories of our memorizing experiences. For example, we may remember the multiplication tables by remembering the time in our life when we learned them, the feelings we had when we learned them, or even a tune or "beat" associated with our recall of them. (Sing, "abcd efg hijk lmnop!")

At the same time, explicit memories give content to our episodic memories. We will be frustrated and maybe unable to recall a story in our life unless we can put explicit names, places, and faces on the memory. But a single explicit memory can cue an entire episodic memory with all its rich detail and understanding!

Foundation for Learning

Remember that we are trying to develop ideas that can support us as we try to become more artful teachers. We are developing a foundation for learning.

Probably the single most important idea for this foundation in this chapter is that feelings always affect reasoning and memory. This influence of feelings runs the entire gamut of possibilities. Feelings can help us remember and make us forget. They can help us recall important events that did happen, but they can also trigger false memories. They are essential for reasoning, and they can hinder reasoning.

As we develop our ideas for changing the brain, we must keep this part of our foundation in mind. Much depends on the feelings of our learners.

Notes

1. W. James, *Principles of Psychology* (New York: Holt, 1890).
2. C. Hannaford, *Smart Moves: Why Learning Is Not All in Your Head* (*Arlington,* VA: Great Ocean Publishers, 1995).
3. Candice Pert, *Molecules of Emotion* (New York: Touchstone, 1997).
4. A. Damasio, *Descartes' Error: Emotion, Reason, and the Human Brain* (New York: Grosset/Putnam, 1994).
5. J. LeDoux, *The Emotional Brain* (New York: Simon and Schuster, 1996).
6. P. D. MacClean, *The Triune Brain in Evolution* (New York: Plenum, 1990), p. 276.
7. S. Kastner and colleagues, *Science,* 282 (1998), p. 108. Also see review of this research by N. Kanwisher and P. Downing in the same issue.
8. I apologize to the reader for what may seem like a cursory encounter with the subject of memory. You should look in other books like Daniel Schacter's *Searching for Memory* (New York: Basic Books, 1996) or Steven Rose's *The Making of Memory* (New York: Doubleday, 1993) for a more satisfying read.
9. Recent work suggests that the process of remembering requires new synthesis of proteins. It is as if the memory itself has been rebuilt. See K. Nader and colleagues, *Nature* 406 (2000), pp. 722–726.
10. *The Emotional Brain,* p. 180.
11. See review by I. Wickelgren, *Science,* 283 (1999), p. 1617.
12. I. Nyberg, R. Cabeza, and E. Tulving, *PET Studies of Encoding and Retrieval. The HERA Model.* Psychonomic Bulletin and Review, Vol. 3, (1996), p. 135.
13. These memories are not necessarily lost. They may return in a flood.
14. These effects are summarized in a review article by R. M. Sapolsky, *Science,* 273 (1996), p. 749.
15. J. L. McGaugh and P. E. Gold, *Psychoendocrinology* (New York: Academic Press, 1989), pp. 305–339; J. L. McGaugh, *Science,* 287 (996), p. 248; review article by A. F. T. Arnsten, *Science,* 280 (1998), p. 1711.
16. D. Schacter and colleagues, *Neuron,* 17 (1996), p. 267.

SUMMARY
OF PART I

In the first section of this book, I tried to draw attention to some fundamental ideas that underlie any effort we may make to help people learn. There may be some surprises here, or there may not be, but my experience is that these ideas become much more real when we recognize that they come from the way the brain is structured.

Here is a summary of the key words that tell us about our foundation: *experience, reflection, abstraction, action, balance, control, danger, pleasure, movement, feelings,* and *body.* Each of these play a role in thinking about how to help people learn, and the chances that learning will happen become less if we ignore one or more of these in our specific plans and efforts at teaching. This is the foundation we will try to build on in the next section.

PART II
KNOWLEDGE, NEURONAL NETWORKS, CHANGE, AND RECOMMENDATIONS FOR THE TEACHER

What is the physical form of knowledge in the brain? How does this physical structure change during learning? What is the first thing a teacher should consider? How do we help people change their neuronal networks?

6

WHAT WE ALREADY KNOW

TO BEGIN, FIND OUT ABOUT
EXISTING NEURON NETWORKS

The single most important factor influencing learning is what the learner already knows. Ascertain this and teach him accordingly.
—*David Ausubel*

A group of professors sat around the large oak table in our conference room, eating pizza and talking. These "teaching conversations" were surprisingly successful. Our teachers seemed to need times like this when they could talk about their successes and their worries.

At one end of the table sat Thom, a frail-looking physics professor. He was a regular, and we could always count on him for clear insights and comments, delivered in his clipped British accent. We deeply respected Thom's intellect; he made us think—and usually laugh.

But today he was not in a laughing mood. We understood that when he suddenly grabbed a handful of papers and, Frisbee-like, flung them across the table.

"These students can't grasp even simple ideas!" he clipped. "Like those papers! I bet you all know that they would keep moving forever in the absence of any resistance! But my students just don't get it! Conservation of momentum is as foreign to them as Chinese!"

I happened to be sitting at the other end of the table, and Thom's papers stopped right in front of me. I, too, noted that they did not continue on their path forever. But I did know what he meant. If there were no resistance from the air in the room, no friction with the table, and no other resistance anywhere, they would indeed still be sailing along.

I gathered up the papers, thinking what I could say. As nominal leader of the discussion, I should respond somehow. But I found myself at a loss. In fact, it wasn't until later, while driving home from work that it came to me.

"I know what I should have told Thom!" I thought. "I hope I can see him tomorrow. We'll have to talk about neuronal networks!"

* * *

Part I laid a foundation for learning. Now I will try to build on this foundation and develop some specific ideas about helping people learn.

This will require us to look deeper into the structure of the brain to examine the stuff of the brain itself, as it appears through a microscope. What we will see is that the brain is made up of complicated cells connected to one another in an immense network of fibers and branches. The cells are called *neurons,* and the connections create *neuronal networks.*[1]

As amazing as these networks are physically, what they represent is even more amazing. In some ways we could say that when we look at pictures of neuronal networks of a human brain, we see a tiny bit of the knowledge the brain once had in its physical form. Neuronal networks are knowledge.

Prior Knowledge

What do I mean when I say "neuronal networks are knowledge"? How can physical structures created by linkage of cells in the brain be equated to knowledge?

You might think this means knowledge is *stored* in neuronal networks. That is true, but it is incomplete. Not only is knowledge stored in the brain, it is produced by the brain through formation and change in neuronal networks. Any change in knowledge must come from some change in neuronal networks

Although he may not have realized it, Ausubel made a profound biological statement when he staked out *prior knowledge* as the beginning of teaching in the quote at the beginning of this chapter. The biological equivalent of his assertion is:

> The single most important factor in learning is the existing networks of neurons in the learner's brain. Ascertain what they are and teach accordingly.

This does not imply that teachers can look into brains and see neuronal networks, but rather that when we find out what our students already know, we are actually finding out about their neuronal networks. We are discovering the connections they have in their brains.

I will develop three important ideas about prior knowledge in what follows. First, prior knowledge is a fact. All learners, even newborn babies, have some prior knowledge. Learners do not begin with a blank slate. Second, prior knowledge is persistent. The connections in these physical networks of neurons are strong. They do not vanish with a dismissive comment by a teacher or a red mark on a paper. Third, prior knowledge is the beginning of new knowledge. It is always where all learners start. They have no choice.

Thom's Students

It should be apparent by now why I thought I should tell Thom about neuronal networks. It seemed that the student brains in Thom's class simply were not prepared for what he wanted them to learn. The things they already knew and understood just weren't doing the trick. They didn't have the right neuronal networks.

It also seemed that Thom might not have considered the idea of prior knowledge, or if he had, he was suspicious of it. That would not be a surprise. Science teachers especially are leery of what students already believe about the physical world and about physics. For example, students may think that heavier objects fall faster than light ones—despite Galileo. They may believe that only moving things generate force, or they may be convinced that jackets have warmth.[2] Their experience has led them to beliefs like this, and those beliefs can be firmly fixed.

Thom might well have felt that he should stay as far away as possible from the prior knowledge of his students.

An Inescapable Fact

The problem for Thom is that he doesn't have a choice. No one can understand anything if it isn't connected in some way to something they already know. Let me illustrate this.

Imagine you land on a desert island and there you find one other person. This person uses a different language and comes from a different culture. Can you communicate? Sure! But how do you do it? You find something that you both understand. It could be a gesture, a wag of your index finger that says "Come here!" It could be a laugh or a sob. But whatever it is, you must find some prior knowledge that you share.

We could think of Thom and his students the same way. His students all have their own personal prior knowledge about conservation of momentum. They have their own beliefs about what "conservation" means and what "momentum" means. They have their own experiences with moving objects and with things that resist movement or reduce it. Whatever their experience, that is where they start.

If Thom is to communicate with these strangers in the land of physics, he must find some prior knowledge he shares with them.

Neurons

When we speak of prior knowledge, we are speaking of something physical. It builds as brains physically change, and it is held in place by physical connections. We could say that prior knowledge is a thing!

That probably sounds strange. We aren't used to taking these concepts of learning and knowing so literally. But I found that this literal way of thinking was an important step toward understanding how to help people learn. It made me realize that I could not banish wrong ideas simply by stating that they were wrong. This was the beginning of a great change in my teaching methods.

But I don't expect that you will just take my claims on faith. They will have no meaning if you do. These suggestions will just be something that you remember rather than something you understand. You will not have a story that connects with the idea, so your emotional brain will not be involved.

We need the story that lies behind all this. And to tell that story we must begin with the characters in it—the neurons.

Neurons are cells. That may not be obvious when we first look them. Generally, they are small, like almost all cells, but as the illustration below shows, they can look more like a bush in your front yard, or a leafless tree in an Ohio winter, than a cell.

It is all the branches that make neurons look so strange. And the branches can make the cell look quite large, as is the case for the neuron at the bottom. The arrows in the illustration point out that there are actually two different kinds of branches. One branch usually looks somewhat different from the others, if we look closely.

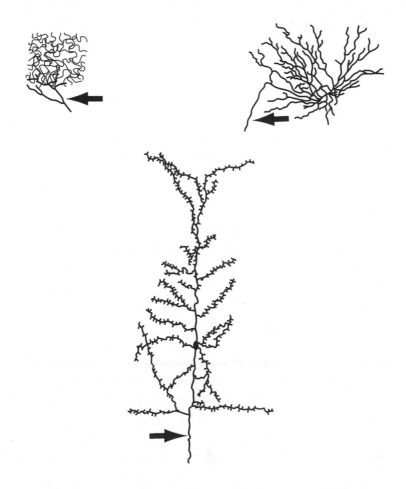

You will notice that the arrows point to a single branch that looks longer and more lonely than the others. These branches are called *axons*.

The rest of the branches are called *dendrites*. In general, the dendrites determine how a neuron looks. These dendrites and the axon branch from a cell body (see next drawing).

This is what our characters look like. What do they do? What is their behavior?

Neurons are sensitive and observant. They pick up signals and send them to other neurons. These signals can come from the outside world in the form of light or sound, for example, or from other neurons. In general, the dendrites pick up the signals and send them toward the center of the cell, the cell body.

Axons, on the other hand, collect the signals coming in from the dendrites and send them together away from the cell body. This process goes on to some extent all the time, and a certain background of this signaling happens randomly.

The last thing we need to know about neurons for our immediate purposes is that they make friends easily. They form connections with other neurons. The axons end by coming up against the dendrites or even the cell body of other neurons. The signals then leap from the axon to the next cell, and if there are enough of these signals, they are carried on in the same way by the second neuron. This place where the signals pass from one neuron to another is knows as a *synapse*.

All of this is very difficult to see in actual pictures of neurons, but the drawing below puts it together in a diagrammatic way. The only things in this drawing I haven't mentioned so far are the bands of material around the axon of the cell on the left. This axon coating is called *myelin,* and it allows the signals to pass much more quickly along the axons, basically jumping from node to node in the myelin covering. When we are first born, many axons in our brain do not have myelin coats, and many never have any. But other axons develop their myelin coating at different times in the development of the brain, and this is an important part of the natural growth in brain abilities and skills.[3]

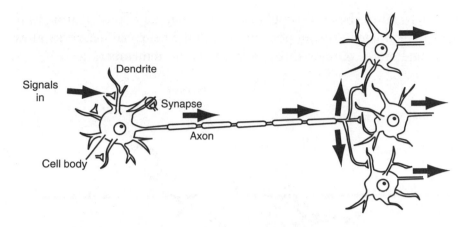

Signals in — Dendrite — Synapse — Axon — Cell body

Neuronal Networks of the Brain

The picture I just described shows a network of four neurons, and it illustrates what I mean when I speak of neuronal networks. You could add in a number of new neurons to this drawing and form a more extended network. In fact, using just this simple drawing your network could get pretty complicated pretty fast! If you count, you will identify nearly 30 unused dendrites in these four neurons; making a single contact with each of them would create quite a tangle of connections.

But that is nothing. When we come to the brain and the actual neuronal networks found there, the numbers of connections, and the tangle of neurons, is truly incomprehensible.

A human brain has about 100 billion neurons (eleven zeros).[4] And estimates range as high as 10,000 connections per neuron.[5] That comes to a total of a thousand trillion connections (that's fifteen zeros) in an average human brain. There are ten to a hundred times more connections in our brain than there are cells in our body.[6]

It is really impossible to visualize all these connections, even in a small piece of the brain. But we can get some idea of their extent by looking at the potential sites for synapse formation on a single neuron. This is shown in the following drawing, which depicts a small segment of the dendritic branches from an isolated hippocampal neuron. Sites that could form synapses are identified by dots. These sites are not actual synapses, but they could become synapses if this neuron were back in its home in the hippocampus, and the neuronal networks grew more and more complex through learning and remembering.

To cell body

A final point is that no matter how many synapses a particular neuron has, it also seems to have the potential to grow more. We will talk about this in chapter 7, when we look at how neuronal networks change.

Neuronal Networks Are Prior Knowledge

I have said that prior knowledge is a thing. Now you can see what that claim means. There is a neuronal network in our brain for everything we know.

Let's look at an example. Each of us knows our name. We recognize it, we know how to say it, and we know how to write it. This is part of our existing knowledge. Our ability to recognize our name comes from neuronal networks in our sensory brain. When Jane sees "Jane" written on the blackboard, a group of neurons in her visual cortex that are triggered by the shapes of the letters in her name always fire together. The visual stimulus, Jane's name in writing, triggers the same neuronal network every time. To her brain, the name *Jane* is a neuronal network.

We can go on. Jane has written her name so often that she does it without thinking. A neuronal network in her memory brain is connected to another one in her motor brain, and she writes Jane without a thought. The motor network for writing Jane is unique; it is her knowledge of how to write her name. And when she signs her checks, Jane uses the larger neuronal network, which consists of a combination of her memory network for her name and her motor brain, which generates the movements of her hand and arm as she writes.

It seems that every fact we know, every idea we understand, and every action we take has the form of a network of neurons in our brain. We know of no other form.

The Divided/Connected Brain

The brain is constructed so that small parts of knowledge are located in small groups of neurons connected to each other in small networks. These small networks are connected with other small networks to produce larger ones, and there does not seem to be any particular limit to these connections. Thus, complex experiences or ideas consist of extensive networks. The brain is a structure that at once is almost infinitely divided and infinitely connected.

These small parts of knowledge are such things as straight lines versus slanted lines, the vibrations produced by playing a single musical note versus another note, or a geometric form such as a cube versus a circle. The small networks are made up of neurons close to one another, and almost every day research brings new information about specific brain functions localized to a particular small part of the brain. We know that there are certain areas for hearing, for creating language, for working memory, for long-term memory, for creating images, for understanding nouns, for understanding verbs, for doing arithmetic, for doing geometry, for recognizing perfect pitch, for remembering the Beatles' *Yellow Submarine,* and for recalling the first bars of Beethoven's *Fifth Symphony.*

Specific groups of neurons fire when we hear middle C on the piano, but different groups fire when we hear C sharp. Specific groups of neurons fire when we see red, but a different specific group fires when we see blue. Different groups of neurons fire when we feel happy, angry, sad, or afraid. Certain neurons fire when we are in love, and others when it's just lust.

Name anything that humans can know, think, feel, or do, and we can find a part of the brain, or a combination of parts, that specializes in that thing. But at the same time, combinations of these neuron groups can also fire at the same time. The more complex the task, the more parts of the brain that are needed, and the larger the neuronal network that comes into play. It is not a stretch to say that *any* neuronal network might potentially become connected with *any* other network, if that connection is a useful one. For example, the network that triggers *Yellow Submarine* can become connected with the network for the name "Jane," if Jane continually hums that tune.

Thus, in cognitive tasks many different parts of the brain can be involved at once. At some complex points in our lives—moments that may try our minds and hearts (i.e., the cognitive and emotional parts of our brains)—large amounts of our brain may be active at once in neuronal networks of incomprehensible complexity.

Progress Report from Thom[7]

Thom and I were eating lunch. We had talked about these ideas for a few days, but he hadn't said anything about teaching. I couldn't stand it any longer.

"Well?" I said. "What do you think? Can you use any of this in your class?"

He looked at me in that penetrating and quizzical way of his. "I hate to give you the satisfaction," he said. "But you're right about one thing. I hadn't thought of my teaching that way. If what students believe is a physical thing, physical connections between real neurons, it sounds more compelling. It might be harder to teach some things than I thought."

"What do you mean?" I asked.

"Well, I just assume that when I explain things in words, or equations, or graphs, they will get the idea. But if those words or graphs have to match up with physical networks in their brains, there's a lot of room for mismatches. Even one word, or a small part of my drawing, could do it. The student could hit a brick wall right then!"

"That can happen," I agreed.

"And what if I try to correct a mistake, or a wrong idea?" Thom clipped ahead quickly. "How can what I say actually change a physical set of connections in someone's brain?"

"It's not easy," I said. "I guess we're learning that from your students."

"Well, it might help if I knew what networks they already have," he pondered. "At least that would give me some clues. I might be able to build on that."

He paused, thinking hard. "Or maybe there's another angle. If I could find out when they *aren't* getting it, when they stumble into a brick wall, at least I would know what networks they *don't* have."

Thom laughed. "Well, one network they don't have for sure is the one for conservation of momentum. We know that much!"

After a quiet moment, Thom asked, "What's known about how these neuronal connections get created in the first place? Can't I make any generalizations? Can't I assume that there are some connections they all have?"

This startled me a little. His quick mind had moved ahead of me. I was still thinking about how something could move forever. Did I have that neuronal network in my own brain?

Neuronal Networks Are the Beginning

Thom had understood one thing very well. Whatever the neuronal networks are in the student brain, a teacher cannot remove them. They are a physical fact. As we will see later, it may be possible to reduce the use of particular networks, or to use other networks in their place, and some networks may die out or weaken with disuse. But no teacher, with a wave of the hand, a red pen, or even with a cogent and crystal-clear explanation, can remove an existing neuronal network from a student's brain.

The useful approach for a teacher is to find ways to *build on* existing neuronal networks. Starting with whatever our students already know and building from there is a biologically based idea for pedagogy. It suggests that we should find out what students believe, and far from disparaging it or trying to ignore it, use it as a tool for teaching. Existing neuronal networks open the door to effective teaching.

Thom's last question then, in an excellent one. Are there common sets of neuronal networks that we can begin with? Can we assume anything about what students already know?

One thing we can be sure of is that the neuronal networks in student brains are related to their own life experience. The things they have seen, heard, touched, smelled and tasted are what connects for them. And things they have tried to do or have succeeded in doing will also be there. There are neuronal networks for the facts of their own lives.

So Thom can generalize, at least a little. He can assume that most of his students will understand when he speaks of things they have all experienced. The objects in their worlds, the language they share, the music, the shapes, textures, smells, and tastes will all be there. Certainly there will be differences, things sensed by one brain but not by another, but this generalization gives us a starting point.

The Importance of the Concrete

As we will see in chapter 8, our brains make physical maps of the world, and the existing neuronal networks are replicas of the physical form of objects in the world, those objects and events that make up our concrete experience. For example, light reflected off an object such as a house or tree comes into our eyes in the same geometric arrangement for us all. (See chapter 8.) The eyes then send that information to the same parts of our visual brains, and the way it is recorded there is a physical reflection of the object itself. So the neuronal networks formed when we sense the outside world are most likely to be similar in each of us; they are created from the same source—the physical world.

How we interpret them, or perceive them, is another matter. Eventually, as we proceed with this book, we may well come to think that almost every brain makes a somewhat different meaning from the same concrete facts. Our perceptions and meanings come from the influence of neuronal networks in other, nonsensory parts of the brain. So, we can't assume anything about meaning.

Despite this personal modification of sensory experience into perceptions, it still seems that a teacher's best chance is to begin with concrete examples. The abstract and theoretical have less meaning if no neuronal networks are associated with the concrete experience of the learner. For example, medical education might start with patients, and arithmetic might start with purchases at the store. Likewise, an understanding of genetics might start with a learner's family traits, economics with the cost of CDs, and civil engineering with concrete examples of interstate highways (pun intended).

These suggestions are really just another way to reaffirm Ausubel's claim. "What we already know" is concrete to us. Our knowledge of it makes it real, part of our experience.

However, especially in higher education, teachers do not necessarily start with the concrete. Our deeper understanding of our fields can lead us to start with principles rather than examples. We may think we should provide students with the "tools" for solving problems before we show them the problems. Or, we may start with the atom rather than the object, the equation rather than the phenomenon, the concept of supply and demand rather than economic stories. We start where *we* are, not where they are.

Beyond the Facts—Neuronal Networks for Ideas

But Thom wants his students to understand an abstract concept, something they never have, and never will, actually experience. What do our ideas of neuronal networks tell us about that challenge?

My suggestion is that abstract concepts are always embedded in concrete experience. For example, observing or riding in automobiles is a concrete experience but that experience is associated with concepts of speed and acceleration. At an even more basic level, the world gives us many examples of multiplicity in objects: cars, apples, people. This concrete information inherently contains abstract ideas of numbers, arithmetic, and statistics.

It's possible that all our brains become comfortable with certain abstract ideas through our real experiences. We may not recognize the abstractions or have names for them, but I suspect they are there. If we accept the proposition that our physical brain is the whole story (which you know is my bias), then it must be true that there are neuronal networks for *all* the ideas that allow us to understand ourselves and the world—ideas like time, shape, novelty, number, causation, extent, qualities, self/other, mass, and hardness. All these come from the world of the concrete.[8]

I propose, then, that Thom's students already have some neuronal networks on which Thom can build. They may not know it, because they have never connected them with the word *momentum*. But they probably know that heavy things are harder to stop than lighter things, and they do know that fast-moving objects can hit you hard, even if they are small objects. They have bits and pieces of the neuronal networks which interest Thom. His job is to discover those bits and pieces.[9]

It is also quite likely that the students are missing networks that tie things together. It could even be something as simple as vocabulary. They may not quite have a good network for the word *momentum*, for example. They may have the parts that need to be connected, but that key last connection hasn't ever been formed. And if we don't know what connections are missing, we won't know how to teach them.

Tangles

Each learner brings his own special set of neuronal networks to class. There's nothing we can do about that. They really can't check them at the door!

These networks are a true tangle, some with branches hanging off one side or the other, some drooping bedraggled on the ground, some sticking bare and brave into the sky, some with weak connections to others, some with strong connections to others. We see this in our experience with students as we come to know about their needs, their misunderstandings, their partial ideas, and their talents and skills.[10]

Our inclination is to straighten out this tangle. We want to correct what we find to be in error, trim up the loose ends, prune out the useless branches, and construct new ones that will be of more value. It's simple! We will just explain what is right and what is wrong, and that will be that!

We cling tightly to this illusion. An example remains vivid in my mind. One of our teachers was complaining bitterly about a certain misunderstanding her students always make, when a second teacher suggested, in total sincerity, "Well, that's simple. I would just list the five reasons why that idea is wrong on the board, and take care of it immediately!"

But we know that this doesn't work. It's not possible to get in and fix things.

This is one of the most important, and yet simple, ideas that biology can give teachers. We must let our students use the neuronal networks they already have. We cannot create new ones out of thin air or by putting them on a blackboard. And we cannot excise old ones. The only recourse we have is to begin with what the learner brings.

Tangles in the Classroom

I learned of another example of the tangle we make of learning through the research of a friend of mine, Kathy Schuh. Her work explores knowledge construction by children, focusing particularly on the idiosyncratic connections they make in classrooms based on their prior experiences. Kathy observed classroom lessons and took notes on the environment and classroom interactions, particularly those comments and questions that seemed to be unique to each child. Then, after class, she asked individual children about the content of the lesson and other things that went through their mind during the lesson.

From this information, Kathy constructed a type of map to show the connections that the child made. One of these maps is shown below. The lesson was about Charlemagne, so you should find your starting point by finding where he shows up on the map. This is just the result for one student in one class, but Kathy studied many students, and the individual maps of different students are all complex and unique.[11]

Of course, we know that this tangle happens in all classes, all the time. Even the most focused of brains finds itself bouncing from neuronal network to neuronal network in a lecture or during a lesson. And the connections are totally unpredictable. A single word can send a mind off through a tangle of neuronal network underbrush.

In Thom's office

When I visited Thom in his office the next day, I found him making paper airplanes and gliding them toward the corner wastebasket. He smiled. "You think I planned this, don't you? Or maybe you think I spend most of my time throwing papers around!"

I grinned and sat down.

"I have been thinking," Thom went on. "Maybe I have a better chance of connecting with the neuronal networks of my students if I use more concrete examples that they already know, like paper airplanes."

He pulled out three airplanes from the wastebasket. One was long and sleek with a very sharp pointed nose. Another was folded with a blunt nose and had wider wings. The third was the worst. Not only was the nose flat, and the wings broad, but the back half of both wings was folded up vertically. That plane was not going to fly far at all!

Suddenly it struck me. "Very clever Thom," I exclaimed. "I bet your sleek plane will fly the longest, because it gives the least resistance. Your students will get that in an instant. Now, if you could only make one with *no* resistance, how long would it fly?"

"Conservation of momentum!" Thom said.

"You could talk about it for a long time, and use lots of equations and graphs, but I bet they will get the basic idea almost immediately with this example," I said.

"Worth a try."

But then he grew more serious. "Still, I'm worried. What will they think! I might lose control and pretty soon everyone will be throwing things around the room."

"Yes," I said. "It will be a challenge to think of ways you can keep them on task."

"That's why I have you," he replied slyly. "But another thing. I've also decided to pay a lot more attention to what they already know. I never did this in a physics class before, but I am going to ask them to write out what things mean to them in English words and sentences. It seems to me that I have been assuming that their neuronal networks are just like mine. But, whatever, I intend to find out!"

"Like what?" I asked.

"Well, for one thing, what does *momentum* mean to them, in their own words? Using their own neuronal networks? Or resistance? Or mass?" He almost seemed excited.

I know I was excited, but I also felt a little wary. "It looks like you have some good plans, but don't expect every student to like them," I said slowly. "They also have neuronal networks about how teaching should be done and about what happens in physics classes. What they already believe could get in the way. . . . Not for all of them, of course," I added quickly.

He never missed a beat. "I know that," he said. "But it's worth it in my judgment. I've got some new connections in my own neuronal networks, and they will be hard to change, too! These ideas have momentum. They can overcome a lot of resistance. Even if they won't fly on forever!" And he laughed as heartily as I ever heard him.

Finding Out about the Neuronal Networks of a Learner

Roger Schank says, "A good teacher is not one who explains things correctly, but rather one who puts things in an interesting way."[12] What this suggests is that such a teacher knows what will be interesting to his students. He knows about existing neuronal networks.

We have talked about starting with the concrete experiences that we believe our students understand. And Thom has the idea that he can find out about existing neuronal networks by asking his students to write out their ideas about physics in words rather than equations. These are both good suggestions, and there may be others we can add to the list.

One method I have used in my small classes is to have students explain their previous experience and ideas about the subject material. Specific questions can be used to get this going. For example, I might ask the students to write out their idea of a gene or draw a picture that conveys their idea. Usually, they are not allowed to use technical terms. Then I ask them to exchange their responses, and each student then tries to explain what they think their classmates are trying to say. Inevitably, as they hear their ideas described by another person, an active discussion will ensue, which uncovers a lot about the neuronal networks of each student. I ultimately try to use the information I get in these sessions to guess what each student will find interesting.

You undoubtedly will think of other ways to learn about the neuronal networks of your students, if you become convinced that it is as important as I say it is. Most teachers are wonderfully creative, once they come around to a new idea—once something fits in with their own neuronal networks!

What We Have Learned about What We Already Know

In these conversations with Thom I've tried to point out some of the key ideas in this chapter. Here are ten ideas that seem worth remembering:

1. All students have prior knowledge that affects how they respond to our teaching.

2. The prior knowledge of students is not an ether; it is physical, real, and persistent.

3. If we ignore or avoid prior knowledge, it will hinder our teaching.

4. Prior knowledge is complex and personal.

5. Students are not necessarily aware of all their prior knowledge.

6. Writing assignments are helpful in discovering prior knowledge of students.

7. Prior knowledge is likely to be concrete; teachers should begin with the concrete.

8. Concepts and broad principles should be developed from specific examples.

9. Teachers should expect and respect the tangles; it is *not our job to* set them in order.

10. Prior knowledge is a gift to the teacher; it tells us where and how to start.

Next Steps

I have said repeatedly that teachers should build on existing neuronal networks. They are a tool to be used. And I have also said that those networks cannot be eliminated. They are persistent and powerful.

But learners do improve and grow in their knowledge. If prior knowledge turns out to be useless, they stop using it and learn new ideas. How do these things happen if prior knowledge is so persistent? What produces change in neuronal networks?

These questions are the topic of our next chapter. As we address them, we will see more clearly how the teacher fits in and why I claim that teachers physically change brains.

Notes

1. I use the term *neuronal networks* rather than *neural networks* because of the rather specific meaning that the latter term has gained in cognitive science. Neural network has come to mean a network of connections in computers rather than those in the head.

2. The subject of so-called "naive physics" has been examined quite extensively. Long lists of the incomplete or inaccurate ideas that students may hold about the physical world can be found in the literature, but educators seem uncertain about what to do about this. To get a sense of this uncertainty, examine M. Reiner and colleagues, or K. J. Pine and D. J. Messer in *Cognition and Instruction* 18 (2000), pp. 1–51.

3. With permission from J. Nolte, *The Human Brain,* 4th ed. (St. Louis: Mosby Inc., 1999), p. 3.
4. The number of neurons in a brain is often described dramatically. However, it should be pointed out that this number is not different than the number of cells in any other tissue. There are approximately 100 million cells in a gram of any tissue.
5. The number of connections per neuron may be as high as 100,000 for some types of highly branched neurons.
6. Occasionally it is noted that the potential number of connections in the brain is higher than the number of atoms in the universe. This "potential" number arises if we assume that every neuron is connected to every other neuron. But this is just a game. As much fun as it is, the brain could not work if this were true, and the added mass from all those dendrites and axons would produce a head at least 1,000 times heavier than it is.
7. As with all the other stories in this book, the first episode with Thom, described at the beginning of this chapter, is based on actual experiences of the author. However, this episode and the final one at the end of the chapter are fictitious. They are conversations I wish I had had.
8. I am not saying that all abstract ideas are demonstrable in the concrete world or through our experience. Some concepts of physics appear to be devoid of any satisfying physical representation, such as the dual nature of the electron or curved space. But from my conversations with physicists, I also suspect that these ideas leave a trace of discomfort even in the brain of the expert. We may be forced to accept them because of a mathematical result, but I'm not sure we ever get really comfortable with them.
9. This is apparently what the Socratic Greeks believed. Education, in their view, consisted of helping the learner discover what was already in the brain.
10. Of course these generalizations apply to all of us, not just students. We look for understanding and order in student thinking because we have created order in our own minds about the subject. But that order is not preordained. Sensory experience brings things to us in a random fashion, and our meaning-making brain connects them up in no particular order. That's one of the reasons our brains work so well. We can take in whatever random nature delivers to us, remember good amounts of it, and eventually make meaning of it, creating our own personal order.
11. Kathy L. Schuh, *Knowledge Structures from a Constructivist Perspective.* Unpublished manuscript, 1998. Figure reprinted with permission.
12. Roger C. Schank, *Tell Me a Story: Narrative and Intelligence* (Evanston, IL: Northwestern University Press, 1990), p. 15.

7

ONLY CONNECT!

HOW TEACHERS CAN CHANGE NEURONAL NETWORKS

Only connect! This was the whole of her sermon. Only connect the prose and the passion, and both will be exalted. . . . Live in fragments no longer!

—E. M. Forster

Mary always sat in the second row on the left of the room—on my right as I faced the class. I remember her from the first day. She had that look: bright, intense, serious, but full of energy. She really wanted to understand!

Science hadn't been Mary's thing up to then. My course was a venture in a new direction, and even though she was bright, she soon hit a roadblock. The topic was protein folding. Esoteric as it sounds, it is almost impossible to understand biochemistry without a grasp of this subject, and Mary really struggled.

One problem was that she kept making the same mistake. It isn't important what the mistake was (that would be too much biochemistry here) but I spent a lot of time explaining why it was wrong. We would go over it and over it, but nothing seemed to work.

Then one day she came into class more agitated than usual. "I figured it out." she said. "I finally found the right connection!"

I laughed out loud when she explained. "Yesterday I saw a duck in the pond by my dorm. All at once, I remembered when I was a kid on our farm. My brothers would put a duck in a tub of water that had a cup of detergent dissolved in it. The duck would begin to swim around, and then it would sink to the bottom, quacking in terror! It was gross!"

"Don't you see, Dr. Zull?" she exclaimed. "The duck sank because the detergent dissolved away the oil on its feathers. That's how a duck floats. The oil on its feathers keeps it on top of the water! That is exactly what happens with protein folding. The oily parts float away from the water!"

She was right. Exactly right! And from that time on, Mary began to excel in biochemistry. In fact it became her career. That connection between a duck and biochemistry changed her life!

* * *

Now we are at the place where we can actually talk about changing the brain. The basic idea comes directly from what we discovered in chapter 6. The knowledge in our minds consists of neuronal networks in our brains, so if that knowledge is to grow, the neuronal networks must physically change.

This is the change that a teacher wants to create. It is change in connections. We may want stronger connections, more connections, different connections, or even fewer connections, but unless there is some change in connections, no learning can occur.

As we saw in chapter 6, in neuroscience terms, changing connections means changing synapses. Surprising as it may sound, there are ways that a teacher can encourage all these types of change in the synapses of her students. It happens naturally, and we can copy nature.

Starting with Change

If you tend to believe that brain wiring is primarily programmed by DNA, you may feel that we have started off on the wrong track. We definitely are headed toward ideas of flexibility in neuronal networks and away from more rigid programming.

Let me briefly try to explain why I think this is the right way to go.

There is no doubt that the growth of axons, dendrites, and synapses depends on expression of certain genes and that individual differences in those genes produce individual differences in neuronal structures— that is, *differences in genes can produce differences in the brain.*

But that is not the same as saying the wiring of the brain is "programmed." The synapses that each neuron will form are not spelled out in a DNA blueprint. Rather, at a minimum, our genes give us the *tools for flexibility* in synapses, and the *basic patterns* of synapses that assure a brain can work (e.g., correct connections between the various parts of the cortex or between the body and the cortex).

Another aspect of this issue is expressed by the following question: How much are our *common* behaviors and preferences determined by genes?

This question suggests that people all share certain genes that make us behave as humans and prefer the things humans prefer. It is a powerful idea and has led to the creation of an entirely new field of study called *evolutionary psychology*. In fact, we have already alluded to this idea in chapter 4 where we spoke of the brain evolving to like the things that were essential for our survival (e.g., liking sugars and fats). When we speak of learning, we encounter this idea again. Maybe everything is programmed; maybe learning doesn't even exist.[1]

But, in the end, that is a technical point. Whatever we call what happens as we gain skills and grow in our ability to think, there is no doubt that it happens and no doubt that this growth is influenced by the people who, by choice or not, become our teachers.

And there is no doubt that this growth in our abilities and understanding is the result of physical growth and change in our brains. It is change in our neuronal networks. When we think of our experience, what we really mean is the experience of our neurons. That experience is not predictable, because it comes from the complex and random events of our lives. It cannot be programmed.

Confronting Complexity

What changes can happen in synapses?

As we will see in this section, one such change is simply adding or losing synapses. In fact, it is possible that the number of synapses changes minute by minute. But it is not just the number of synapses that can change. Each synapse can also change the strength and pattern of its signaling. For example, a synapse that fires in a regular pattern can begin to fire in bursts. And, even more dramatically, synapses can totally change character; they can change from excitatory to inhibitory.

Given all the synapses and the different ways they can change, it is easy to feel overwhelmed. Things can look frighteningly complicated. But complexity like this is common in biology. For example, the number and diversity of different forms of life, literally millions of species each with different shapes and behaviors, seems impossible to understand or remember. But it turns out that this complexity can become almost unimportant once we appreciate the unifying idea of natural selection. The details of the structure of any organism are the result of evolution and are part of the story of survival for that living thing. All organisms can be understood by use of the same conceptual framework. They are all different, and yet underneath they are all the same.

This combination of unity and diversity is also true for our brain. If we focus on the details, we will be swamped and confused. We can't look at every synapse or every neuron. But if we recognize the unifying ideas, we will not feel so helpless.

Where we are going next, then, is actually very simple. It turns out, the things that produce change are fundamentally the same for all synapses. And they are things we can understand. The two things that change synapses are (a) *how much they are used* and (b) *how important the signals are*. In this chapter we will build on the first of these, and in chapter 12 we will talk about the second.

The Strong, the Weak, and the Silent

Not every synapse that can be seen with the microscope is actually sending signals. Some synapses are strong, some are weak; in fact, some appear to be so weak they seem *silent*. They can be seen as physical structures, but they don't send signals often enough, and reproducibly enough, to be effective.

We should note that the terms *strong, weak,* and *silent* are a little misleading when it comes to synapses. It is more accurate to say that different synapses fire more or less frequently. A *strong synapse* is one that fires in many rapid bursts when it is triggered, and a *weak synapse* is one that fires only a few times. The individual signals are not strong or weak, but how often they fire makes them seem that way. Silent synapses may fire randomly once in a while, but not in any consistent way. In fact, neurons are firing periodically all the time. From the moment of their development in the womb, our networks of neurons are blinking on and off in a starry night scenario. The patterns of blinking change, and those changes come about as different stars become part of different clusters through change in the connections between them.[2]

This range of synapse strength allows for learning. A weak synapse that has been firing only infrequently can become strong and start to fire much more often. A silent synapse can gain its voice, and a strong synapse can become mute. When a silent synapse begins to fire, it produces a new neuronal connection, and when a loud synapse quits speaking, we lose a neuronal connection. Synapse change is neuronal network change.[3]

Origins of Change: Nature

Neuronal networks change continually throughout the normal development of animal brains, which, of course, includes us. This change begins when neurons first form in the primitive brain of the embryo and continues until we die.

Much of this change is simply biological growth and development. It will happen regardless of our individual experiences and learning. Just as other parts of our bodies grow and change naturally, so does our brain. This type of change depends partly on our genes, but it also comes partly from other, so-called "epigenetic" processes that aren't inherited but are caused by physical and cellular events.[4] Of course, much of this biological change comes along at specific ages as we grow.

Origins of Change: Nurture

As certain as we are that change in the wiring of our brain is directed by genes, we are equally certain that sensory experience changes our neuronal networks.[5] This has become a basic tenet of neurobiology and has been shown in many different ways, ranging from experiments done decades ago with simple animals like sea slugs to more recent ones with mammals and with people.

Neuronal change that is produced by experience is sometimes called *plasticity*. The wiring of the brain is plastic in the sense that it can be remodeled, or physically molded. Sometimes this is dramatic. For example, in deaf people, the auditory parts of the brain can be invaded by neurons from the vision part. Or, if a monkey loses an arm, the sensory neurons that map the arm can form new connections with the neurons used to map the face.[6]

These types of change are huge, neurologically. Whole areas of the cortex are changed. But change in synapses can also be demonstrated with single neurons. If a neuron is stimulated to fire frequently, its synapses may grow stronger. Silent synapses may even begin to fire if the neuron is active enough. And, most dramatically, totally new dendrite branches may grow and totally new synapses may come into existence.

You can see an example of this growth of potential new synapses in the picture below, which shows the appearance of new "spines" on a dendrite of a neuron that was electrically stimulated by an experimenter. Each of these spines is a potential synapse site, and as the figure shows, they begin to show up within minutes of stimulation.[7]

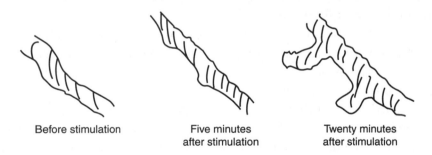

Before stimulation   Five minutes   Twenty minutes
                         after stimulation   after stimulation

The growth of new branches like these explains the results from Marian Diamond's experiments with baby rats. If the rats are raised in what is called an "enriched environment," which means they have lots of things to do, look at, hear, and touch, then the dendrites of neurons in their cerebral cortex become much more branched than when they are in a less complex environment. Lots of sensory input produces complex and extensive new branching of neurons.[8]

All these and many more experiments show that experience changes the wiring in our brain because it changes the activity in our neurons. When neurons are more active, they can make more synapses.

The Simplest Change—Developing Our Gifts

Genetic, epigenetic, and experiential events provide each of us with a unique brain. Each of our brains is skilled at some things and not skilled at others. What those skills are depends on the complex mix of our biology and our experience in the world. Most of us have brains that are very good at some things we all value, things that could serve us well in our lives. These are our gifts.

One of the most basic kinds of change in our brains is the change that builds on what we already have—our neurological gifts. There is no simpler way to learn than to practice things we already know. Synapses get stronger with use.

I am reminded of a story Terrance Deacon tells in his wonderful book, *The Symbolic Species*. He describes his visits to an aquarium where dolphins were trained to perform their amazing leaps and dance on their tails. Deacon recounts how he inquired whether dolphins learned these thing so well because they are particularly smart. Surprisingly, the answer was "no!" Rather, it turned out that dolphins are trained by rewarding them for things they already do naturally in the wild. Everything they eventually end up doing is an offshoot or an exaggeration of something that they do with no training using neuronal networks they already have.[9]

This seems to be a good neurological way of thinking. Neurons that are repeatedly used grow stronger synapses and more effective neuronal networks. And the more they fire, the more they send out new branches looking for more new and useful connections. The more experiments they carry out, the more likely they are to get a new connection, like the dolphin that finds a rumba in her beat while dancing on her tail!

I can't think of a better example of what I am trying to explain here. So often we conceive of teaching as starting with our own knowledge rather than that of the learner. Even when a person is showing us directly what her personal neuronal networks are like, we still plunge ahead with our plan for how to teach her. We truly and deeply, but totally erroneously, believe that her existing networks are of little value. We ignore what may be our best opportunity to change a brain by refining and exaggerating the valuable connections already there.

Part of the art of changing the brain is recognizing the existing neuronal networks in a learner and inventing ways for her to use them. She will do the rest.

My Student Mary and a Famous Neurobiologist

The story at the beginning of this chapter about my student Mary offers an example of the development of new synapses. Here is how a neurobiologist might explain her connection between a sinking duck and protein folding.

Mary had neuronal networks for ducks, oil, water, floating, and sinking from her childhood experiences. She also had neuronal networks for proteins and biochemistry from her experience in my class. When some of these networks began to fire at the same time, when she saw the duck on the pond while she was thinking about proteins, these two networks became physically connected.

Networks that fired together got wired together.

This idea was proposed more than fifty years ago by one of the pioneers in neurobiology, Donald Hebb. Actually, it was also Hebb who suggested that when synapses are active, they get stronger, but he extended this idea in a subtle but important way.[10] Suppose that two neurons (A and B) have synapses with a third one, neuron C. The synapse between A and C is strong, and whenever A fires, so does C. But the synapse between B and C is weak, and so when B fires, C does not usually respond.

Hebb proposed that if A and B both fire at the same time, not only will the A–C synapse get stronger, but so will the B–C synapse. In fact, if this happens often enough, B will begin to fire C on its own![11] Hebb's theory might explain Mary's learning. I have tried to illustrate this in figure below.

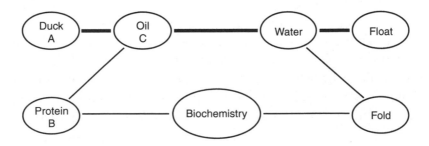

The heavy lines in the figure represent existing neuronal networks in Mary's brain. These were established in her childhood. The lighter lines are connections that formed once she understood protein folding. When Mary saw a duck while thinking about proteins, neurons A and B both fired on C at the same time, and the connection between B and C became active. She now had the connection she needed to understand protein folding.

Possibly the most interesting thing about this model is that when that new synapse is established, a new neuronal network comes into existence. This network now includes protein, oil, water, and folding; thus, it is a *combination* of the new and the old. The oil and water networks are an integral part of the new network, but they came from Mary's childhood experiences. Those old experiences are forever tied to her new understanding and mastery of biochemistry.

This seems to be how we learn. We continually add new experiences to our old ones. We blend the old and the new, and in blending we create whole new networks. We construct our understanding using part of what we already know and part of what is new.

So we find a new challenge for teachers. Part of the teacher's job is to find ways to combine the established networks, or parts of them, with new networks—to build new concepts using a mix of the old and the new.

Searching for Connections: What Can a Teacher Do?

How can a teacher know what new synapses will help someone learn? No one could have known what network Mary was going to use, and it was just chance that she found the right connection at all. What does teaching have to do with it?

Again, we find ourselves thinking about teaching is a different way. Rather than seeing our job as giving students new information, facts, or concepts, maybe we should put more effort into finding the old. Otherwise, the new may be of no use!

How can we do that? First, I think, we have to remember how personal and individual these old networks can be. As a result we should use a broad brush in our search for relevant past experience. This would include the possibility of using different sensory avenues, including images, music, and different forms of language such as poetry or dialogue. I will say more about this in chapter 8.

It also seems possible that if we are creative, we may help our students find the useful neuronal networks in their own brains. For example, we might ask, "What does this make you think of?" Or, "is there some part of this that rings a wild bell for you? What is the first thing that you thought of when we began this topic?" Or, we might turn to our learner's peers. Asking various members of a class to describe the connections they have made may well cue other students in the class. They are more likely to have the same concrete experiences. Such a conscious effort to direct the student's thoughts toward what may already be in her brain could produce the simultaneous firing of synapses needed for new connections.

Maybe if I had asked Mary what she thought of when we talk about oil and water, she would have answered, "Ducks!"

Losing Synapses

Neuroscience gives us many examples of strengthening existing synapses and growing new ones. But there is another side to this learning coin. It seems likely that learning also involves loss of synapses!

For this confounding fact we must thank Peter Huttenlocher who has spent a lot of his time actually counting synapses in the brains of people of different ages. In the graph below I show you my reconstruction of one part of this work, the changes that take place in the numbers of synapses in the visual cortex from birth to seventy years of age.[12]

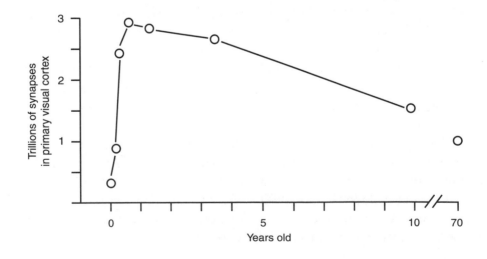

There is a huge increase in the numbers of synapses in the visual part of a baby's brain over the first few months. But then things change. Sometime around the first year, the number of synapses begins to decrease, and that decrease then continues throughout life. Unless we want to argue that we don't learn anything through vision after one year of age, it seems that learning goes on at the same time that we are losing synapses.

Furthermore, the loss of synapses is not trivial. For example, between age four and ten, about a trillion synapses are lost in the visual cortex. Tens of billions of synapses in the visual cortex are lost just between eight and sixteen months of age.

It is easy to misunderstand what these data mean. We may find ourselves thinking that up to eight months or so, it is *all* synapse increase, and after that time it is *all* synapse decrease. But that is virtually impossible. It is much more likely that synapses are being lost all the time, and others are being formed all the time. It's just that up to eight months they are being formed much faster than they are being lost; then things turn around, and we begin to lose synapses faster than we make them.

In the years that we are probably learning the most, we may be losing more synapses than we are gaining!

Learning by Losing

Earlier we talked about how synapses can weaken, become silent, or even disappear when they aren't being used. But what is the value of disuse? Is it possible to have too many connections?

Gerald Edelman gave us our best ideas about these questions when he described a theory for learning based on selection of synapses rather than production of synapses.[13] He proposed that, at first, brains do produce more synapses than they need. The explosion of synapses following birth may not be as much for learning itself as it is a *preparation for learning.*

Suppose that in its early development our brain produces all the synapses it needs to do anything it could ever do. It even produces synapses for things it will never do, such as recognizing all the sounds in all the languages of the world. Maybe, as the Socratic Greeks believed, all knowledge is stored in our brain, at least for a brief time. Learning, then, would simply be the process of keeping the connections that are useful to us in our individual lives and becoming aware of them. That would depend on our experience in the world. We would keep the synapses that are strengthened by our experiences and our culture, but those that were not useful would not be used much and might even eventually die out. For example, we would keep the connections that we use when we recognize the sounds in our native language but lose those that allow us to recognize sounds in a language we never hear. In this model, learning is really just *selecting* the synapses that we need and getting rid of the rest. Or, if we don't get rid of them, they simply sit on the shelf for possible later use.

This theory came from Edelman's realization that, in biology, things are almost always achieved by selection. Rather than having to create entirely new ways or tools to meet a need, living things just use what is at hand. This is just like natural selection and evolution, so Edelman's theory has been called "neural Darwinism."

Selection and Teaching

Edelman's ideas suggest something important about teaching. If learning is change in neuronal networks, that change might not depend on instruction. If by *instruction* we mean some process of providing specific directions for the steps in learning, then instruction cannot be responsible for establishment of neuronal networks. We just don't have the instruction manual.

This is a question of philosophy for the teacher. It suggests, again, that rather than directing and instructing learning, we should give the learner incentives and support in using what she already has in her brain. She will learn by selecting the right neuronal networks from among those that already exist.

And if she does begin to fire some new networks, that will come by giving her new experience and showing her new things, not by instruction and explaining.

The "Wrong" Connection

If learners are to build on their existing knowledge, the teacher must look out for the factually, or conceptually, wrong knowledge that exists in all brains. Here is a specific example of the wrong connection from my teaching experience.

When I was trying to teach about reactions in the body that go very fast and other ones that give off a lot of energy, some students would become confused. The wrong connection they had was that fast reactions must be energetic, and vice versa. Neither of these is true.

In neuroscience terms, I would now tend to say that these students had an existing neuronal network that was simply wrong. This network might be written, Speed = Energy. I would dearly have liked to get rid of it!

How might we do that? It's not easy. That connection is strong. It has probably been there from early childhood, when their parents said something like "Look at her go! She sure has a lot of energy!"

I found it relatively ineffective to stress the mistake. When I continually corrected it and drew attention to it, if anything things got worse. I found myself wondering if I wasn't actually strengthening the wrong connection by continually talking about it. Maybe my constant repetition of "energy does *not* equal speed" actually reinforced the existing, wrong network. Or maybe my students just heard something like "energy, blah, speed, blah, blah."

This is all speculation, of course. But there is research on the alternative approach. Ylvisaker and Feeney call it "errorless learning."[14] In working with brain-damaged children, they found that repeated use of the correct connections was an effective way for the children to learn. Their approach then is simply to ignore what is wrong and focus on what is right. This is one of those experiments I intend to try with my students. It may be better to ignore an error than to correct it!

Incomplete Networks

We might feel uncomfortable about this errorless learning approach. Simply repeating what is right may leave us feeling rather empty. A recording could do that! Isn't there a more proactive approach?

I think there is. Rather than trying to remove wrong ideas or ignore them, maybe we can build on them.

Let's go back to our energy/speed example. First, we should remember that the "wrong" connection came from some experience, so in some fundamental way it must not be "wrong." Active people do have a lot of energy. So this is where we should start. The problem is that this is not the end of the story. So we might tell our learner, "That's right, but there is more! Think about a hand grenade. It will just lie there in its bin with dozens of others, but it is packed with energy! And which has more energy: a glacier pushing the side off a mountain ten inches in a year or the fly buzzing around your ear so fast that you can't even swat it?"

As we enrich the experience of the learner, we begin to realize that sometimes the "wrong" connections are just *incomplete*. In our example, the connection between energy and speed is just a part of the total picture. Wrong by themselves, these incomplete networks can become a small, but essential, part of a complex and sophisticated network that is dramatically right!

Better Networks from "Wrong" Facts

Once when I was talking with some middle school teachers, one of them suddenly burst out, "What am I going to do with my students? I am trying to teach them about Martin Luther and the reformation, but no matter what I do, they all think that I am talking about Martin Luther King!"

Sometimes we find that people just have their facts wrong. They may *know* that the religious man named Martin Luther—who lived centuries ago, preached things that stirred people up, was hated by people in authority, but eventually changed the world—was Martin Luther King.

I have shown you an illustration of these connections below. The solid lines show all the connections that are already there. It will probably be very hard for people with these networks to realize that something is wrong.

How can a teacher help to make the right changes in these brains? We probably should not do what we are most likely to do. We should not say, "Oh, forget about Martin Luther King! This is not about him. Please pay attention to me! We are talking about Martin Luther."

One aspect of the problem is that children do not have a clear idea of time. Centuries ago is just a *long time,* and Martin Luther King lived a long time ago, too, in their experience. We could work with that and try to modify their neuronal networks about time. That would be a useful lesson and is certainly worthwhile, but we shouldn't be too optimistic about any quick changes. Some people never get a clear idea of historical time.

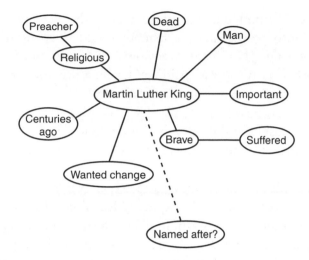

But it is possible that our constructive approach might be powerful in this case of the wrong fact. Suppose that the teacher says something like, "Yes! Martin Luther King was a lot like Martin Luther. In fact, why do you think that Martin Luther King's parents named him that? Why didn't they name him Sam King?"

This is the dotted line in the illustration. It suggests that since many of the neuronal networks and their connections work for both MLK and ML, our students may gain almost immediate understanding of Martin Luther by starting with these networks. They can be a tool for teaching rather than a barrier.

And, of great importance, if they know all these things about Martin Luther King, we may finding them asking, "Why was Martin Luther so important?" "When did he die?" "What is a century?" They may become motivated to understand more. Existing neuronal networks provide *both* the foundation for new learning and the emotional motivation for that learning!

Stopping the Signal, but Keeping the Network

At the beginning of this chapter I mentioned that the neurotransmitters released by some synapses actually inhibit firing of the next neuron rather than excite it. Signals from these neurons have the effect of interrupting a network.

This might sound like the place where the teacher's instruction could come into play. Maybe a teacher could turn on an inhibitory synapse by saying, "No! That is wrong!" But it doesn't seem to work that way as far as we know. Adding the network for a negative to a neuronal network doesn't block the network; it just makes it more complex.

But awareness of inhibitory pathways and their modulation can give us insights of a different nature, which we haven't encountered so far.

One example of this comes from experiments with barn owls.[15] These owls are very smart. They quickly learn how to find mice in the barn by using their visual brain and their hearing brain together. This precise coordination of hearing and sight is learned through experience. And they can adjust their learning if necessary. If we put little spectacles on our owls to distort their visual information, for example, they will stop using their accustomed neuronal networks and use *new* networks to work with the new sensory input.

Two questions interest us in this example. Where does the new network originate? And, what happens to the old network?

You already know possible answers to the first question. It could be selection, or it could be new network growth, but either way, new experience triggers firing of new neurons, and the synapses in those networks get stronger. Old networks for hearing and the new ones for vision fire at the same time and become part of a new, larger, "hunting network."

It is the question about the old network that is more provocative. It turns out that if we take the spectacles off, the owls begin to use the old network again. Either it is still there, intact, or it can be quickly recreated.

The experiments eventually suggested the first of these possibilities. It turned out that the old network was just inhibited. It was still there, apparently intact, but it was blocked from acting. As the authors of this paper said, there seems to be "experience-driven changes in patterns of *inhibition* as well as adjustments in patterns of excitation."

This is very interesting for the teacher. It suggests that our brains may contain networks that have not been used for some time but remain intact. They may just be inhibited and so might be put back into use at some future time.

This could be an opportunity, and it could be a danger. If old networks begin to seem attractive again, teachers may find that they come back online quite readily. If we present the "old" challenges to the learner, she may well rediscover the "old" solutions. If they are good solutions, fine; but if they never worked, we don't want them back.

For example, I decided to stop lecturing several years ago, and my students have been active and engaged in class ever since. But once in a while I slip back into that lecturing habit, and the minute I do, my students also slip back into that stupor that made me abandon the practice in the first place!

Neuronal Networks, Metaphors, Analogies

In chapter 1 I referred to Lakoff and Johnson's book, *Philosophy in the Flesh*. I think this work marks an important step toward understanding thinking and learning.[16] I would like to describe briefly a neuronal model for their idea and make a few suggestions about how this model can be of use in helping people learn.

As we have noted, Lakoff and Johnson say abstract ideas and thoughts arise from physical experiences of our bodies. In a way, nothing is really abstract. Our ideas are based on the concrete actions of our bodies. For example, they extensively develop the metaphor "life is a journey" to show how our abstract thoughts about life, with its past, present, and future, are derived from our bodily experience of journeys.

I would like to build on this idea and make a couple of suggestions for helping people learn. It seems that metaphors are sets of neuronal networks that possess specific physical relationships to each other in the brain and thus embody the concept of the relationship itself. Let me try to explain this using the metaphor "life is a bowl of cherries." Some of my friends say that I see more in this metaphor than is really there, but let me tell you what I see anyway.

The meaning this metaphor has for me is described in the illustration below. On the left are the meanings of the metaphor, and on the right the neuronal networks that provide this meaning are represented. First, we have a concrete object, a bowl of cherries, which we perceive visually in our vision brain and emotionally in our pleasure brain. In sequence, these perception networks are linked with others for eating and taste, suddenly hitting that pit, which is a surprising blow to our pleasure, eating more cherries, running out of cherries, and finally finding the bowl empty.

"Life is just a bowl of cherries"

Eat cherries

Looks good ← Hit the pits

↓

Depleted

Action brain/
pleasure brain

Visual brain/
pleasure brain ← Somatosensory brain/
danger brain

↓

Vision brain/danger brain

If we substitute *life* for the bowl of cherries, we see the powerful, but still abstract, idea of the metaphor. Life is filled with things that look good and are good, but which can surprise us with nasty blows and which eventually run out.

The power of the metaphor comes from the physical relationship of the neuronal networks from which it is constructed. The network itself—the specific connections between these specific parts of the brain, the *arrows* in our diagram—give meaning. Any concrete example that has the same type of neuronal network can be used to create this conceptual, or abstract, idea of life.

This is why metaphors, parables, and stories are so powerful when we want to teach a concept. We cannot understand anything unless we create internal neuronal networks that reflect some set of physical relationships that accurately map the relationships in the concept. At a minimum, we must be sure that our students have connections of this sort. We must push them to tell us their metaphors or stories.

The same is true of analogies. Again, we should provide students with physical analogies for ideas, and we should ask them to tell us their analogies. If they don't have any, it is quite possible that they have not learned. If they show us mistaken analogies, we get insight into their prior knowledge (existing networks). And if they have good analogies, they become useful teaching tools for everyone!

Helping People Learn

Oliver Wendell Holmes said that "once we stretch our mind around a new idea, it never returns to its former shape." This fits much of what I have been saying about how we learn. As new and different networks of neurons fire because of our sensory input—our experience—these networks constantly change. They form new connections and lose others. The brain physically changes.

Let's review some of the specific ways teachers can change brains:

1. Watch for inherent networks (natural talents) and encourage their practice.
2. Repeat, repeat, repeat!
3. Arrange for "firing together." Associated things should happen together.
4. Focus on sensory input that is "errorless."
5. Don't stress mistakes. Don't reinforce neuronal networks that aren't useful.
6. Try to understand existing networks and build on them. Nothing is new.
7. Misconnected networks are most often just incomplete. Try to add to them.
8. Be careful about resurrecting old networks; error dies hard.
9. Construct metaphors and insist that your students build their own metaphors.
10. Use analogies and similes, too.

You may notice that this list is a combination of older ideas and newer ones about teaching. For example, it includes practice and drill as well as construction of knowledge. This is important because it illustrates how studying the way the brain works gives us independent insight into teaching. We can see where the time-honored practices of educators might be retained and even increased and where the newer concepts of constructivism are also essential.

Neurobiology has no educational philosophy, and that is a good thing. If we follow what the brain is telling us, we can free ourselves from the education wars!

Notes

1. As strange as it may seem, this proposal has been debated for many years. The debate started with Noam Chomsky, *Rules and Representations* (New York: Columbia University Press, 1980); also see review by E. Bates and J. Elman, *Science* 274 (1996), p. 1849.

2. I am indebted to Professor Hillel Chiel for this image.

3. Other things can change, such as the myelination, but the most important change, and the one that seems to happen fast enough for learning, is the nature of the synapses.

4. The development of the pattern of veins in our legs is an example of an epigenetic process. We all have genes for vein production, but the genes do not control the pattern. That pattern is influenced by physical things in our physical experience, such as pressures from the surrounding tissues when we move in the womb. This experience differs for all of us, so we all have different vein patterns, even identical twins with the same genes.

5. The classic study demonstrating change in neuronal networks produced by experience is probably the paper by D. N. Hubel and T. N. Wiesel, *Journal of Neurophysiology* 28 (1965), p. 1041. This experiment showed that the wiring of the visual cortex in kittens was altered when there was no sensory input to the eye. There is also a *Scientific American* article by the same authors, vol. 241, (1979), pp. 150–162.

6. H. J. Neville and colleagues, *Proceedings of the National Academy of Sciences* 95 (1998), p. 922; a brief summary of cortical plasticity is presented in F. E. Bloom, C. Nelson, and A. Lazerson, *Brain, Mind, and Behavior,* 3rd ed. (New York: Worth Publishers, 2001), p. 344.

7. M. Maletic-Savatic and colleagues, *Science* 283 (1999), p. 1923.

8. M. Diamond and colleagues, *Journal of Comparative Neurology* 123 (1964), p. 111; M. Diamond and J. Hopson, *Magic Trees of the Mind* (New York: Plume Publishing, 1999).

9. Terrance Deacon, *The Symbolic Species* (New York: W. W. Norton, 1997), p. 108.

10. Actually, as Steven Rose explains in his book *The Making of Memory* (New York: Doubleday, 1993), it was an Italian physician named Tanzi who first put this idea in writing more than 100 years ago. He doesn't get full credit because this was long before the neuronal basis of brain function was known and no one could understand how his suggestions would work.

11. D. O. Hebb, *The Organization of Behavior* (New York: Wiley, 1969).

12. See P. R. Huttenlocher in *Human Behavior and the Developing Brain,* edited by Geraldine Dawson and Kurt W. Fischer (New York: Guilford Press, 1994), p. 142. Brain tissue was obtained from people who died of accidents at different ages; Huttenlocher's study represents averages of many different people over the time span of a lifetime. It does not represent what happens in a particular person. The data shown are for the visual cortex. Similar results have been obtained for other parts of the cortex, but with different time frames.

13. Gerald Edelman, *Bright Air, Brilliant Fire* (New York: Basic Books, 1992), p. 81.

14. M. Ylvisaker and T. J. Feeney, *Collaborative Brain Injury Intervention: Positive Everyday Routines* (San Diego, CA: Singular, 1998); also see L. Turkstra, *Seminars in Speech and Language* 22 (2001), pp. 150–151.

15. W. Zheng and E. I. Knudsen, *Science* 284 (1999), p. 962.

16. See G. Lakoff and M. Johnson, *Philosophy in the Flesh* (New York: Basic Books, 1999). This work was preceded by a number of shorter books, the most important of which is probably *Metaphors We Live By* (Chicago: University of Chicago Press, 1980).

SUMMARY
OF PART II

In this part of the book, I have tried to be more specific about what happens when we learn and how teachers can benefit from that knowledge. The most important point, I believe, is the idea of building on existing knowledge—existing neuronal networks. Even when these networks seem to be in error, they can still be of use for teachers. In fact, they are the most valuable source of information, telling teachers what may be missing and what is necessary to make them useful.

Again, let me remind you of the key words or phrases that recall the most important concepts in this section: *neuronal networks, prior knowledge, construction, concrete experience, tangles, inherent gifts, associations, errorless, build don't destroy, metaphors,* and *analogies.*

Now we are ready to revisit the parts of the cerebral cortex that we discussed in Part I. Using the concepts we have developed in Part II, we can now see how they may be applied to our five regions of cortex: sensory, back integrative, front integrative, motor, and limbic.

PART III

USING MORE OF THE CEREBRAL CORTEX TO DEEPEN LEARNING

How can the teacher take advantage of the power of the sensory cortex? How can we challenge the back integrative cortex to produce deeper comprehension? What are ways that we can encourage the learner to use the frontal integrative cortex in construction of her own knowledge? What do we mean by action, and how can we help the learner actively test her ideas and complete the loop of learning? What models of teaching most effectively engage the emotional brain and thus provide optimal learning?

8

SENSE LUSCIOUS

USING THE POWER OF THE SENSORY BRAIN
TO HELP PEOPLE LEARN

How sense-luscious the world is!
—*Diane Ackerman*

I still remember the lecture of my life.

I had taught biochemistry for many years, and I knew it backward and forward. So I agreed with no hesitation when my colleague, Chris, asked me to fill in for him on the spur of the moment. He wanted me to lecture about mitochondria, the so-called "power plants" of the cell, and there was no subject I understood better.

I was totally relaxed as I walked into the class. This was a group of premedical students, and as usual they were wound up and ready to go—and I was ready for them!

In the next fifty minutes, I gave a brilliant lecture on how cells get their energy from sugars and fats. I had no notes, but I covered the board systematically from left to right as the period progressed. Everything was organized in my head, and it just poured out the end of that piece of chalk. Nuances were crystal clear. The underlying concepts were powerful and yet obvious. I was hot!

At the end of class, I put my chalk down, dusted my hands on my pants, and asked for questions. I was slightly surprised that there weren't any, but I attributed that to the clarity of my lecture. Only one student stayed, and that was just to butter me up. "That was a wonderful lecture," she said. "I think I really understood!"

It turned out that Chris needed me for the next class, too, so I used my second meeting with his students to check out what they had learned from my brilliant lecture. And, naturally, I wanted them to see how much they had learned!

You may have guessed the outcome already. The lecture of my life was followed by one of the greatest surprises of my life. As I probed their understanding with increasingly easier questions, I was met with complete silence. Even my student fan had nothing to say.

Finally, I was relieved to see a hand go up at the back of the room. "Yes?" I responded eagerly. "Dr. Zull," he said, "could you explain about mitochondria again?"

*   *   *

In chapters 2 and 3 I talked about the brain's natural cycle of learning and the idea that the back and front parts of the cortex play much different roles in this cycle. I also suggested that teachers should balance their teaching so that students use both the front and back cortex. And I promised you that I would come back to this and talk more about my ideas of *how* to teach in that way.

Now I will try to deliver on that promise. This and each of the following chapters will focus on how teachers can challenge a particular part of the cerebral cortex.

This chapter is about the part of the back cortex that first receives sensory input, the so-called *sensory cortex*. Actually the sensory input from different sense organs goes to different parts of the brain, so I am not referring to just one part of the cortex when I use the term *sensory brain*. Rather I am talking about any region of cortex that is the first to receive input from one of the senses. For example, the auditory cortex and the visual cortex are both part of the sensory brain.

In terms of the learning cycle, the sensory brain is where our concrete experience is first recorded in the cortex. The sensory brain gathers the raw materials for reflection, abstraction, and action.

We can underestimate the richness of these raw materials. Ackerman is right when she says that the world is "sense-luscious." As we live our lives and have our experiences, our brains are literally awash in signals both from outside and inside our bodies. One important thing we will see in this chapter is how powerful our sensory brain is. There is really no need to invent any special, nonphysical theories about how we sense the world. Our physical brain is more than up to the task.

Even though we live in a luscious mix of light, sound, and sensation, I am going to focus mostly on sensory experience through light—the sense of vision. The basic ideas we will encounter are illustrated best by vision, and once we see how we see, it is easy to extend those concepts to the other senses. Vision is central to any concrete experience that we have. In many ways, our brain is a "seeing" brain.

Revisiting the Back Brain

Let's review what we have said so far about the back cortex, using the illustration below. During concrete experience, physical information from the world and from our bodies enters the brain through the sense organs (eyes, ears, nose, skin, mouth, internal organs, joints, and muscles). It is then sent in parallel to the emotion monitor (amygdala) and the specific parts of the cortex for each of the senses (visual cortex, auditory cortex, somatosensory cortex, etc.). If the amygdala recognizes the experience as dangerous, it will trigger an instinctive body action, such as jumping back or freezing. That is the extreme response. Normally, both the emotional and cognitive content of experience are sent on to the cortex to be processed by the integrative cortex in the parietal and temporal lobes. This is where cognitive meaning begins to form. In this chapter we will talk mostly about the sensing part of this process, the part that proceeds to integration and meaning.

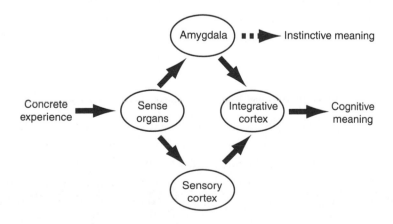

Seeing Things

When we understand something, we say, "I see." This is no accident. The brain's ability to visualize is arguably the most significant aspect of cognition. When we try to help people learn, we want them to "get the picture."

Thus, we will begin our discussion of the sensory brain with vision. What happens in our brain when we see things?

Part of the answer to this question is that different neurons in the visual brain see different *parts of things*. The brain first senses the visual world in little bits, but each bit is detected at the same time. We say that the information for each bit is sent in parallel with that for the other bits.

This "disassembly" of visual information actually begins in the eyes, even before any signals reach the brain. Certain cells in the eye sense the *color* of objects, and other cells sense the *form* of objects. Each of these two types of cells sends its signals to different neurons in the sensory brain. Still, the information for color and form all arrive at once in the brain because they travel on parallel pathways.

The first neurons in the visual cortex to receive signals from the eyes respond to specific aspects of that input. To register the form of something, the bits of information consist of edges, or lines, which run at different angles. Added up, they produce an outline of objects and features in the visual field. Basically, every object we see becomes a set of lines, or edges. For example, when we look at a window, our brain sees vertical and horizontal edges for the window frame. Certain neurons in the brain respond to the vertical edges, and other neurons respond to the horizontal ones. And if through that window, we see the branches of a tree angling up from the tree trunk toward the sky, that perception depends on neurons that respond to edges going at an angle.

Details

One way to represent what our early visual cortex "sees" is illustrated below, showing the letters *O* and *C* as sets of edges at different angles. This is crude representation but it makes an important point. The difference between the two letters is detected instantly, even though the actual physical difference is very small. Details make all the difference!

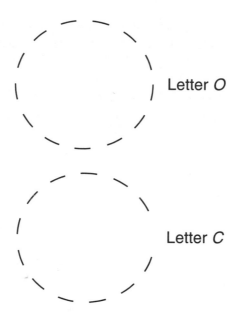

Letter *O*

Letter *C*

Our brains become accustomed to discerning details like this, but they can also make mistakes if we get careless. I was reminded of this recently when my daughter *Bess* won a small amount of money in the Ohio Lottery. Instead of *Bess*, her check was made out to *Ben*. I was puzzled by this, until I wrote the two words side by side and realized what tiny details separate the two words as I had written them:

The differences between the letter *B* in both words were ignored both by my brain and by the brain of the person who wrote out the check. But the differences between the *ss* and the *n* were important to each of us. They made the difference between Bess and Ben. I leave it to you. Which is which?

A Teacher Looks for Details

The fact that the brain is fully capable of seeing great detail and nuance is encouraging for teachers. We shouldn't doubt for a moment that our learners *can* see the fine points. And when it seems like they can't, we should look at ourselves for the remedy. Here is an example.

* * *

I was teaching about energy changes in chemical reactions, which chemists call ΔG. (The "Δ" stands for the "change" in energy, and the G for the amount of energy.) As we got deeper into the subject, I explained that under some special conditions, this energy change is called ΔG *prime,* written $\Delta G'$.

This seemed fine with my students until the test came along, and I soon discovered that several of them never even noticed the *prime.* And when I deducted points for this omission, they accused me of being picky!

I had been called "picky" before. It fits right in with another common accusation, which is that I give my students "busy work." In both cases, I put importance on something that seemed trivial to my students. The details that I knew were important were hardly visible to them!

This time, rather than shrugging off the indictment, I decided to do something about it. I decided to change my teaching.

The change I made was based on my growing understanding of the sensory brain. I was coming to appreciate its ability to sense even the smallest details, and I decided that my students should be able to focus on those details if I worked harder.

Actually, the changes I made were minimal. First, I just paid more attention to the *prime.* I wrote it with colored chalk for awhile, and every time I said "delta G prime," I would stop and say, "delta G *prrrrime!*" Second, I began to pay more attention to details in my preparation for classes. I consciously looked for places where little things make a big difference. Third, I explained that I was doing this to my students, and I asked them to do it, too.

I was surprised at the effect this had. It became almost a game; who can find the important little things? Who would notice some small thing first? For example, one day a student noticed that I was writing my deltas a little smaller and wondered if this was important. My students began to use their sensory brain in a more effective way. They grew to realize that a detail can mean everything, or it can mean nothing. The trick is to know which is which.

Novice, Expert, and Details

The experience I just described led me to recognize something that seems important. Whether we are an expert or a novice, our brains basically sense the same things. The difference is that the expert knows which part of his sensory data is important and which part isn't. The brain of the chemist knows that the *prime* is important, but the size of the delta isn't. The chemistry novice, on the other hand, sees every little thing as being of equal value. To him, it is still all just sensory input.

We have known this for a long time. In his 1840 essay, *On the art of teaching,* Horace Mann wrote, "The removal of a slight impediment, the drawing aside of the thinnest veil, is worth more to him [the learner] than volumes of lore on collateral subjects." And later Mann noted, "the mind of the teacher should migrate, as it were, into those of his pupils."[1]

This brings us back to the importance of seeing things as the student sees them. We must see through the student's eyes. This means that we must look back and see our subject as it was at first, when it was just sensory input!

It remains a mystery why some teachers do this well and some don't do it at all. My guess is that many of us have never even thought of it. And it may be that sometimes we are just carried away by our own engagement with our subject, so much so that we almost forget the student.

In any case, I can testify that a conscious, persistent effort made a difference for me. I am better at seeing what the student sees now that I have thought about it.

Attending

Seeing details requires attention. But paying attention is not easy. Many barriers keep us from paying attention.

One such barrier is the amygdala. As I outlined earlier in this chapter and in chapter 5, sensory input is continually screened for possible negative emotional content by the amygdala. If we instinctively sense difficulty or threat, our actions will not be controlled by our sensory cortex that breaks things down into details, but by our survival shortcut through the amygdala, which is fast but misses details.

Another, possibly even more common, barrier to attending is our own misunderstanding of what it means. What should we do when we pay attention?

At one of our teaching discussions with university faculty members, I asked that very question: "What do you do when you try to pay attention?" They wrote their responses on a slip of paper, which I then read to the group.

Here are a few of them:

"I try to focus on the subject and ignore what is peripheral."

"I sit still, look right at the person, and listen carefully to their words."

"I set aside my sexual fantasies and try to focus on what is being said." (Yes, this was an actual response!)

Clearly, attention is about focus. It also seems to suggest being physically still, which presumably helps us focus. However, as Ellen Langer points out in *The Power of Mindful Learning*,[2] these notions about paying attention may not work very well. If we look hard at one thing, the image becomes blurred and our mind finds itself in a struggle to just keep focusing. We find ourselves focusing on focusing itself.

This is absolutely biological. Paying attention does not mean unrelenting attention on one focal point. Our brain evolved to notice details by *shifting* its focus from one area to another, by repeatedly scanning the surroundings. This was better for survival. The brain is more likely to notice details when it scans than when it focuses. We exhaust our neurons if we make a constant demand on the same ones for too long. We rest them by using different ones for a bit and then coming back to the details that seem important.

An example of this is shown in the figure that follows, which is an experiment on the movement of the eyes when people studied a photograph entitled "Girl from Volga." The strange looking image on the right shows how the eyes move as they focus on different regions of the picture. The lines show the eye movements and the dots are the regions of the picture on which the observer focused (where movement stopped). Thus, the dark areas are the places that were examined the most. The experiment clearly shows that the eyes do not stay focused on any one area of the photograph for long, but instead jump from place to place, returning more frequently to areas of interest. Rather than holding our eyes still, or boring in on one area, we "study" the picture by *moving* our eyes.³

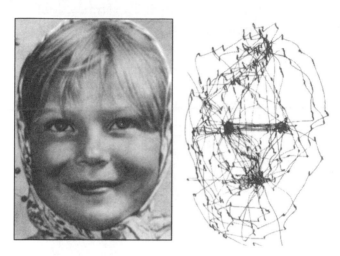

Importantly, these eye movements are unconscious. It is just the way our visual brain works. It looks for details, not by attending to one area for a long time, but rather by returning to areas of greatest interest more often.

It seems then, that instead of asking people to pay attention, we might ask them to look at things from many different angles. Instead of sitting still, we might ask them to move around so they can see details. In fact, Langer experimented with this approach. She asked students to study a famous painting by walking back and forth in front of it instead of sitting still. Her experiment was very biological, as you can see. She just took advantage of what the brain does by itself. The outcome seemed good for this theory. Students who studied this way remembered more about the painting than those that sat still in front of it and "paid attention" to it.

Seeing the World Is Mapping the World

We have seen that the visual brain breaks things up into little bits. Now we can turn to what is at once one of the most remarkable, and the most necessary, functions of how the brain organizes these bits.

Basically, the physical arrangement of the neurons that fire when we see an object is a map of the physical structure of the object itself.

It is difficult to explain this effectively with words, so let's use the power of the visual brain. The illustration below depicts one of the experiments that demonstrates this idea. The strange looking object at left is part of the brain of a monkey; it is an *actual piece of the visual cortex*. The dark spots on this piece of brain show places where the neurons have been particularly active. These are clusters of neurons that have fired frequently while the monkey looked at a specific object.[4] That object was the "half-wheel" shown on the right.

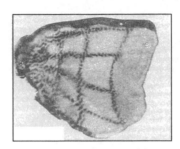 

This result is striking. The most active cells are arranged in a geometric pattern that contains all the physical relationships of the image itself! Every line in it has a corresponding line of active neurons in the brain. These lines converge at the center, like those in the image, and they cross one another in an exact replication of the image.

This and other experiments have shown that the visual world is literally and physically mapped in our brains. The networks of neurons that fire when we see something retains the physical relationships that characterize what we see. Our concrete experience of seeing is retained in a concrete form of physically connected neurons in the brain.[5]

What Images Give Us

We can visualize the world with our eyes closed. Neuroscience doesn't have a complete explanation of these images yet, but there is little doubt that they begin with physical maps consisting of connected neurons in the brain. Our brains are full of such networks, and it seems certain that what we call thinking and remembering is based on them.[6]

How rich these images are! We have an image of a person walking, but that image also brings an image for *motion* itself into our consciousness. An image of two trees beside one another activates the neuronal network for the concept of *comparison* and for *number.* An image of one person above another is an image of *status.* An image of a core in an apple is an image of *enveloping,* or including. In fact, images give us the concepts on which we construct language itself: verbs, nouns, prepositions (whether one thing is *on* or *beside* another), number, gender, and even articles (e.g., whether it was *the* dog or just *a* dog).

Physical objects in the world contain conceptual relationships, and so, then, do the neuronal networks of our brain. When we realize the centrality of images, it isn't hard to understand why they are by far the easiest thing for the human brain to remember. Memory experiments with pictures have produced amazing results. For example, people can recall seeing hundreds, even thousands of pictures, even when they have seen the pictures for only a few seconds. Researchers in this field have even suggested that there is *no* upper limit to the number of pictures that the brain can store![7]

Our concrete experience contains much of the information we need for understanding, because it produces images for our brains to analyze, rearrange, manipulate, and turn into action. We have maps of our experience in our brains, and we can run through these maps like the frames of a moving picture. We can switch to a brain video of our life anytime we wish.

The Best Image

One of the most important and powerful aspects of experiential learning is that the images in our brains come from the experience itself. These are by far the richest images. They are undiluted and direct, rather than being transported or filtered through text, film, TV, or lecture. They contain data from all the senses at once, rather than just vision, or just sound. They are "sense-luscious."

My guess is that this richness influences the emotional brain. Experiences have a "feel" to them, and getting our images by direct experience feels better. "You had to be there," we say when we are at a loss to convey the entirety of our experience in words.

We are also more likely to trust the sensory input from the experience itself. I suspect that this confidence and trust in our sensory input of the "real thing" has a calming effect on our amygdala. And a calmer amygdala means clearer thinking.

I am reminded of the first time I went to a major league baseball game. The minute I entered the stadium, I sensed electricity in the air. The excitement was palpable. And as I watched the players warm up, I was amazed at the things I sensed. The ball literally whistled through the air. There was incredible beauty in the throwing action of the players, which I had never noticed when I watched games on TV. I could see the completion of the throw and the fluidity of the players as they moved effortlessly into their next motion. It was all one big ballet, and I could sense its wholeness, rather than being limited to what a camera man would choose to show me. There was freedom in this experience. It felt clear, complete, and safe. It was the best image I could have.

Images and Academics

Given the centrality of images, it seems that teachers could make extensive use of images to help people learn. If we can convert an idea into an image, we should do so. And whenever possible, we should require our students to show us their images. It should go both ways.

It is easy to see how certain subjects can be conveyed with images. For example, a great deal of chemistry or biology can be taught completely with images. Other academic subjects may seem more difficult at first, but with creativity it seems likely that almost anything a person would want to learn can be put in the form of an image.

Take mathematics. It is full of images. Calculus produces images of motion and change in motion and of filling up spaces. It may be one of the most image-dependent subjects. And exponents give dramatic images of growth, attrition, explosion and fading away.

The figure that follows illustrates how Rob Dunn, a professor of music at my university, uses images. He converts music into visual maps. This figure represents Rob's image of the first line in Strauss' *Also sprach Zarathustra*.

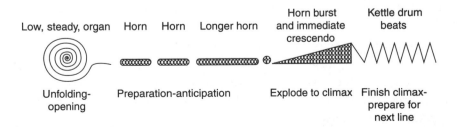

This image suggests the dynamics, the structure, and even the instruments themselves for this dramatic piece. It begins with the unfolding of a steady sound from the organ, followed by intense horn sounds of different lengths, and ending with six loud drumbeats. The images also suggest the character of the sound. Horns tend to be steady clear bands rather than thin lines, for example. And the images reveal the strategy of the composer in leading the listener, generating excitement, and holding our attention. The visual image is a pedagogical tool for helping students understand the composition and a learning tool for enhancing recall and aiding discovery about the music.[8]

Teaching as Showing

In one of the teaching seminars I recently attended, the speaker described some experiments in which a teacher was helping children learn. The speaker repeatedly said that the teacher provides "support" for the learner. So I asked him what he meant by "support." What did the teacher actually do?

His answer was amazingly simple. He just said, "show them." Just let the student see what you consider to be a good answer or a good example.

This rang a bell with me because I had just discovered that the origin of the word teacher seems to be an old English word *techen,* which meant "to show!" A teacher is one who shows. And, of course, it is entirely consistent with what we have said so far about the visual brain. People see what we show, and when they truly see, when their eyes are opened, they will not need our explanations.

Some of you may protest that a teacher does more than just show things to his students. It doesn't seem satisfying to think of teaching that way. Anyone can do that!

I think not. If our task is to show, then we must decide what we are going to show and how. Here are some points to consider.

First, we must think carefully about our choices in *what* we show. It won't be enough to simply throw something together at the last minute. We have to decide what are the best examples of the things we believe to be most important. What do we really want our students to learn? We need to choose things that show fine points as well as the big picture. We should show what we hope our students will eventually be able to do themselves.

Second, I think we should stay close to the raw image of concrete experience whenever possible. This is the level where we share the most with the student, where our brains come closest to sensing the same thing. We should give the student opportunities to have concrete experiences directly, if possible. Field trips, internships, research projects, true hands-on experiences, collaborations, role playing, and other active learning methods are effective for this very reason. And we should share these experiences with them. The point is to bring the teacher and the student as close together in their concrete experience as possible. Then they will have the same images, and the teacher can understand "what the student already knows," as we discussed in chapter 6.

Third, we should point out the important parts of images. In many cases we don't need to say why these parts are of interest or explain things. We just need to encourage students to "Notice this part." Or ask, "Did you see that part?" Students must notice the important things in order to have useful images. Often, the kind of things we look for have become second nature to us, but by experiencing how we look at the details and seeing what we think is important, our students can begin to form the habits of observation and study that work best in our field.

We can be creative in this "showing." We can even show students what happens when mistakes are made. For example, we can show them how important it is to add acid to water rather than water to acid. We don't have to explain it. They will get the picture themselves.

Show more, share more.

Hearing Things

Of course, concrete experience involves more than just seeing things. In fact, one of the most important points about experiential learning is that it engages all of our senses. But when we look at the other senses, we still find ourselves coming back to the main points we found with vision. Let's look at hearing to illustrate this.

First, our auditory cortex gets its sensory input in little bits, just as with vision. The bits are not edges, but rather frequencies or pitch. Different cells in the ear respond to different pitches, and those cells are wired to specific cells in the auditory cortex. This means that our hearing is also sensitive to details. All the points we made about the importance of details in teaching apply to what the student hears as well as to what he sees.

The brain also attends to sound in a way that is similar to vision. We cannot focus on a particular sound to the exclusion of all others for long. If we do, it loses its significance. Rather, we listen intensely to new sounds for a short time, and then others become more interesting. Our brain expects movement in sound, not fixed attention on one sound.

In fact, if we hear a repeated sound for awhile, it becomes mesmerizing—even tranquilizing. Eventually we begin to ignore it; we literally do not hear it. This is called *habituation,* and it is a characteristic of neurons and networks of neurons. The synapses actually fire less frequently if we hear the same sound over and over. This explains why we can live in an apartment by a major freeway, and after a few weeks we do not even hear the traffic.

Nothing demonstrates habituation more than a lecture. Unless we break up the sound every few minutes, we are almost certain to induce habituation in a learner's brain. Even when we think we are breaking it up, we all have "our way" of speaking, and the learner gets used to our way, whatever it is, with time. You may have noticed how interest picks up when a new person begins to talk in a class or a lecture. That interest holds up for a short while, even if the speaker ultimately turns out to be "boring." At first, it is enough that he is new.

A third similarity to vision is that our sense of sound hooks into our image networks. We hear where things are, when they happened, and what they were like. This information is all assembled into a sound map, which, like a vision map, retains many of the actual physical features associated with the experience itself. This is why we can close our eyes, listen, and "picture" what is happening.

The Special Powers of Sound

Sound also has special powers that enrich our concrete experience in ways that vision cannot.

One of these powers is that sound can go around the corner. We can know things that are happening in hidden places if we can hear them. We can make the world aware of our hidden opportunities, or dilemmas, through sound. And we can communicate our identity to an

inattentive world through sound. As in *Horton Hears a Who,* we can
cry out, "We are here! We are here!" Even more remarkable, we can
call out, "I am here! Jim is here!" This ability is natural and quite
sophisticated in the animal world. For example, dolphins seem to communicate their "names" to each other by specific sounds.[9]

Using sound is also an immensely personal way to communicate.
We cry, we laugh, we scream, and we talk. Our friends recognize our
voices when we phone them, and they can tell how we feel from the
way we sound. Our sounds are generated by our personal voice apparatus, which is of unique shape, size, and conformation. We all sound
different. We truly speak with a different voice. And it is hard to hide
how we feel when we talk. Despite our best efforts at deception, our
feelings often come through.

Because brains can both produce and detect sound, and because it
is personal and emotional, sound is a natural vehicle for learning. We
see this in the animal world as well. Birds learn their songs from other
birds and can learn many different sounds from people. Whale songs
seem to evolve with experience, somewhat like language. And preliter-
ate human cultures preserved their history with stories and songs,
because they were learned so easily.

A Note on the Other Senses

Even though I said that we would limit ourselves to vision, I can't end
this section on sensory experience without briefly mentioning the
potential value of the other senses for the teacher.

Probably one of the reasons that the experience itself is the best sensory input is that it contains more than just sound and sight. Concrete
experience produces a rich blend of all the senses. We feel the experience.

There is no more powerful sensory stimulus of the emotions than
smell and taste, and as we saw in chapters 4 and 5, emotion is key to
learning. So it seems obvious that providing smells and tastes will help
people learn. This doesn't happen often in school learning, but I think
it could. For example, we might incorporate the smell of a burning tire
when we talk about friction in a physics class. Or we might bring in the
odors of putrefying flesh (organic chemists know which chemicals to
use) when we describe a civil war battlefield. I am sure you can think

of many other good possibilities for enriching the sensory content of academic subjects.

The sense of touch can also enrich learning. One of my colleagues in the neuroscience department has a sealed plastic bag filled with cooked oatmeal that she uses when she talks about the brain. As she is talking, the bag of oatmeal is being passed around the room, and students who hold and squeeze that bag have a vivid memory of how it would feel to hold a fresh human brain in their hands.

In fact, touch and vision are similar in their mapping capabilities. We can close our eyes and determine how an object would look by feeling it. Blind people use the vision part of their brain when reading Braille, and once a blind person examined how I "look" by touching my face and head.

There is also the sense of body position. We know if we are seated or standing, relaxed or tense, leaning forward or slouching. We feel the weight of objects held in our hand, their heft and balance. And we feel the strain if we are working. This sensory input into our brain becomes a part of our maps of concrete experiences.

Finally, we sense our feelings. We sense whether we are afraid or confident, excited or calm, attracted or repelled in all our experiences. Emotion is part of our sensory experience, providing flavor and quality to the maps in our brain.

I have no doubt that we could do better in helping people learn if we paid more attention to all of these.

The Lecture of My Life and the Concrete Experience of the Classroom

By now it should be easy to see why the lecture of my life was such a dud. I really didn't consider any of the things we have been talking about in this chapter. My students had very few of the images that I had. There were far too many details they could not notice and had not practiced. And I didn't show them anything at all about mitochondria; I showed them a professor passionately engaged in his subject. That is not without value, but it does not help a student learn about metabolism!

In many ways, my lecture was like the Gary Larson cartoon in which Ginger the dog is listening carefully and hopefully to her master. He says, "O.K. I've had it with you, Ginger! Be a good girl and stay out of the garbage!" And in the second panel, we see what Ginger hears: "Blah, blah, blah, Ginger! Blah, blah!" Poor Ginger is just getting sound—no meaning.

As we noted in chapter 2, a classroom is, first of all, a concrete experience. The sights and sounds that a student finds there first enter his brain through the senses. It can be mostly sound, even "blah, blah, blah." It can be a visual image of a teacher either standing still or moving around enthusiastically. It can be an emotional image of support or threat. It can be the sound of chalk on blackboard and the sight of symbols appearing and disappearing on that board. It can be a series of images on a screen in a dark room, accompanied by a droning voice or an excited voice.

Or it can be images, sounds, and feelings that connect with what the student already knows. It can be watching an expert model how to solve a problem. It *can be* learning. But *it is* concrete experience; *it is* sensory input to his brain.

Notes

1. Horace Mann, reprint of essay *On the Art of Teaching* (Bedford, MA: Applewood Books, 1989).
2. E. Langer, *The Power of Mindful Learning* (Cambridge, MA: Perseus Publishing, 1998).
3. With permission from A. Yarbus, *Eye Movements and Vision* (New York: Plenum Press, 1967).
4. A small amount of radioactive sugar was injected into the bloodstream of a monkey in a darkened room, with the image of the half-wheel projected on the wall. Looking at this image triggered specific neurons in the animal's visual brain; these specific neurons need more energy than others and thus take up more radioactivity sugar. These more active neuron clusters appear dark in the image. Taken with permission from R. H. B. Tootel and colleagues, *J. Neuroscience* 8 (1988), p. 1551.
5. The same can be said of sensory input by touch.
6. See A. Kossyln, *Images and Brain* (Cambridge, MA: MIT Press, 1996).
7. Ibid., p. 130. Other studies suggested the astonishing result that the human brain can search for more than 50,000 images per second in long-term memory!
8. With permission (R. E. Dunn). For more examples and discussion of the use of images in "Creative Thinking and Music Listening," see R. E. Dunn, *Research Studies in Music Education* (July 1997), p. 42.
9. V. M. Janik, *Science* 289 (2001), p. 1355.

WAITING FOR UNITY

HELPING PEOPLE COMPREHEND
THEIR EXPERIENCE

It is unity that doth enchant me.
                    —*Giordana Bruno*

Eric was a new math instructor and eager to try out his theories of teaching. But he ran into trouble. Shortly after the semester began, nearly half of his students dropped out. So he came to talk to me. And I listened—patiently, I hope.

"Those students are lazy," he began, and I braced myself for an intense and emotional conversation! "I do give them hard problems," he went on. "I want them to learn that they can think! But they just give up. If they can't solve a problem right away, they just quit!"

"You know how I solve a hard problem?" Eric rushed on. "I just let it stir for a few days. I think about it on and off. I don't expect immediate revelations. So why should a student expect an answer right away?"

Then he continued. "Usually the breakthrough comes when I am not expecting it, maybe in the shower in the morning or when I'm walking the dog. Things just come together. There is this beautiful unity! It's never planned. It just happens."

Now he was excited. "It's thrilling. Almost as good as sex!" He laughed. "Well, hard problems do require foreplay! Problems that can be solved instantly are no fun!"

He thought for a minute and then went on. "You know what?" he said. "I wonder if my students even think about math outside my class. They probably never take time to reflect or puzzle over a problem."

I thought I should defend the students, at least a little, so finally I spoke. "They do take a pretty heavy load," I ventured.

It was quiet for a minute, and then Eric spoke, more slowly. "That's a good point. I forgot that. When I was in college, I took at least six courses every semester. And I got good grades because I was fast. No one ever rewarded reflection!"

This seemed to depress him, and when he spoke again, I could see why. "I'm afraid my theory won't work. College students don't have time to think. In fact, we probably reward the ones who think the least."

*   *   *

The previous chapter explored how the back cortex gets information in small bits and then reassembles it. Important parts of this reassembly take place in the integrative back cortex. In terms of the learning cycle, this integration process is what we expect to happen during "reflective observation." As implied by the term *reflective,* it may take considerable time to get everything integrated and see the full meaning of our experience. We have to think about things (reflect) and examine the images in our memory (observation). We stand back from our experience, look it over, and think about it. And what we look for is an image that fits *all* of our experience. We look for unity.

The task for the teacher is to help her students in this search. But it is inherently private, and we cannot enforce it directly. Our work is to give assignments that require reflection and that induce learners to reflect on the right things. In this chapter we will examine what those things are and how the integrative back cortex puts those reflections together.

What's to Integrate?

The following illustration is a reminder of the structural relationship between the major regions of the sensory cortex and the integrative cortex in the back cortex. The three sensory areas for vision, hearing, and touching are shown because these parts of the cortex give us most of our cognitive information about the world. As we noted in chapter 8, these three senses tell us things like shape, spatial relationship, and location. They provide what we would call "objective" information.

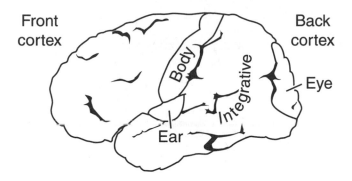

The point of this drawing is that the integrative cortex is adjacent to—in fact, right in the middle of—these three dominant regions of sensory cortex. So it is a short journey for signals to travel from these sensory regions to the integrative back cortex.

In fact there is a lot of overlap in what we can learn from these three senses. For example, the shape of something can be determined by feeling it and looking at it, and the location of something can be determined by listening to it or looking at it.

However, we do need to remember that each sense gives us unique information too, and the integration of *all* this sensory input is needed for us to comprehend the objects and events that make up our concrete experience in the world.

What and Where

A great deal of what is known about the integrative parts of the back cortex comes from the visual system, so we will build on that information.

Signals from the visual cortex travel to the integrative regions in the back cortex via two different routes. As is illustrated in following figure, one way is upward and forward and the other downward and forward (the upper and lower routes). It turns out that the upper and lower areas of the back integrative cortex are responsible for very different things. The upper route leads to understanding *where* things are. It analyzes spatial relationships and pays particular attention to how things are arranged especially when we want to copy that arrangement (i.e., mimic something).

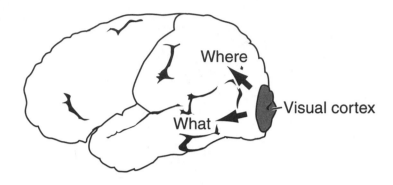

This upper pathway is also part of what is called the "attention network." It becomes active when we are trying to pay attention. This makes sense, since paying attention to something first requires that we find *where* that thing is located.

The lower integrative area does something different. It analyzes the neuronal maps for information about *what* the brain is seeing and puts images in categories. Is it a person or an object, alive or inert? The *what* region also goes beyond recognizing categories to identify specific objects within categories. For example, this region is responsible for recognition of individual faces. It not only tells us *what* but *who*.

There are other important things that happen in the integrative back cortex, but we will postpone talking about them while we consider how this idea of *what* and *where* might be used in helping people learn.

Beginning Comprehension: Categories and Relationships

As we saw in chapter 8, the neuronal maps produced in our sensory brain retain the relationships of the physical world that created them. So these relationships continue to be preserved as the signals are passed on to the integrating back cortex. This allows for identification of categories as we noted previously. The best hypothesis seems to be that the brain knows things belong in the same category because those things trigger similar combinations of neuronal networks.

Knowing what we see is not the same as naming it. For example, apes can distinguish dogs from cats,[1] but they do not seem to use language. Naming and knowing are separate and use separate parts of the brain.

Knowing *what* is an important step in beginning to comprehend our experience, but knowing *where* may be even more important. Knowing where things are gives us relationships. We can only know where things are, or where parts of things are, in reference to something else. For example, we know a chimney is on top of a house, but the relationship could also be stated by saying that the house is underneath the chimney. We can use either one to explain where the other one is. The relationship is important, not some absolute coordinates. There are no absolutes in relationships.

Spatial relationships tell us the detailed structure of the material world, and this structure leads to function (as we discussed in chapter 3). If we are to comprehend what surrounds us—our world and the objects in it—it is hard to think of something more important than knowing relationships.

Teaching How to Sail: Lesson in *What* and *Where*

Here is a story about my efforts to teach my friend, Tim, to sail a small boat. I hope it illustrates some important ideas about thinking of *what* and *where* when we teach.

*   *   *

Tim was excited about sailing. He had loved watching the sailboats as they skimmed over Lake Erie's sparkling surface. What a wonderful way to relax on a blue summer day!

So I agreed to teach Tim how to sail. I began Tim's education by giving him some new vocabulary.

"See that rope," I said, pointing up the mast. "It's called the halyard."

Tim nodded and repeated, "Halyard."

"And that one," I said, pointing to a coiled rope laying on the deck. "That is the sheet."

"I thought a sheet would be a sail," said Tim. "What about that expression 'three sheets to the wind' or something?"

"Nope, the sheets are ropes," I said. "The sails have names like *mainsel, jib,* and *spinnaker.*"

Tim shrugged. "OK," he said.

Shortly we motored out of the harbor and into a 10–15 knot breeze from the north, which was generating a 3–4 foot chop—not dangerous, but enough to keep us on our toes!

I headed into the wind and shouted to Tim. "OK, pull on the halyard."

The excitement was growing, and Tim looked around eagerly for a rope. Of course, he grabbed the sheet! It was the first rope he saw.

So it went on. It won't surprise you to hear that I ended up doing the sailing myself on this day. Between his excitement, his confusion of sheets with sails, and the strange word *halyard,* Tim was not much help out on that rough water.

But while we were out there, I was thinking about my pedagogy. There must be a better way to teach a novice! And I decided to try a different tack (pun intended) when we got safely back.

"Tim," I said as we rocked gently in the harbor. "Forget *halyards* and *sheets.* Just study the boat for awhile, and pay attention to *where* things are. Look at everything, including all the ropes, but don't worry about *what* they are. Just notice as much as you can about *where* they are."

Tim learned there was a rope that went up to a pulley at the top of the mast and back down. It was obviously meant to pull something up the mast. And he saw another rope attached to the corner of the sail, obviously meant to pull that corner in and let it out. When he saw where things were, their purpose became obvious.

Later that week, we tried again. And yes, we both did much better. When I shouted, "Raise the sail," he pulled on the rope attached to the top of the sail. And when I cried, "Let out the sail," he released the rope that let the corner of the sail swing wider away from the boat. We never used the words *halyard* and *sheet,* but we sailed well!

And, my satisfaction was complete when, the next time we sailed, Tim suddenly asked, "What did you call that rope again? The one that raises the sail?"

*   *   *

I have tried to make three points in this story. You will recognize the first one because we talked about it in chapter 8. The best teaching is often just showing. I showed Tim the boat and let him think about what he saw.

The second point is that with Tim, my teaching worked better when I did not start with the names of things. Tim knew *what* things were—for example, he knew about ropes, and he knew *where* they were—but he did not need to know their names right away.

The last point is that when he understood how things worked, Tim asked for the names. And the names came to symbolize concepts rather than just sounds. First he created meaning, and *then* he needed vocabulary.

More about Where

The meaning of *what* and its utility seems fairly obvious, but it seems worthwhile to think more about the idea of *where*. It means more than is at first apparent.

Where can mean more than the physical location of objects. In a story, for example, it can mean where in time. It can mean *when!* As we picture the story in our minds, we keep track of the time line by remembering what came first, second, and third and keeping these events lined up in that relationship in our minds.

Where can also mean a personal relationship. Where does my spouse fit into my life? It's not always an easy question; it requires comprehension to answer!

Where also tells us how the characters fit into a story. Only when we have a clear understanding of how the characters relate to one another, where to place them in relation to each other, can we understand the story itself.

And there are degrees of *where*. We might be close to a friend, but closer to a lover. The relationship might be powerful and direct, or subtle and tangential.

Where also helps us understand ourselves. We find deeper comprehension when we put ourselves in another's place, when we rearrange *where* we are. Comprehension deepens as we understand more and more about *where*.

Two Sides of Where

Earlier I said that the *where* region of the back cortex is part of the attention network.[2] This part of the cortex comes into action when we pay attention, look for things around us, or watch for something important to show up.

For many years it has been known that our awareness of the space around us is primarily the responsibility of the upper right side of the integrative back cortex. People with damage in this area don't pay attention to everything in the space around them. They may neglect part of it, and so this problem is called a "neglect syndrome." For example, if they are asked to draw the face of a clock, they may draw just the numbers on the right side of the clock. They are unaware of the numbers on the left side.

However, it turns out that we use the same area on the left side when we pay attention to specific objects, or limit the region that we attend to by drawing a boundary around it. If we pay specific attention to our hand, rather than just to the general space around us, or if we draw a circle around something, the left hemisphere becomes heavily engaged.[3]

In other words, there is general attention (right side) and specific attention (left side). Both tell us *where,* and we use both when we pay attention to things.

This is also the kind of *where* we use when we are analyzing movements we need in order to reproduce an action, to mimic something. The brain maps the location of each part of the movement. But this seems to be separate from the general awareness of space. In fact, the general neglect syndrome is now thought to be caused by damage to the area of the right brain that is between the upper and the lower pathways.[4]

All this may seem confusing, but there may be a way to simplify and make it useful for helping people learn. This simpler picture is that we should give our students assignments that require them to use these different parts of the brain, assignments that ask them about spatial issues—both the big picture and the details.

For example, we might ask our students to describe the big picture, the context, of the battle at Gettysburg. This might include geographic aspects, the big issues of the war, and the general locations of the armies over the entire battlefield. But we should also ask them to focus on specific events during the battle, such as individual soldiers, particular moments that were turning points, or the locations of particular bridges or trees and their role in the moment-to-moment ebb and sway of the battle. To fully use the upper pathway, we might ask them to act out specific events or construct a map showing Lee's battle plan.

Math and Where

One of my colleagues often grumbles about the way his students go about solving quantitative problems. "They have no sense of whether their answers are reasonable or not," he complains. "They don't even notice that one meter is a ridiculous answer for the size of a molecule. They just do the calculation and write down the answer they get. They never think to estimate!"

I have not been totally surprised by this lament, since most of his students are in the premedical curriculum and thus believe that they will never actually have to do quantitative calculations. But I have been surprised to hear similar things about engineering students. "They just memorize the equations and get the answer," one of these math teachers said. "Sometimes they seem to have no concept of why they are using any particular equation or why that equation works for them. They just plug and chug."

I am sure you recognize this problem. It is very much like our old issue about the difference between memorization and understanding. But there is another way to think of it, a way suggested by brain imaging studies.

These brain studies show that when we make calculations of exact answers to math problems, we use a different part of the brain than when we try to estimate possible answers. In fact, the calculation of exact answers activates areas in the front cortex more than any region of the back cortex. And, of great interest, the area of the front cortex most active during arithmetic calculation is the same as the area that is associated with production of language (which we will discuss in chapter 10).[5]

But when we try to estimate answers, we depend on our old friend, the *where* pathway in the upper back cortex. When we compare things to each other, we envision *where* they are, relative to each other. For example, on a size scale, molecules are *in between* atoms and cells. This is a fact that would be helpful to the premedical students I mentioned earlier. It is an example of why one would even want to know the size of a molecule—to see *where* it falls.

These ideas remind us that the actual process of calculating and getting answers is not a reflective activity. It uses the front cortex more than the back cortex, according to the imaging studies I mentioned previously. It seems that calculation is more like a language activity, where the rules and pathways for action are already known. It is just application of those rules and pathways. It is action centered.

But understanding the answer obtained by calculation and getting its meaning is more back-cortex focused. It requires reflection.

With this in mind, a teacher might focus on making math more reflective. Calculating a right answer is important, but it does not generate understanding. To support learners in understanding the result of a calculation, we should challenge them to think about the answer, to recall things in their life that are related to that answer, and to examine where their answer puts things in relation to each other.

Speed and Learning

The issue of math and the emphasis on speed brings us back to the point Eric made in the story I told at the beginning of this chapter. Reflection can take time.

Even the quickest learner needs time for reflection. She must let her integrative cortex do its thing. If she doesn't, her ideas and memories will be disconnected and shallow. They may be adequate for the moment (to pass a test, for example) but still transitory and ultimately unfulfilling.

However, I find that many of my colleagues think that the smartest students are the quick ones. An engineering professor startled me one day when he said, "The only difference between an A student and a B student is speed. The A student catches on faster." Setting aside the implication that there are categories out there (baskets labeled "A Student" and "B Student"), or the other notion that the teacher's job is to find out who is fastest, I remember protesting that the better student was the one who thought the most deeply. And thought takes time!

A dramatic example of this disconnect between intelligence and speed is a story about Neils Bohr, the brilliant physicist who won the Nobel Prize for his work on the structure of atoms. Apparently, Bohr was a slow thinker. In fact, the story goes, he had to take someone with him when he went to the theater, because he couldn't follow the plot of a story fast enough. Whoever went with him was required to explain the plot as it went along![6] He was always searching for unity.

Fast Brain/Slow Brain

It is easy to see why some teachers are infatuated with speed. Indeed, the sensory brain is very fast. We sense things quickly. And so we may believe that learning is also fast. Bang! Bang! Bang! It happened, we paid attention, now it's over, and now we know!

Most of us realize this is not how learning happens. Our own learning experience has taught us the value of time. And physical differences between the sensory brain and the integrating brain explain why this is so.

One reason that sensory input is fast is that many of the neurons that deliver information from the sense organs are coated with myelin. This means that the signals can go along nearly 100 times as fast as they could without this coating. It is important for survival that we evolved ways to get information fast.

Another reason sensory input is fast is that it requires only a few neurons—perhaps as few as three or four—for information to reach the sensory cortex. The access routes are shallow and wide. A lot of stuff can get to the brain quickly.

Third, the numbers of brain neurons actually engaged in direct sensory input is relatively small. You may have noticed in our drawing earlier in this chapter that the primary visual, auditory, and somatosensory cortex added together still takes up a smaller fraction of the cortex in the back than does the integrative cortex.

All these things contribute to the speed of sensory input. However, they all change once the brain needs to integrate information. First, most of the neurons in the integrative brain are not myelinated, so information travels slower. Second, the routes for information transfer become much more complex in the integrative brain. It appears that the sensory information can reach almost all parts of the integrative brain, and indeed, if things are to be integrated, they must all be eventually brought together physically. Third, there are just more neurons available for integration than for sensing.

We get our data quickly, but it takes longer to see the unity in it. In some things, it may take a lifetime! This difference is not lessened in the "information age." As we discussed in chapter 3, the great speed with which we can now get information is not necessarily a good thing. Information can come too fast for understanding. It can become the enemy of unity.

Reflection

Our physical picture for integration is that signals from different areas of the back cortex spend time just bouncing around through all the existing connections there. Some of these connections are distant, and some are weak. Some may fire right away, and others may only fire after the original input has wandered around a long time in this thicket of neurons. Pathways with the weakest of connections may still eventually be activated, but we may have to wait.

Reflection is searching for connections—literally!

Another physical image of reflection is helpful. Remember that reflection is a physical process, a bouncing back and forth. For example, light reflects off the window and comes back to us. However, it comes back in a somewhat altered form. It is changed by the process of reflection. It may be weakened, scattered, or contaminated with light from some other source. And the more things reflect back and forth, the more complicated they get—the less they are a pure copy of the original and the more they mix into the rest of the world.

We need reflection to develop complexity. We may start with a direct and sometimes relatively simple concrete experience, but that experience grows richer as we allow our brain the freedom to search for those still unknown connections. And as we find those connections, our brain changes. We attach the networks of our present experience to those that represent our past experience.

The art of directing and supporting reflection is part of the art of changing a brain. It is the art of leading a student toward comprehension.

The Stuff of Reflection

Let's try a small experiment. Set this book aside for a minute and reflect on what you have just read. Then try to sneak up on your brain and see what it is doing.

When I do this, I find two fundamental things. One of these is what we call *mental images*. Whatever the topic, my brain has vague but identifiable images of it. These images slip by in a flash sometimes, and if I try to focus on them, they may disappear. But I can't seem to think of anything without an image of that thing in my mind.

The other thing that I always find is language. Or perhaps it would be better to say I find elements of language. I may find fragments of sentences, or I may be speaking mentally to myself. I may be playing with words, tunes, or songs. I may find myself saying names of things or counting. I seem to count a lot and sing a lot. Inside my head!

To me this is the stuff of reflection: images and language.

The Images of Reflection

The images I see during reflection are not images produced by my eyes. In fact my eyes usually drift out of focus when I am reflecting, and in actuality I am not seeing anything in the outside world. I may even close my eyes. The images I see are internal ones. They are coming from my own brain!

We now know what parts of the brain are active when we think of an image. You could guess what these parts are by remembering that an image is a reassembled, or *unified*, set of neuronal connections. For example, the image of O we discussed in chapter 8 is a combination of segments of the letter. Our image is an intact O, not the separate edges that our sensory brain initially perceived. It is the integrated image.

When we reflect, we bring up images from our past experience, and these images are what we see in our mind's eye. But, in one of the most satisfying discoveries from brain imaging studies, it turns out that the part of the brain we use to see images with *our mind's eye* is the same part that we use to see them with *our real eyes*. This is shown in the following illustration, in which the parts of the brain used to perceive images with the eyes are identified with triangles, and the parts used when we call up images from memory are labeled with circles. (There is also some involvement of the front cortex, and we will talk about this in the next chapter.)[7]

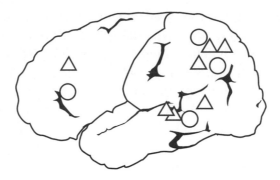

In fact, the parts of the brain activated when we bring up images from our memory are the *what* and *where* regions we identified earlier in this chapter.

Making Meaning: The Past and the Emotions

For the most part, things have meaning when they remind us of something in our past. When they don't, we are just puzzled.

But there is another requirement. Even if we experience something that has happened to us before, it is hard to make meaning of it unless it engages our emotions.

The images we assemble in our mind's eye came to us first through our real eyes. The neuron networks in the integrative back cortex that arise from our real experience are the only source we have, or at least, they are the major source. If we are to create a mental image of some new thing, we try to do it with parts of old things. There are no totally new images.

You may feel this is wrong. Don't creative people produce truly new images? For example, isn't some of modern art truly new? Images in such paintings often do not remind us of anything we have ever seen before.

But let's look at this example of modern art for a minute. In the movie *Pollock,* Jackson Pollock is asked, "What is modern art about?" And he explains it something like this: "Artists have always focused on their passions. The Greeks created images of the body, the Egyptians of their Pharaohs, the medieval painters of the Crucifixion, and the Impressionists of nature, color, and light. Modern artists do this, too, but their passions are no longer external. In this age we care about what is inside us, and that is what we paint."

This made a lot of sense to me. If a Pollock painting is an image of what was inside him, I can understand that. He was disturbed, enraged, confused, passionate, complex. And when I look at his paintings, I may feel the same way.

Or I may not. My response to Pollock depends on my own experience. Paint splattered all over the canvas makes me feel confused and frustrated because that is what my experience has taught me. Whenever I have experienced any image like this, it was because something was broken, spilled, or chaotic. Without the neuronal networks for those past images, I may not respond at all to Pollock. His work may have no meaning for me.

The Ultimate Reflection

Reflection is a search for connections. The search can continue consciously, as we will discuss in the next chapter when we talk about control and the front cortex. But this search also goes on subconsciously, even when we sleep.

When we reflect, we seem to do better if we shut out sensory experience. That way our brain is not distracted by receiving new information at the same time it is working with old information. We may close our eyes when we are thinking, or if we do not close them, they still drift out of focus. And we often begin some "mindless" activity, like pacing, knitting, scratching our head, or rubbing our chin. We do things that do not require our attention, because our attention is inward.

Of course, reflection like this is the ideal. In real life there are constant interruptions, as the sensory input from the world makes its way into our brains against our will. The phone rings or someone enters the room, and we throw up our hands in exasperation. "Let me think," we demand!

But when we dream, we escape these distractions. In fact, an important part of dreaming is that sensory input to the brain is cut off. Our sensory brain does not get any signals; we do not see, hear, or feel (by touch) things. Another important aspect of dreaming is that, to a great extent, we are paralyzed; our body cannot act out during dreams. For example, we may run in a dream, but our body does not move.[8]

In general, dreaming is the activity of an isolated brain. In dreaming, the brain cannot sense events outside itself, and it cannot produce responses to what is going on inside itself.

Imaging studies have shown that the back cortex becomes more active in dreaming and the front cortex less active. This is one reason I have suggested that reflection is a back-cortex activity. When we dream, we put our reflective brain to work. It sees images and hears language. And, of utmost importance, the amygdala is also active in dreaming. We seem to be monitoring the emotional content of our internal experience, and we certainly have intense emotions while we dream.

This seems like the ideal state for reflection. Isolated from sensory input or the need to plan any actions, the experiences of our life cycle through the networks of neurons in our memories. And the emotional content of these networks dominates. This is the stuff of meaning!

The results of these studies lead some sleep researchers to postulate that dreams help us make connections. In this theory, the connections we make in dreams are important, central ones. They give us insight into the big picture. We discover what is important to us, because we dream about what matters most.[9]

Education and Dreaming

For comprehension we need time. We may need several days, weeks, or even years. Sleep and dreaming may help, so when we have an important decision to make, we ask for that time. We say, "Let me sleep on it."

It would seem, then, that in institutions where learning is the goal, there should be more thought about sleep and dreaming. This idea is problematic, of course. Even if we were able to decrease our emphasis on speed and information and increase the possibilities for reflection, we still would have to give our students the kind of experience that would produce dreams—experiences that engage their emotions. As we discussed in chapter 4, our experiences must matter in our lives if we are to learn from them. This happens when a young person gets to graduate school or gets a new job, but in the K-16 period, most of the educational experiences seem too thin to make this type of impact. Students are exposed to several subjects each day, and the way they encounter these subjects often does not have much emotional impact.

You can consider what changes we might make to address this challenge. We might teach only one subject at a time; for example, we might spend a week on mathematics, then a week on reading, and so forth. It would also help if we make the learning experience intense enough and connected to life so that our students actually dream about it. That may sound like a dream itself, but it suggests how seriously we have to take emotion if we want to foster deep learning.

Language and Image

Earlier I said that when we free our mind to reflect, we call up images from our memory. But I also pointed out that in addition to images, we probably also call up language (or sound). Words, tunes, and voices may run through our minds.

This may sound different than images, and indeed language has special characteristics that make it a wonderful tool for learning and an almost essential tool for demonstrating what we have learned. But at its heart, language is also about images.

First, language is a tool to produce images. If one picture is worth a thousand words, one word also can produce many images. In fact, I could argue that each individual brain produces a somewhat different image from the same word. My image of "girl" will probably be different in some way from yours.

But the category "girl" does have particular common elements, so an important part of learning is our ability to produce an image that contains the common features. If I ask you to show me your image of a girl, and you draw a tree, we have a problem.

Very often, learning is about forming the right images when we hear or read language. And the right images can be precise. As we become expert in some subject, our images become more and more exact and complex. A freshman in chemistry may think of an electron as a negative particle, but a more advanced student will think of it as the region in space where negative charge is most likely to be found. A novice may think of a poem as a limerick or a nursery rhyme, while a poet will think of a Shakespearean sonnet or T. S. Eliot's *The Wasteland*.

When we show that we have a precise and complex image for a word, we demonstrate deep learning. We demonstrate comprehension of the language of our field.

Asking for Images

A teacher can help build in reflection by asking students to produce exact images that demonstrate the *whats* and *wheres* in her subject. Here is an example from my own experience.

*   *   *

Harold was a student in my biochemistry course for nurses. Quite early in the semester, I saw that he was struggling. I noticed that as I was drawing the structures of even simple molecules on the board, his pen would stop moving. He would look around, and his attention was obviously not on the image I was producing on the board.

Eventually, there came a test, and Harold did not do well. Not surprisingly, I noticed that his chemical structures were very difficult to decipher. They looked vaguely like they should, but only vaguely. So I asked him to come talk to me in my office.

"Harold," I said, "let's talk about some structures. I think you can do much better."

He looked at me wide-eyed, but said nothing.

I plunged ahead. "Can you tell me what a carbonyl group is?" I asked.

And surprisingly, he answered correctly with little hesitation. "It is a carbon atom with a double bond to an oxygen atom," he said.

"Great," I said. "So why don't you draw a carbonyl group on the board."

Reluctantly, he took up a piece of chalk and faced the small board in my office. Slowly, he drew a large C, for carbon, and a large O for oxygen. And then he did something I had never seen before. Slowly, he drew two wavy lines. But neither line was connected with both atoms. Then he looked at me with what I can only describe as a sad combination of hope and desperation.

It hit me. Harold had no image of a carbonyl group. The image for this simplest of structures just wasn't in his brain. He had memorized the language to describe the structure, but it did not link up with a useful image. He simply did not comprehend the language he was using.

Gently but firmly, I began to insist that Harold draw structures for me. We started back at the beginning, but *he* drew the structures rather than me. And in one of my more satisfying moments, I was able to give him a passing grade at the end of the course.

*   *   *

Comprehension often requires us to make images out of language. This is possibly the ultimate in integration by the human brain. We integrate the sensory input of reading and hearing language and make complex internal images from it. And if our student does this well, we have some of the very best evidence that she has learned.

The Other Side of Language

Language comprehension is a function of a region of the cortex that is just behind the auditory cortex in the back cortex. In most people, but not all, this region is found in the left hemisphere, and damage to the left side of the back cortex can make it hard for people to comprehend language.[10] This shows up in confused speech and in the inability to identify confused speech. For example, they might say things like "I think mung, but log of net and unged in a little wheat duhvayden."[11] Not only do they produce language like this, but they would not notice if you spoke that way, too!

However, this process of understanding the cognitive meaning of words and sentences is only part of understanding language. As I mentioned, it is controlled by just one of the two cerebral hemispheres, most often the left one. But there is another language function in the same general area of the *other* hemisphere, which may be equally important.[12] This area understands the meaning of language that comes through emphasis on particular syllables—the rhythm, the pitch, the tone, and the inflection. These aspects of language together are called *prosody,* and they are of immense importance for meaning.

Here is an illustration of prosody.

There are different ways we might say the simple sentence, "You look great," and I have shown you three of them below. In each case the meaning of the sentence goes beyond the vocabulary and the grammar. We learn more than just the facts.

You look great! (Others may not.)

You **look** great! (Maybe you aren't acting great. Or, maybe you aren't feeling great.)

You look **great**! (I'm surprised? I'm happy? Put in your own meaning!)

This is meaning beyond the dictionary and grammar. It may not be stressed in school, but without it, our understanding of language would be flat and simple. At best, the images would lack richness and complexity, and at worst we may totally misunderstand.

I suspect that a great deal of the art of changing the brain has to do with the effective use of prosody. Teachers who convey deeper meaning by their powers of expression, both semantic and prosodic, have a better chance to reach their students. We should emphasize the use of the right language brain in schools. We should integrate the cognitive aspects of language with prosody. Possible approaches would be to read aloud, to ourselves and to others (not just to children), and ask people to read aloud to us.

Maybe we are *too* focused on the symbols and rules of language; maybe we forget the power of the brain to go beyond them.[13]

Overrelying on Language

Few of us doubt the importance of language for learning. We probably focus on it more than any other subject in school. But it seems to me that this continual stress on language has a pitfall and that many of our students find themselves trapped in it.

Let me illustrate this with another short story.

*   *   *

Recently while listening to National Public Radio in my car, I heard a woman interviewing an author who wrote a book about what it was like to grow up as the child of a union factory worker. This author described how in school she felt that others were "looking down their nose at us."

The interviewer, an obviously intelligent and verbal person, then asked a question: "Do you think that they looked their nose down at you all the time?"

Yes, you read it right. I would have concluded that I had just misheard what she said, but then she did it again, and again. There was no doubt. She was saying "looked their nose down at you."

The author was too polite to make the correction, or perhaps she disbelieved her own ears. But I laughed out loud in the privacy of my car. "She doesn't know what it means," I thought.

Now maybe I was too unkind. Maybe she was dyslexic or had some other language disability that she had overcome with great courage. But the alternative that occurred to me was that she had no image of a person raising their eyebrows, drawing their head back, and literally looking down at another person right over the bridge of their nose.

Rather what she had was a memorized phrase. She had language, but since she had no image, she could not arrange the language correctly. It was about nose and looking but that was as far as it went.

* * *

I tell the story because I think that this is a risk in the way we educate. We stress language so much, but we do not attend to the image that the language is meant to create. And so students think they understand when they have the language. If they know the word for something, they may believe that they understand the thing itself.

This shallowness is a danger when we try to teach things to students before they have the right images. When we try to teach the structure of DNA to high school students, but they have no image for how atoms bond to form molecules, we are just giving them names of things. They can't have the image.

But they think they do! So when they show up in college and we try to teach them about DNA, they are upset. "I already know that," they claim. But they only have the language, not the image.

Unity

I hope you feel a sense of unity from our discussion of the back cortex. But even if this is not the case, I still hope you understand my primary goals in what you have read here. I wanted to show how the functions of the back cortex all work together to produce comprehension. The integration of *what* with *where,* emotion with fact, big picture with precise detail, symbolic language with prosodic language, and language with image, together all play their part in the development of deep understanding by a learner. And this all takes time.

If this fits together for you, I believe you may see your way to becoming a more artful teacher. You may well invent new ways to help students reflect and integrate their experience, new ways to use the power of their back cortex.

But whether I have succeeded or not, it clearly is time to leave the back cortex and move on with the learning cycle. Having comprehended its experience, the brain is in a position to do something about it. If true understanding has been gained, we will be able to make plans and develop new ideas about what that experience implies for the future. Our new unity can now lead to new hypotheses and creative ideas. The learner can take ownership of what she has comprehended, and in doing so she will be transformed from a receiver and understander to a *producer* of new knowledge that she can share with others. The change in her brain can lead to change in the world!

Notes

1. D. J. Freedman, M. Reisenhuber, T. Poggio, and E. K. Miller, *Science* 291 (2001), p. 312; also see the review of this work on p. 260 of the same issue.
2. The "attention network" refers to a group of parts of the brain that work together to enable us to pay attention and control our attention. It includes regions used to move the eyes, as we described in chapter 8 (superior colliculus), regions that control the flow of sensory information to the cortex (the thalamus), parts of the frontal lobe that play a role in deciding where to direct attention, and the parietal lobe of the integrative back cortex, which we are talking about in this chapter.
3. D. L. Arrington, and colleagues, *Journal of Cognitive Neuroscience,* supplement 2 (2000), p. 106.
4. H. Karnath, S. Ferber, and M. Himmelbach, *Nature* (June 21, 2001), p. 950, and M. S. A. Graziano on p. 903 of the same issue.
5. These studies are reported by S. Dehaene and his colleagues in *Science* (May 7, 1999). Dehaene has also written a book on mathematics and the brain for the layman, *The Number Sense* (New York: Oxford University Press, 1997).
6. I am endebted to my colleague Mano Singham for this story.
7. With permission; this illustration is described by Posner and Raichle in *Images of Mind* (New York: Freeman, 1999). The original studies were conducted by Kossyln and his colleagues and are described in *Science* 240 (1988), p. 1621.

8. Of course this is not universal. Sometime we do act out parts of our dreams. We may strike out, cry out, or even walk in our sleep.

9. E. Hartman, *Dreams and Nightmares* (New York: Plenum, 1998); also see the series of articles on sleep, dreams, and memory in *Science* 294 (2001), pp. 1047–1063, which includes papers both supporting and disputing a role for dreaming in memory consolidation.

10. F. Bloom and A. Lazerson, *Brain, Mind, and Behavior,* 2nd ed. (New York: Freeman, 1988), p. 283.

11. In 1874 Carl Wernike described brain-damaged patients who could not comprehend language. These patients all had damage of the cortex directly behind the auditory cortex, and eventually this region came to be called *Wernike's area.*

12. Until recently there have been no apparent structural differences between the right and left part of the language comprehension cortex. However, it is now known that the clusters of neurons in Wernike's area are farther apart than those in the prosodic region of the right cortex. This suggests that the left brain in this area has room for more *connections* between neurons and, by inference, can analyze things in more specific and finer detail. In contrast, a smaller number of connections on the right side could lead to a more vague but broader image—the big picture. This could explain why the right side gives us context rather than the precise structure of language. See A. W. Galuske and colleagues, *Science* 289 (2000), p. 1946, and comments on this work by M. S. Gazzaniga on p. 1887 of the same issue.

13. In *The Man Who Mistook His Wife for a Hat* (New York: Summit, 1985), Oliver Sacks tells a humorous story about prosody, in the chapter entitled "The President's Speech." He describes brain-damaged patients who could not comprehend the cognitive meaning of the speech but who understood the prosodic meaning very well—in fact better than people with undamaged brains. So while most people took the president's speech very seriously, those with brain damage saw through the speech and laughed uproariously.

THE COURAGEOU

CREATING KNOWLEDGE BY USING
THE INTEGRATIVE FRONTAL CORTEX

The shrewd guess, the fertile hypothesis, the courageous leap to a tentative
conclusion—these are the most valuable coin of the thinker at work.
          —*Jerome Bruner*

From the first day of class, Veronica always had her own ideas.
Some of the other students thought she talked too much, but their dis-
approval did not stop her. She just couldn't help talking about her ideas
of what things meant.

It wasn't that she didn't listen. In fact, she was an intense listener,
and she always noticed the gaps and assumptions in what I would say.
To me, Veronica was just an immensely engaged student and a joy to
teach.

One day, however, I noticed that she was unusually quiet. I couldn't
tell if she was sad or sullen, but something was eating at her. So after
class I invited her to my office for a talk.

"You seem different today," I said. "Is anything wrong?"

"Not really, I suppose. At least nothing cosmic," she replied. But
then she went on quickly. "Dr. Zull," she said. "You know how you are
always encouraging us to develop our own ideas and use the learning
cycle? Well, I have been really excited about that, because I love to
think about things and try to invent my own hypotheses about what
they mean. I love the abstract hypothesis part of what we do!"

She stopped for breath, then went on. "Well, I have been trying to use the cycle in my other classes, too. But yesterday, I really had a shock."

"What do you mean?" I said. "You had a shock?"

"Well," Veronica replied, her face turning pink, "one of my teachers suddenly began criticizing me for telling him my ideas! You know what he said?"

"I think I am going to find out," I replied.

"Yes," she exclaimed. "He said that he didn't want to hear our ideas. He said that he would explain things, and it was a waste of time for us to think about our own ideas. He said that he knew exactly what everything means, and we should just learn what he tells us!"

And, then, she broke into tears.

* * *

As we discussed in chapters 2 and 3, if we are to learn and grow, there must come a point where we change from receivers of knowledge to creators of knowledge. Instead of reproducing the work of others, we must begin to create our own. This is where humans excel. Our ability to create makes us the best thinkers in the world.

Creating takes place in the front cortex. So, our next step is to examine some of the things that happen there. This will help us recognize what this process of creativity is about and how it seems to work. It will also bring us face to face with one of the teacher's greatest challenges—the necessity of giving control to the learner. If we can't do that, we can become an impediment to learning rather than a support. The passive student will just forget what we taught and the ones who care will become sad and angry, which is why Veronica cried.

Front Cortex Summary

The following illustration reminds us of the role of the integrative front cortex in learning. This part of the cortex is most active in solving problems, creating ideas, and assembling those ideas into the symbolic form that we call language. In addition, this part of our brain oversees everything, makes decisions and monitors its own progress.

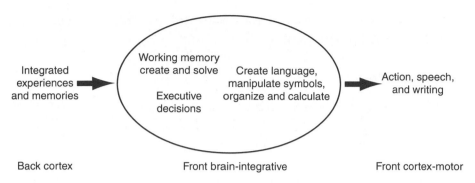

The eventual outcome of these activities by the integrative front cortex is action by the body, which includes speech and writing. But we will discuss those actions in chapter 11. Here we will focus on the circled items in the drawing and on how to help people learn by helping them do these things—indeed, by insisting that they do them!

A Difficult Step

This adventure into the unknown land of new ideas can seem quite risky when compared to the safe and cozy back integrative cortex. It is easy to simply receive and integrate information, when we don't have to do anything or even tell anybody about what is tucked away in there. In contrast, the whole point of the front cortex is commitment and action. To plan a venture into the future, basing everything on our ideas and hypotheses, can be frightening. Our thoughts are still abstract. We have not seen them played out in the real world before, and this lack of concreteness increases the risk. They are just ideas, and they could be wrong. Often they are wrong!

Further, since these abstract ideas come from the individual brain, they are bound to be different from the ideas of other brains. Abstract ideas may generate conflict. There will be trouble if we all have different ideas. This is why we have religious wars.

But despite the risk, we still fall in love with our own ideas. We love them even when they are irrational and factually mistaken. They contain our experiences, our reflections, our judgments, and our labor.

Abstract ideas are at once the most powerful and the most dangerous product of the human brain.

Starting to Work

Creating abstract ideas requires our brain to begin working. The free ride of just receiving sensory input and waiting for connections to appear is over. Making something new is a whole new thing. It is tough and it requires energy.

So, it is not an accident that one of the main functions of the front integrative cortex has been labeled *working* memory. The work begins with remembering a few things for a short time, from seconds to minutes or sometimes a few hours. The purpose of remembering these things is to use them for developing an idea or solving a problem. This is the working part.

Of course, short-term memory is useful on its own. For example, we use it when we want to remember a phone number until we can dial it or an e-mail address until we type it on the computer. We use short-term memory for these momentary challenges, all the time, every day.

But if we are going to create anything, it will take work.

Mundane Work

I have given a rather grand view of working memory and new ideas. But the fact is that we use working memory to solve the most mundane of problems that we encounter in our daily lives. Here is an example.

* * *

As I am eating my breakfast, my wife reminds me that I have a doctor's appointment. I check my calendar and see that the appointment is at 10 A.M. Then I remember that I also promised to get groceries today, and that I have to prepare for my class, which is at 2 P.M. So I go to work with these facts. I hold them briefly in my working memory and line them up in different ways. I estimate about how long each of these tasks will take: half an hour for groceries, an hour for the doctor (they always take longer than we hope), and two hours to prepare for class. I then place those estimates in my working memory while I develop my plan. (Notice that now the exact times of the events are not relevant.

So I forget them for the moment.) I decide I have time enough to go to the store first, then the doctor, then prepare for class.

*   *   *

I could go on, but I hope this is enough to illustrate how we use short-term memory to hold a small number of facts that we then manipulate in order to make decisions and develop plans. We must do this whenever we solve any problem.

Finding Abstraction

The example I just gave is so ordinary that you may have trouble seeing how there is any abstract thinking at all. After all, isn't abstraction what great minds do? Doesn't abstraction imply theories like the expanding universe, the wave behavior of electrons, or the philosophy of Kant?

The first definition of *abstract* in my dictionary goes as follows: "thought of; in absence of any particular instances or material object; not concrete." So I think I am on solid ground when I claim that the ideas and plans of the front cortex, no matter how ordinary, are still abstract. My idea about how to organize my day was based on a plan that had yet to be tested in the concrete world. It was just an idea!

What Working Memory Is Not

It is easy to think that memory works like a relay race, where information is passed first to short-term memory and then on to long-term memory.

But this is not a very useful metaphor. In fact, working memory and long-term memory involve separate pathways in the brain. It is possible to hold quite a bit of information for a while, if we work hard and pay attention to it, but that information can disappear, sometimes rather quickly. It may never find its way into long-term memory. In school, cramming for exams is the classic example of this breakdown between working and long-term memory.

And we all know that long-term memory can form immediately in some cases. As we discussed in chapter 5, we may remember for a long time things that happened only once if they produce strong feelings.

Although they are separate, working memory is not unrelated to long-term memory. When we use things in working memory to do some work, to create something new, then that new thing can become part of our long-term memory. For example, if we meet a new person and try to remember his name, we often forget it. But if we associate that name with a bit of information about the person, making it part of a little story that contains a cue or two, we may well remember the name for a long time. It isn't the name that we remember but the story, with its cues.

When we create stories, theories, generalizations, poems, songs, and so forth, they contain details that once were in working memory. But now we have done the work and we can remember what that work produced. We remember because we made it!

Distributing the Work

Like the back integrative cortex the front integrative cortex divides up its work. Different parts do different things. One example is that, like the back cortex, separate areas of the front cortex work with the *where* and the *what* of things.

The following illustration depicts a summary of different parts of the brain that have been reported to be engaged in working memory for spatial *(where)* information and working memory for object *(what)* information.[1]

The open circles in the figure identify regions that are active when spatial working memory is in use, and the filled circles are regions that are active when object working memory is being used. In general, spa-

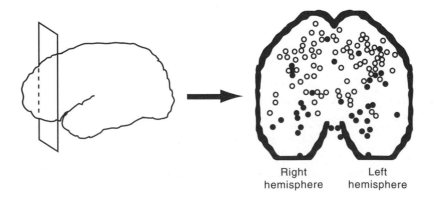

Right   Left
hemisphere   hemisphere

tial working memory more frequently engages the upper part of the front cortex and object working memory the middle and lower parts (note that this is similar to the distribution of the *what* and *where* regions in the back cortex, discussed in chapter 9).

These results remind us again of the importance of working both with spatial and object information when we are teaching. But now we must go beyond the suggestions we made in chapter 9 about recognition and analysis of *what* and *where*. Now we will want to ask our students to invent their own ideas, their hypotheses, about spatial relationships and about object features that define categories. For example, with spatial relationships we might challenge them to tell us how Lee might have deployed his troops differently at Gettysburg or how the atoms in a molecule might be rearranged in space while still following the rules of chemistry. With objects we might require our students to propose structural features for a transition species (a missing link) in evolution. Or we might ask them to engineer a new type of vehicle (a new structure) for use in hunting terrorists in rough mountain terrain.

Students should use the spatial working memory and the object working memory parts of their front cortex to make full use of the mental power they possess.

Limited but Powerful

Working memory is a curious thing. In some ways it seems remarkably limited, but in another way it is virtually unlimited.

Working memory is limited in capacity, tenacity, and time. It can only hold a few (about seven on average) isolated items, such as unrelated words, at once. And it doesn't hold tightly to anything. All it takes is a slight distraction to knock something out of our working memory.

At the same time, we use working memory to help create new ideas, and there seems to be no limit to those ideas. They just pour out of us! The power of this limited part of the brain is almost inexhaustible.

This might seem like a contradiction at first, but when we think about it, the contradiction seems to disappear. In fact, to be creative we need constant influx of new ideas. If working memory held tenaciously onto its contents or had a much larger capacity, it could be a disadvantage.

We can think of this as a card game. The deck must constantly be shuffled if we are to deal out new hands. Flexibility of the content of the hands is the only way to get anywhere. But the hands need not be large to be varied. In fact, small hands are important, because they allow us to focus on specific possibilities. It would be hard to see a straight flush in a hand of fifty cards, but in a hand of five cards, it is easy.

If working memory could hold more information or hold it longer, we might not be able to reason as well as we do. We might waste time on irrelevant things, not notice the important things, develop overly complex plans, and ultimately find that our thinking was greatly slowed, maybe so much that we couldn't survive.

Working Memory and Teaching

Let me give you a few of my own ideas about the role of the teacher in supporting working memory.

Probably the most obvious point is that we should be careful not to overload working memory. A classic error of college teachers is to keep shoving information in one end of working memory, not realizing that they are shoving other data out the other end. The teacher has a large number of facts enmeshed in his lectures, but the students are only getting isolated facts. And recent research suggests that the more things we have in working memory, the harder it is for us to focus on what is most important.[2]

If we want our students to process what we are telling them, we have to limit the number of items they need to process. I try to keep it to three or four pieces of information at most. For example, when I am teaching about making chemical solutions, I ask my students to remember just two concepts and two specific terms. The concepts are volume and weight, and the terms are liters and grams. They can then manipulate these four pieces of data in a variety of ways to develop their ideas and solve problems about concentration.

This view of working memory suggests that the teacher should break things up. This is a good thing. Not only does it limit the load on working memory, but it also uses the natural inclination of the brain to analyze large or complex objects by examining the parts. It jumps from point to point. The brain likes breaks and takes them naturally.

Breaking things into smaller units may seem more difficult with some subjects than with others. If we are teaching history, we may want to develop a complex image for the student to assimilate as a whole. It might take the whole class period to build up this image, and breaking it into smaller pieces may feel artificial. But we should remember that the learner's brain is breaking it up anyway. In fact, good students probably find their own imaginative ways to keep the parts of things divided into small groups that fit together naturally. They may be doing this for us.

Breaking things into simple components may seem like "dumbing down." Isn't this an insult to the intelligence of our students? We aren't in kindergarten, are we?

But this argument misses the point. When we are new at something, we are all basically in kindergarten. As we discussed in chapters 6 and 7, we can only start with what we have. So if our students already have prior knowledge about the subject, they can attach new things to those old networks, and they easily become part of the long-term memory. But if they are asked to hold new things in isolation, then working memory is engaged, and working memory does not expand with maturity or experience. If it is new, it is new! We are all novices at something, and the limits on our working memory are, on average, all the same.

The Hard Part

As I noted earlier, creating new ideas has two steps: *short-term storage* of information and *manipulation* or rearranging that information to form new relationships. This manipulation of information in working memory is what creates new knowledge for the learner. As he organizes things in new arrangements and attaches them to the networks that represent his prior knowledge, each learner creates his own understandings. The conscious rearranging and manipulation of items in working memory comes closest to what we call *thinking*.

This manipulation process is carried out by a part of the front cortex that is often called the brain's *executive*. Brain imaging studies suggest that this executive activity engages more of the front cortex than working memory does. This is suggested in the following illustration, which shows the regions of the left front cortex that are most active when the brain is just saving some language information for a short time (shown on the left side), and those parts that are most active when we not only save but also process (work with) the information at the same time (shown on the right side). It probably takes more of the brain to think than to just remember.

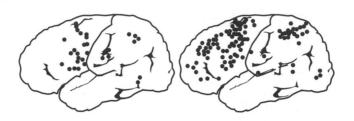

The Parts of Executive Work

Executive processing can be broken down into its parts, too (depending on who is doing the dividing). Let's look at two parts that seem to be crucial: (1) attending to relevant information, and task management, which requires mentally manipulating the relevant facts in order to achieve a goal.[3]

Maybe another story will help illustrate these two parts of executive processing.

* * *

Once I asked my eight-year-old son to water our garden, while my wife and I were on vacation. I told him how to hold his finger over the end of the hose to produce a nice spray (I had lost our nozzle), which plants need more water, how long to water each plant (count slowly to ten) and how to coil up the hose on its hook when he was done.

And we went away on our vacation.

I expected my son to use his executive processing skills to water the garden. I expected that he would attend to the information I gave him and manipulate that information to figure out how to do the task.

And he did. But when we came home from vacation, I noticed immediately that the hose was stretched out on the ground, and further, the plants that needed heavy watering were not doing well. In fact, they were wilted and lying nearly flat on the ground.

It was only with the greatest TLC that I eventually saved them.

*   *   *

My son's executive brain had dealt with this assignment in a different way than I imagined. There were at least two differences, one in attending to relevant information and one in manipulating that information.

The attending part had to do with taking care of the hose. To him, how the hose was put away was not relevant, so he didn't attend to it. He didn't use it as part of his plan. After all, he was just going to take the hose down and water again tomorrow. Why bother with putting it back every day? So he worked with the problem, minus that bit of information.

But he also manipulated the information in a way that I had not anticipated. This had to do with those extra thirsty plants, and when we discussed it, I understood. "Well," he said, "I thought that the best way to get more water on those plants was to not put my thumb on the hose. Then the water would come out stronger."

His manipulation of the facts produced a plan, an idea, for watering the garden that went like this: turn on the water, pick the hose up off the ground, count to ten for all plants, put thumb over hose for most plants, take thumb off hose for more needy plants, turn off the hose, and drop it on the ground.

It turned out that the idea didn't work very well, but it was *his* idea. I couldn't criticize. He was just going through the learning cycle!

Executive Processing and the Teacher

To help students with the executive processing part of working memory, a teacher may find it useful to focus separately on the *attending* part and the *task management* part.

Attending seems easier. It simply requires sorting out the relevant from the irrelevant. Of course, every learner has the power to choose what he believes is relevant; just as my son didn't put the hose back, those choices may not be the same as the ones we would make. But we can tell them, and show them, what *our* choices would be.

Another thing we can do in helping students attend to the important parts of a problem is to point out that they are doing this in their own brain, anyway. We can ask our learners to list the important facts, or steps, needed to solve any particular problem or to generate a particular idea. We can ask them specifically what information they need to do the task and compare our own list with theirs.

Task management is probably the most personal. How a learner manages and manipulates facts and information depends greatly on the learner's past experience, on his existing neuronal networks. So if we are going to help at all, we must pay a great deal of attention to the topics we discussed in chapters 6 and 7.

An example is my son and his ideas about water coming out of the hose. I should have realized that he did not have enough experience to know that putting his thumb over the end of the hose does not significantly reduce the amount of water coming out. He had no neuronal networks for this.

But, of course, we cannot know all the neuronal networks in another brain. And, in any case, in this part of the learning cycle we often must stand back and give the learner freedom. We try to save time by explaining things, but as I have noted many times, our explanations are often ineffective. Meaning develops when the learner *actively tries* his own ideas. More about this in chapter 11.

Trusting the Brain to Think: A Story

Using the executive brain is the essence of what we call thinking. So I have been encouraging you to let your students think on their own. Despite my bravado, the truth is that I still have difficulty giving my learners this much freedom. In fact, I sometimes have trouble trusting that they will think at all. This happens most often when I am trying to convey a concept, and it isn't working. I begin to think they can't think.

But, almost always I find out that I am wrong and that the problem lies elsewhere. Here is an example.

* * *

I had been working hard to teach the idea of cloning to my students. One thing I wanted them to grasp was that clones already exist in the world. All identical twins are clones. Duplication of genetic content of a human egg is not some strange new event in the reproductive world.

I was amazed at the difficulty I was having. First, they didn't actually understand what twins are—different people with the same genetic information in their cells. Explaining that didn't seem to help much. My students still talked as though clones would be a terrible new thing. They seemed to lack the power of deduction. If twins are clones, then clones are not new at all.

One particular student seemed to have the most trouble. She had struggled in the class, and I admit that I had begun to form some negative opinions about her. But then, I was brought up short by this student.

I was talking about how genes are contributed from both the mother and the father when they make a baby and how each sibling gets a different combination of those genes. And suddenly my nonthinker spoke up. "You mean that I am different from my brother because I have different genes?" "Yes," I said abruptly, still terribly frustrated.

"Well, then, twins must be clones, since they have the same genes. So there are lots of clones in the world. What's the big deal?"

* * *

I have had enough experiences like this to realize that when we worry about students thinking, we could be missing the boat. They probably have just not noticed some key thing. Once the facts and concepts get through, the thinking part of it can seem easy, almost trivial. "Of course there are lots of clones in the world!"

Natural Thinking

Even though it is hard to put into practice, I believe we should trust our students to think. Thinking is natural. It is what the human front integrative cortex does, just like sensing is what the sensory brain does. We all sense. We all think.

A lot has been written about how the brain thinks. It is a great topic for theorizing, and I do not pretend to make any new contribution to this subject here. But I do encourage you to not be intimidated by high-flying theories of unexplained (and maybe unexplainable) reasoning and calculating machinery in the brain. We are not going that way here. Rather, we will take our normal down-to-earth, physical perspective.

As with sensing and comprehending, I believe that the brain relies on its experience in the physical world when it thinks. The executive brain orders up images of physical experience, holds bits of those images in its working memory, attends to the parts that are relevant, and arranges (and rearranges) those parts in ways that are consistent with physical experience. For example, it arranges them with regard to time, size, complexity, spatial features, numbers, or probability. In this I believe I am following Lakoff and Johnson, whose ideas were discussed in chapter 1. (See ref. 2 in chapter 1.) I cannot help but believe that underlying this mystery of thinking, we will find mundane mother nature and her solid, physical facts.

Natural Thinking and Probability in Life Experience

So what would be called "natural thinking"? What kind of thinking would be produced by nature?

If we look for ideas about this question in our common life experience, one of the answers we get is related to probability and statistics. I am not talking about fancy equations here, but, again, about the mundane. For example, if something happens a certain way a lot of times, it probably will happen that way the next time. On the other hand, if a certain thing has never happened in our experience, then it is unlikely to happen in the future.

Another common experience is that things are hard to predict. Even if we know that something will probably happen, we also know that sometimes it may not. Experience tells us there are a lot of different possibilities. Life is variable!

The extreme form of this variability is complete randomness. A lot of what goes on has no apparent pattern. We are always trying to find reasons for our experience, but often—most often possibly—there are no reasons. As they say, "stuff happens!" This experience becomes the idea of randomness.

Here, then, are four basic ideas of statistics: *probable, improbable, variable, and random.* They all come naturally to the brain because that is the way life is. These natural ideas of probability are related to thinking and reasoning and, hence, to learning.

Statistical Learning

We don't pay much attention to events that seem random. For example, a leaf falling from a tree may catch our attention, but if other leaves continue to drift down once in a while we conclude that they are falling at random. We go on with our lives. But if we notice a few falling one day, many more the next, and even more on each succeeding day, we take notice. Fall is here, winter is on its way

Patterns get our attention. They are probably not accidents.

We use this approach from earliest childhood. It is how we learn. Sometimes it is called *statistical learning*. For example, babies learn language statistically. They notice that the sounds in speech are not random, and their developing brains quickly recognize that the sounds are broken into parts, and that the parts do not appear randomly.[4]

This statistical learning is also linked to our belief in causality. If a baby pushes on his bottle, and it always moves, the 100 percent probability of this outcome equals a certainty. And a certainty is equivalent to a cause. The baby believes that pushing causes movement because he can always produce movement by pushing. The so-called abstract concept of causation is actually just a word for our concrete physical experience that the bottle always moves!

We could discover many rules of logic by this approach. For example, the neuronal network for the idea of "necessary but not sufficient" probably comes from the physical experience that concurs with that idea. If the baby pushes on his bottle one day and it doesn't move, then he has the experience that something else is needed to move the bottle. It may be that the bottle is resting against the side of the crib. In that case, pushing is necessary, but not sufficient.

Can We Teach Reasoning?

If reasoning and logic are a natural product of the brain, we might ask if reasoning can be taught. And if so, how would a teacher go about it?

My colleagues are of various minds about this question. Some believe that "reasoners" are made, and some that they are born.

Those of us who think reasoning can be taught often believe that people will learn to reason if they learn to do whatever it is *we* do! This is a humorous idea, if we can laugh at ourselves! I fell prey to it for a long time. In my mind, learning biochemistry was equivalent to learning reasoning. But I began to doubt this when I realized that many of my colleagues were making a similar claim. I found that teachers of physiology, physics, math, Latin, and philosophy all staked out this reasoning terrain as their own. "Any student who gets an A in my course has really learned to think!" was our boast.

And it is not just teachers who feel this way. We hear the same thing from employers who joke that since their new employees just got a college degree, it is time for them to learn to think. And, equally funny, we hear it from parents, who cannot understand why their children can't think at school, when those same children have seen lucid thinking for their whole lifetime from their parents at home!

Of course this is not a new frustration. We have always worried about teaching reasoning. Plato championed the study of geometry as the answer, and medieval scholars pushed the use of syllogisms. But now it seems that all this effort has been based on a false belief about learning; the belief that if we teach someone the rules for a particular kind of reasoning, they will apply those rules in a general way to everything else.

Fortunately, this does not seem to be the way the brain works. I say fortunately, because it relieves the teacher of all that responsibility. We do not need to blame ourselves if our students do not show wonderful reasoning skills after taking our course. It is not our fault!

General rules of reasoning are not easily taught. An explanation for this is suggested in chapters 6 and 7. Neuronal networks grow by building on existing networks, so our entrée to reasoning in one subject comes through the neuronal networks for information in that subject. Often we don't have the networks that connect one subject with another. They have been built up separately, especially if we have studied in the standard curriculum that breaks knowledge into parts like math, language, science, and social science.[5]

A Useful Exception

There seems to be one very interesting exception to this lack of transfer of reasoning skills between subjects. This exception was described by Nisbett and his colleagues, a few years ago, in a study on teaching reasoning.[6]

For the most part, this study confirmed that it is hard to teach reasoning by learning rules, such as the rules of logic—with one striking exception. And that exception is our old friend, statistical reasoning, or the "laws of large numbers." These laws, of course, are those that we just discussed in the preceding sections, laws that say that if something has happened a large number of times, it is likely to happen again (and the converse).

I won't go into the details here, but consider this quote from Nisbett's article: "These results support the view that people possess an abstract version of the law of large numbers and that improvements to it can transfer to a wide range of problem content." You can check the paper for details, but it is the comment that "people possess an abstract version of the law of large numbers" that interests us here.

What might that abstract version of the law of large numbers be? Of course, I believe it consists of the rules of experience that we discussed previously. It is natural thinking. People already possess the neuronal networks for these laws of probability, because they are part of life. The connections are already there.

Our understanding of neuronal networks and the empirical evidence about teaching reasoning both suggest that we might consider much greater use of ideas of chance, probability, and statistics if we want to enhance the ability of our front cortex to reason logically. Rather than focusing on formal logic, math, or biochemistry as the route to reason, perhaps we should build on students' statistical experience in life.

Front to Back—and Back

From our discussion so far, it may seem that the integrative front cortex acts alone as it gets ideas and solves problems. But nothing could be farther from the truth. In fact, its executive capabilities include sending commands and requests to most other parts of the cortex.

Many, if not most, pathways of signaling in the brain include a combination of neurons that send signals in one direction and neurons that send signals in the other direction. I would like to give a couple of direct examples of this and show how it enriches our concept of experience and thus of experiential learning.

We know that sensory information from the back cortex is sent on to the front cortex. This is the direction of signaling we have been talking about through most of this book. But in chapter 9 we also saw the reverse. The front cortex seems to send signals to the back cortex, when we recall images. In its executive function, the front cortex tells the back cortex to remember particular things, both images and language. This control by the front cortex is specific for the right and left hemispheres. That is, recall (retrieval) of facts, which we call *semantic memory,* is directed by the left-front hemisphere, while recall of stories, called *episodic memory,* is directed by the right-front hemisphere.[7]

Another example of this front-to-back signaling has recently been described in monkeys. Specifically, when a monkey has to hold a visual experience in its working memory (front cortex) for a few seconds, neurons in the visual cortex (back cortex) fire more frequently.[8]

This back-and-forth between our idea brain and the back cortex expands the concept of *experience,* which was developed in chapters 2, 3, and 8. Experience can be more than just the sensory brain receiving signals from the outside world. Since the sensory brain can also receive signals from the front cortex, it seems that this may represent another route for experience. Our front cortex ideas become part of our experience. We might call this, *internal experience.*

For the teacher, recognizing this internal influence of the learner's ideas on his sensory and reflecting back cortex may be of great importance. When a student has missed or misunderstood a key sensory experience, it may be that this is the impact of his idea brain on his perceptions. We may have to track down such misperceptions carefully and with understanding. The learner loves his ideas, and their impact can extend deep into his perceiving brain. It happens to us all!

Learning by Copying

We now turn our attention to a more specific function of the front cortex. This function engages the executive brain but appears to have evolved for a specific function of great value in survival. That function is copying and mimicking, and I have chosen it because it seems to have special relevance for teachers.

Humans and other animals mimic what they experience. We mimic sounds, actions, and ideas. In fact, we could argue that virtually nothing in our brain originated there. We lift ideas and actions, left and right!

How does this happen? How can we generate a plan of action based on observation of that action?

I don't have a detailed answer to this question, but I can tell you about some interesting discoveries seem to be part of the answer. One of these discoveries came from research with monkeys showing that certain neurons in the front cortex fire both when the monkey *observes* a particular action and when it *does* that action—the same neurons! For example, specific neurons in the frontal cortex fire both when a monkey sees a picture of a hand grabbing a banana and when the monkey grabs a banana.[9]

Appropriately, these neurons have been called "mirror neurons." They reflect an observation by reproducing it as an action. They seem to be responsible for the old adage, "Monkey see, monkey do!"

Brain imaging studies have confirmed that there are regions of the human brain that behave in a similar fashion.[10] So, if you ever doubted it, it seems that neuroscience confirms our natural instinct to copy things. The brain is wired to copy what we observe.

Is It Mine? Deciding to Take Ownership

Our theme in this chapter is taking ownership of knowledge. But now we are talking about copying. So we might ask, "Can we own something we have copied?"

I think there are three things to consider here. First, we could ask if we really learn by mimicry. Perhaps we just get the basic idea or the raw materials for learning by observing others; it is how we manipulate this information that makes it ours. For example, we might hear someone swearing and learn a few pungent phrases, but we don't really learn to swear until we create our own forms, uses, and mannerisms for application of profanity in our life. In the executive processing model that we used earlier in this chapter, hearing swearing gives us facts to attend to (new swear words), but it is the way we organize and apply those facts to produce a cloud of blue haze that makes one a true and unique profaner!

The second consideration is different in nature. And it draws our attention to another feature of the front cortex that is of great importance. Indeed, it is one of the most difficult features to explain in physical terms. This is the process of *making a decision.*

Taking ownership of things we have observed involves more than just the process of copying or mimicking them. It requires a decision by our own front cortex. We *choose* to copy, consciously or subconsciously. We can reject as well as select, but whichever way we go, one could argue that is the point at which we take ownership.

Finally, it seems that mimicry still requires that we construct an abstract idea of our own. We imagine how it will be. If we mimic something we have seen and take a little bit of something else we heard, we can assemble a new form of ourselves. It seems fair to say that, yes, we do own this imaginary new form of ourselves.

Mirror Neurons and Cheating

This discussion of mirror neurons naturally brings up cheating. People will copy the work of others.

I am not saying that plagiarism should be condoned because we have mirror neurons in our brains. But I do think the edges can be fuzzy. Our natural instinct to copy is at work all the time. We see a behavior we admire, and we decide to mimic it. We see, or hear, a turn of phrase that seems compelling, and we start using it. Even strongly held opinions often turn out to be copied. We hear someone assert a view in an impressive way, and we decide to take on that view, not because we have analyzed it for ourselves, but because we liked how someone else explained it. We may even copy the conviction as well as the opinion!

Teachers actually encourage students to copy certain things. For example, we want them to mimic how *we* work. If they approach a project or problem exactly as we would, we think that is good. We show them a complex analysis or a derivation, and when the test comes, we assess their performance according to how closely it mimics our own. We grade students based on how well they have internalized what *we* think!

We don't want them to give it back to us verbatim, however. We want *our* ideas in *their* words. We see a big difference between memorizing a derivation and actually understanding it. But that difference may not be big, or even apparent, to the learner.

All this suggests that we must be careful in how we handle issues of plagiarism. For example, I am told that oriental students may believe that using an exact quote demonstrates comprehension. If the quote is used in the right context, does that not show understanding? And if a number of quotes are strung together by a student, is the whole quote original? Or what about parts of quotes? Can't these be lined up by a student, just as he would make a sentence by arranging *words* or *scripts* he copied from others?

We all have mirror neurons. We need to be exact when we explain when students can use them and when they can't. But it may not be easy to draw that line.

From Mimicry to Language

Mirror neurons fire only when a *specific* action is observed. For example, some mirror neurons fire when the action is grasping something, and others fire when the action is tearing something. These mirror neurons almost sound like "verb neurons." They fire when the *idea of grasp* or the *idea of tear* is triggered in the brain.

If this is starting to sound a little bit like language, you should not be surprised. Mirror neurons and mimicry neurons are localized in an area of the brain that has been associated with language for decades. It is known as *Broca's area,* and it is heavily wired to Wernike's area for comprehension of language in the back cortex. In fact, the connection between these two key language areas is made via one of the major fasciculi (arcuate fasciculus) that we described in chapter 3—the connections that are important in balance.

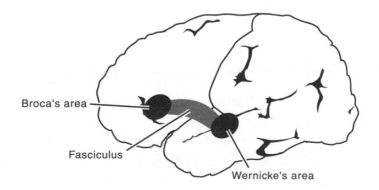

Broca's area

Fasciculus

Wernicke's area

Broca's area is where spoken language is assembled prior to being actually spoken. People with damage to this area of their brain generally can understand language but cannot produce coherent sentences or phrases. They can speak words and some phrases clearly, but they cannot assemble them into meaningful speech.

Are mirror neurons the same neurons that we use to assemble language? Did language originate as a form of sign language, where gestures and other body actions were received and passed on to others by mimicry? Did these body gestures begin to include movements of mouth, tongue, and diaphragm, thus leading to spoken language? Is this how human language was born?

Of course, we don't know for sure, and may never know, but this seems to be the favored explanation for language at the present time in our understanding. We may owe the single most powerful tool our brains possess to our ability to copy what we see and hear.

Assembling Language—Planning for Action

In chapter 11 we will talk more about the production of language through action, the actions of speech and writing. But before we actually produce language, we must plan for it. We must assemble ideas into logical relationships that make up the grammar of our language, and that is a function of Broca's area.

Constructing language is making a plan for action. It is a major part of what the front brain evolved to do. Let me try to give you an example.

Let's say that you are studying the civil war, and an image begins to form. It is an image that you have assembled yourself, and you begin to feel fond of it. You want to share it, using language.

So you assemble the language you will use. You identify the parts of your image and put them into working memory. You hold them there and begin to arrange them in an order that shows their relationships to each other. You identify any objects or people in your image with nouns. You express the most fundamental relationship between these objects by using one as object and one as subject. You refine these relationships by using prepositions and other language organizers. And you explain the dynamics of the image with past, present, or future tense verbs.

You create a sentence: "I think it is unlikely that the civil war was fought over the issue of slavery."

Before you speak this sentence, it is an abstract idea in your mind. It is a plan for speaking—for action. The first part of the idea is just that you will say something. Your subject will be the civil war and the issue of slavery. So you will need nouns like *war* and *slavery,* verbs such as the past tense of *to be* and past tense of *fight,* and some other relationship words. And, as a last thought, you will need to assure people that you realize you are just telling them what you think.

Much of this is partly assembled already with phrases such as "I think," "civil war," and "issue of slavery." But the way these will be organized is up to you. You are creating your own idea of how to express your thought—how to describe your image.

Of course this all happens very quickly, and we are not aware of what the brain is doing. Sometimes it even seems that we need to speak in order to know what we think. But, if we keep careful track of things, we can follow our brain as it speaks, gets a new connection (which produces a new idea or correction), speaks again, and cycles round and round. And in the middle of it all sit the neurons in Broca's area of your brain, spinning away at assembling your ideas into speech.

Demanding Language

In my experience, unskilled use of language by the learner is one of the greatest challenges for a teacher. This challenge is discussed by Robert Leamnson in his book *Thinking about Teaching and Learning.*[11] One approach that intrigued me was his idea of insisting that students speak to him about the academic content of the subject using complete, grammatically correct sentences.

This comes close to the idea I have in mind. It requires learners to carefully assemble their plan for speaking. This plan must have specific content, and that content must be arranged in a way that accurately conveys the image that is in their brain. No clear image, no clear plan!

But assembling the plan is how the image gets clear. When we have to identify the relevant parts of our image and manage the task of arranging them in a logical sentence, the image is brought sharply into focus. A specific plan makes things clear.

No matter how much they object, I believe learners take a huge step when they assemble their images into specific language. With some exceptions, I think we should insist that they do it.[12] If language is a plan for action, then our insistence that a learner explain something "in your own words" takes on a new meaning. It means "tell me *your* plan for action." And it means more than just *words*. It means, "in your own *sentences,* in your own *paragraphs!*" It means that you want to see planning, and you want it to lead somewhere.

But if we do that, we have to think about our own habits. We have to assemble our own plans for action. We need to plan carefully what we will say to our learners. It is quite a different thing to ask students to assemble a plan for how they will speak than it is just to ask them "what they think."

When we ask "Any questions?" we are also asking for a student plan for action. We are asking students to assemble some language that expresses uncertainty or confusion. But our manner and phrasing might mislead learners. Maybe we shouldn't be so flip. If language is as important as we say, we might take the time to use it better ourselves. We might think of more effective ways to elicit the kind of response we want. For example, we might say to our learners, "Take some time to identify anything you feel uncertain about and then, describe this uncertainty and its origin in complete sentences."

And, finally, if we take the assembly of language as seriously as this, we may well want to change our timing. We may take it more seriously ourselves and not expect instant answers. Developing a plan takes time—a few seconds at the very least and probably several minutes in many cases. But it is worth the time. Good questions take time, and so do good answers.

My Student Veronica

Let's finish this chapter by going back to the story about Veronica.

If creating new knowledge is a key part of learning, then it seems that we must allow our Veronicas the freedom to develop and express their ideas. But where does this leave the teacher? If we have worked with something all of our lives, we probably do know "what it means." Or at least, we know what we, and the other experts, all agree that it means. Isn't it our responsibility to explain these things to our students? Indeed, isn't it a waste of time if we allow them to thrash around without benefit of our insights?

This leads us to our next subject. Learners may need guidance in developing their ideas. And the learning cycle tells us the nature of that guidance. Any ideas we produce must be tested by action. We must guide our learners toward developing *testable* ideas. We are not just looking for any old action, but for action that is the direct result of ideas produced by the learner.

In chapter 11 I will try to explain what I mean by this and how teachers can lead their learners in this direction.

Notes

1. E. Smith and J. Jonides, *Science* 287 (1999), p. 1657.
2. J. W. de Fockart and colleagues, *Science* 291 (2001), p. 1803.
3. Smith and Jonides (note 1) suggest that these two tasks are the most fundamental and interrelated, but they also identify three others: planning a sequence of steps in the subtasks, updating and monitoring progress, and coding the representations in working memory as to time and place in the process.
4. J. Saffran and colleagues, *Science* 274 (1996), p. 1926; also see review and comments on this work by E. Bates and J. Elman, p. 1849 of the same issue.
5. This separation of neuronal networks can be striking. I am reminded of a story told to me by New Zealand educator Neil Fleming. A chemistry teacher was trying to teach about chlorophyll, and his students seemed confused. Finally, the teacher said, "Don't you remember about chlorophyll in biology? You know. Photosynthesis by green plants?" And then a student suddenly sat upright and piped out, "Oh, you mean *that* chlorophyll!"
6. R. E. Nisbett and colleagues, *Science* 238 (1987), p. 625.
7. T. Shallice and colleagues, *Nature* 368 (1994), p. 633; L. Nyberg, R. Cabeza, and E. Tulving, *Psychonomic Bulletin and Review* 3 (1996), p. 135.
8. H. Super, H. Sprkreijse, and V. Lamme, *Science* (July 6, 2001), p. 120.
9. G. Rizzolatti and M. A. Arib, *Trends in Neuroscience* (1998).
10. M. Iacoboni and colleagues, *Science* 286 (1999), p. 2526.
11. Leamnson, R., *Thinking about Teaching and Learning* (Stylus: Arlington, VA, 2000).
12. There are obvious exceptions, such as learners with speech difficulties. We should not ignore other ways that students can demonstrate understanding. But language is still the most widely used and central vehicle for making ourselves understood.

II

TEST BY TRIAL

USING THE MOTOR BRAIN
TO CLOSE THE LOOP OF LEARNING

Knowledge must come through action;
you can have no test which is not fanciful, save by trial.

—Sophocles

Samuel was brilliant. I could tell that from the first. He seemed to understand everything instantly. And he was motivated. If there was ever a promising student, it was Samuel.

It probably won't surprise you to hear that he was also pretty cocky! He was used to being right. His thoughts and ideas were always better than those of his peers.

My moment of crisis with Samuel came after the first test. He hadn't done well with one of the problems, and I suspected that he would not like his grade much. It was no surprise when he showed up in my office, graded test in hand.

"What is wrong with this answer?" he challenged me directly. "I understand this problem exactly, and I know that I have done it right!" He looked at me defiantly.

I took a deep breath. "Well," I said, "let's work it through and see what we can find."

"I don't have to work it through," he said. "I never do. I understand it without all that. I never work them through. It is a waste of time for me!"

"Well, then," I answered. "Would you do it for me? Show me what you are thinking?"

Reluctantly, he began to do the problem on the board. I watched the board carefully at first, but then my attention wandered for an instant, and I saw his face. And as I watched, his face began to turn pink and then bright red. Contrasted with his jet-black hair, the image was unforgettable. Samuel had seen his error—an experience that was new and powerful for him.

"I see what happened," I said quietly. "Of course you know how to do the problem. You just forgot something. When you actually wrote it out, you saw it instantly."

I hoped that he would overcome his embarrassment, but it was too much to ask right at that moment. Without a sound, Samuel picked up his test and bolted from my office.

* * *

What Samuel discovered was something obvious but at the same time often ignored by learners. He found that there is a great difference between imagining that we have done the problem and actually doing it. No matter what ideas our front cortex has created, we cannot know if they are true until they have been tested in a concrete and active way. Until we do that, as Sophocles said, our knowledge is "fanciful."

Testing our ideas through action is how we find out if we are on the right track. But there is another reason that action is a key part of learning. Action makes the learning cycle a cycle. Physical movement is needed to link our abstract mental notions with *new* concrete experience. Biology backs up this dual role for action in learning. This is one place where the connection between body and brain, which we discussed in chapter 5, is obviously relevant. The brain gets ideas so the body can act. At the same time, the action of the body provides sensory feedback to the brain. It is through action that the biological wholeness of learning becomes apparent.[1]

What Is Action?

As we have seen in earlier chapters, the *doing* part of learning is the natural last step in the biological sequence that characterizes nervous systems:

Sense ⇒ Integrate ⇒ Act

In fact, action is why nervous systems are useful and why they evolved. Thinking of actions that might help us survive is important but useless unless we carry through, unless we act.

Biologically, action is what happens whenever the muscles in our body move, either contracting or relaxing. When this happens, some part of our body must also move. This is a broad concept, and it may not fit well with some of our preconceptions. For example, we may think of action as something dramatic and obvious. But, according to this biological definition, people can be active while appearing quite still.

A good example is reading. To read, we must use the muscles in our eyes for focusing and for following the words on the page or screen. Each eye contains a small lens that is continually adjusted by small muscles in the eyeball, allowing us to focus on what we see. And, each eyeball is turned up, down, or sidewise, by other small muscles, thus allowing us to follow the words along the page. The lens changes shape, and the eyeball moves as we read. Reading is an intense, focused use of the motor brain. Reading is action.

Ideas Without Action

Like my student Samuel, we often have great confidence in our ideas. This is certainly true for me. When I have some new experience and develop some ideas about it, I automatically believe I have learned something and I am quite sure that I know what I have learned. So I often put off, or simply ignore, the testing part of learning. "That was really interesting," I think. "I really learned a lot!"

But as my life has gone on, I have noticed that this kind of learning doesn't work out well. If I never get around to actually doing something about those ideas, they seem to die. They may rest in my brain for a while, but ultimately the life goes out of them.

Since I am writing in the fall of 2001 following the terrorist attacks on the United States in which the two towers of the World Trade Center were destroyed, let's use that historical context for an example of ideas without action. Since the Taliban in Afghanistan supported the terrorist attacks, you feel that you would like to understand more about the reasons behind this terror. You decide to read Rashad's book, *Taliban*.

As you read and as you reflect on the book, you find yourself getting some ideas about the Taliban, Afghanistan, and maybe even America. You may decide that even though you now understand things better, there is nothing in this book that can in any way justify the terror. Or you may arrive at a different conclusion. But whatever you begin to think about terrorism, you have arrived at that point by going through the learning cycle, including the *experience* of reading, your *reflections* on what you have read, and developing your own *ideas*.

So what happens now?

You might argue that this is enough. You learned some things you value. You might use this knowledge sometime, but for now you will not do anything in particular about it. It is nice to have. You feel enlightened and even enriched.

But I would argue that you can't claim you have learned, just yet. Rather you have what Alfred North Whitehead called *inert ideas*, ". . . ideas that are merely received into the mind without being utilized, or tested, or thrown into fresh combinations."[2] And your learning will remain inert, without life, until it is tested.

Forms of Active Testing

You may resist this. "Of course I learned something!" you may protest. "I learned a lot about Afghanistan!" And if you do protest, then I would immediately feel better. In fact, I would drop my argument completely, because the minute you rise in defense of your learning, you have begun to test it.

Active testing can take many forms. Defending your inaction is a form of active testing. Even just reading another book on a related subject would be active testing. Any action that is inspired by your ideas qualifies as active testing. This is true because that new action will produce new experience, and learning can then continue.

How else might you test your ideas? You might talk to someone about the book. In conversation you would have many chances to explain what you learned and to hear what another person thinks of it. Or you might test your learning more directly by checking out what you could find about the Taliban on the web. And if you were very determined, you might seek out a friend from the Middle East to ask some questions.

If you are inclined to be more analytical, you might develop active testing to an art form. You might set up controlled experiments, so that you could be assured of the outcome. You might plan your actions in careful and rigorous ways, and you might repeat the testing many times to be sure that the results are statistically significant. You might actually revel in this part of the learning cycle.

You could also "live out" your active testing. The Taliban book might raise your awareness of the importance of education or of women's rights, and you might take up one of those causes. That could be the most rigorous test of all.

In fact, it seems that life is a continual process of active testing of our ideas and hypotheses. Learning comes from those continual adjustments that we make in our actions as we have new experience and new ideas.

Motor Brain, Language, and Active Testing

You may have noticed that active testing is often based on language. We may have a conversation about our ideas or we might even talk to ourselves. We may write things down. Writing makes us be specific about our ideas, and is one of the best "active tests." I may think I have a good idea, but I don't know for sure until I write it down. Putting my images into language is a rigorous test!

In fact, any use of language requires movements. Speaking requires the use and control of a large number of muscles in the face, tongue, mouth, and hands. Babies first begin to produce spoken language in the reflexive movements of the mouth, throat, and tongue, so the first sounds produced seem to be the same regardless of what language the baby will eventually learn.[3] These are simple actions like moving the jaw up and down and "bunching" the tongue, and they lead to baby sounds like "yaya" or "wawa." A little more tongue constriction or opening of the nose produces those exciting moments where we hear our baby say "dada" or "mama."

Sign language is more obviously about movement. In fact, some theorists suggest that sign language was the precursor of actual speech in evolution. And recent research shows that hearing babies (babies who can hear) whose parents are deaf learn the arm and hand movements of sign language before they learn either sign language or spoken language. They babble silently with their hands.[4]

Speech may demand more of our motor brain than any other action. It requires coordination of the contraction and relaxation of more muscles in more complex and rapid patterns than anything else we learn to do. In fact, the motor brain dedicates almost half of its neurons to control of lips, jaw, tongue, vocal tract, and breathing apparatus (all needed to produce sounds).

Language is the primary way we change our ideas into actions.

Making Learning Physical

Language isn't the only way we test our ideas, of course. We may act them out, we may show them in gestures, or we may make drawing of plans or images. Regardless of how we test our ideas, the outcome is some physical process that alters the physical world around us. If we speak, we produce physical vibrations in the air, sound. If we write, we make physical marks on paper or physical images of words and sentences on a screen. If we draw, we create a physical object that reflects physical light in specific and defined ways.

When we test our ideas, we are changing the abstract into the concrete. We convert our mental ideas into physical events. Action forces our mental constructs out of our brains and into the reality of the physical world.

However we test our ideas, the physical nature of this testing is almost always a clarifying process. Making an image concrete, by converting it into the precise form required for language, helps us see the details in our image, or it makes us invent those details. We struggle to find the right words, discard some of them, add others, or recognize a flaw in our idea as we see it in concrete form. And we may notice that something is missing, a gap in our thought that we would never have seen without converting our abstraction into physical form.

If we act on an idea by changing our behavior or undertaking something new in our life, we see the idea expressed in the physical form of body action and sensory interactions with people and objects in the world. In our effort to express our ideas, we create concrete experience. And that experience gives us information about the validity of our ideas; it is active testing in the most direct and concrete form possible.

Ultimately, physical testing is the final arbiter of truth. For example, Einstein's theory of relativity was just an idea until it was tested with physical experiments. If the experiment disagrees with the theory, it is the theory that must be changed.

Inside Out and Outside In

What I have just described is a model of learning that depends on interactions between the physical constructs of neuronal networks inside the brain and the reality of the concrete world. There is the world inside the brain and the world outside the brain. We must bring them to terms with each other if we are to learn.

Nowhere is this idea more apparent than in the learning cycle. Our experience with the concrete world gives us connections and ideas inside our brain, and these internal ideas and connections allow us to understand and manipulate the outside world—allow us to survive.

So we learn both by getting information from the outside through our concrete experience and by putting information back to the outside by our actions. We learn from outside in, and from inside out.[5]

These ideas are illustrated in the following figure, which divides the learning cycle into the parts that happen "inside" and those that happen "outside" the brain.

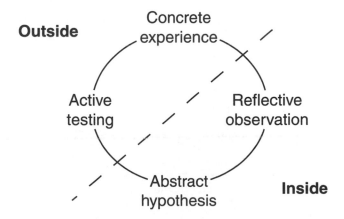

Active testing is the inside-out part of learning where our ideas encounter the concrete world. Without that encounter, we cannot say if our ideas are right or wrong. We cannot say that we have learned.

Sensing while Moving

Signals from the motor brain produce movement by our muscle tissue. But the movements are not the end either. In fact, there is no end—it is indeed a cycle. Movements are sensed. Action produces sensation. As we learned in chapter 8, this happens through various specialized structures throughout the body. The brain knows what its body is doing. So action closes the loop of learning. It generates new concrete experiences, and the cycle begins anew. It becomes a spiral, producing progress toward understanding with each turn.

This is not just high-sounding theology. It is a biological process. One way it comes about is through actual sensory organs buried in the muscles themselves. This is shown in the following illustration, which is a diagram of a sensory organ called the muscle *spindle organ*. As you

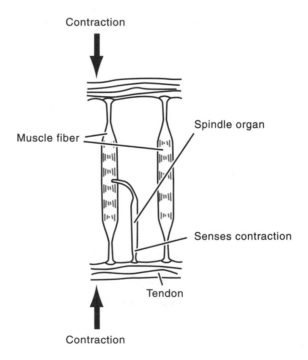

can see, these spindle organs are lined up right in the midst of surrounding muscle tissue.

In fact, the spindle organ is both muscle tissue and nervous tissue. *It both contracts (weakly) and senses contraction.* When surrounding muscle fibers contract and produce movement, the spindle organ is directly compressed and this compression triggers the neuron part of the structure to send signals back to the brain about what movement is occurring. The action of the muscles produces the sensation of the spindle organ, a direct physical connection between action and sensation.

The combination of signals from these sensory structures, together with pressure receptors scattered throughout our joints and body, tell our brain what actions have been, and are being, carried out. They send back information about the directions in which we are moving our position, the amount of effort we are expending, the degree of tension in particular muscles, the rapidity of contraction, the intensity of contraction, and the rhythm of contraction and relaxation.

Of course, a similar, although not as direct, connection exists between all movement and sensation. If something moves within our visual sensory field, we see it. If someone speaks within our auditory sensory field, we hear it. Although the message must travel over a distance, through the outside world, if there is action, we sense it.

This is the fourth stage of the learning cycle. It is closing the loop of learning.

Entering the Dynamic of Learning: A Story

The remainder of this chapter will focus on teaching, so let me turn to a teaching story.

* * *

Professor Wall taught philosophy. He even looked philosophical, stocky and serious with heavy black eyebrows that moved up and down while he thought and when he talked. And he looked determined!

Prof. Wall wasn't an exciting lecturer, but he was compelling. He just carried the class along as, bulldog-like, he grabbed hold of the material and wouldn't let go.

Most compelling of all, Prof. Wall listened to his students. He *wanted* to hear our philosophies and our ideas.

But I wasn't used to discussion classes. I was used to leaving class, going to my room, and studying, using the book and my lecture notes. That was how I tested my ideas and understandings.

I started out in Prof. Wall's class the same way. I took good notes, listened, and studied.

My friend Fred was also in this class. And Fred was more aggressive. He began to get into the discussions right away.

I knew Fred well. He was smart, but I didn't think he was any smarter than me. But he was getting all this attention from Prof. Wall, and it bothered me.

One day I couldn't stand it any more. We were discussing the British empiricists, and Fred had been the center of attention again. So I raised my hand. And when Wall called on me, I discovered that he took me just as seriously as any other student. He listened carefully and asked a question about a part of my idea that I hadn't expressed very well. I clarified the idea in better language, and when he understood, Wall nodded and suggested that I pick up a book on Hume (one of those British empiricists) in his office after class.

I was filled with confidence as Prof. Wall and I exchanged ideas. We were having a conversation, a comfortable back-and-forth as though we were peers. As the class went on, I could see that Wall was headed in exactly the direction I had suggested. My ideas were good!

That was the most successful class in my college life. It wasn't *what* I learned that made it successful. Rather, it was the fact that learning came alive for me. I had entered into the action.

A Requirement

Many things made my experience in Prof. Wall's class valuable, but the one that meant the most was that he wasn't looking for an answer. He was looking for a process. When I speak of active testing of ideas, I mean that the testing itself is where we find the value.

This seems especially important. Too much testing is designed merely to elicit an answer. When the answer is the goal, the test may not produce actions that are of value. It may be useless for learning.

I found a powerful example of this when I read a recent article about the SAT, the standardized test used in selecting students for college. The article described how students can prepare for this test by practice and by analyzing patterns in the answers. Test takers are trained to analyze the answers without ever thinking about the question![6] As I thought about this article, I began to realize that with all the emphasis on testing and the possibility that the right answer can be obtained without knowledge, it should not surprise us that learners in schools often think that the answer is the goal—a disembodied answer, if you will, disconnected from knowledge about the question.

Of course, this cannot happen with true active testing. When it is the process we are looking for, this type of testing becomes *formative*. Its value is in the learning that takes place, not the answer. We should insist on seeing the process! We must see how the learner *gets to* her answer.

Whose Ideas?

Another thing my experience in Prof. Wall's class demonstrated was that, as has been the case with almost everything we have discussed in this book, the learner is in control. I was the one who had to act. Active testing must be done by the learner. It is her motor brain that must produce the action.

True, Prof. Wall could have called on me with his own question. But that would not have been active testing of my ideas. It would have been testing his ideas!

Only the learner knows her own hypotheses, so only the learner can test them. Part of the art of changing the learner's brain, then, is the art of eliciting action. But since the learner is in control, she will not act unless she wants to do so. In my case, my feelings about Fred were important in generating my own action, but Wall knew nothing of that. Once again we see the personal nature of learning and the places where emotion comes into play. We will address ways a teacher can deal with this challenge more in chapter 12.

Feedback: The Teacher Becomes Important

It is a great opportunity for the teacher when a learner tests her ideas. Now the teacher can give relevant feedback. If the learner has given you her own ideas, it is a valuable gift. She has engaged you in her learning, and there is great potential for growth in her understanding. You, the teacher, have become important.

You might be surprised that I say this. I have stressed the independence of learning so frequently that you might have come to think that the teacher is almost irrelevant. But I believe there are key moments when the teacher is of great importance.

Our ability to seize these moments depends on how we prepare ourselves. If we come to class thinking only of our own goals, we may miss the moment. But if we come ready to discover what our students have been thinking, we may see the door open for us to have a major impact on learning.

This is what happened in Prof. Wall's class. He focused his efforts on dealing with what his students had on their minds. But at the same time we all knew that his first love was philosophy. We knew that if we wanted a conversation with him, it would have to be about philosophy. But if that conversation took place, we knew the reward would be great. We would get feedback about our ideas from an expert.

Of course, this can only work when the teacher takes students seriously. And that is not always easy. Sometimes student's ideas are poorly developed. But still, as we discussed in chapters 6 and 7, we must start with those ideas. Our art is the art of understanding the student brain and of building from there.

Active Testing while Listening

Taking notes in a class can be one of the most helpful forms of active testing. If we just copy what the teacher says or does, it is not of much value, except for the reinforcement. But if we translate what a teacher says into our own words, we are doing one of the most effective versions of active testing. Once we have developed our notes by writing down our own ideas, we can get feedback by looking at a book or asking the teacher to critique them.

The practice of listening to a teacher, making meaningful connections, converting those connections into our own ideas, and writing down those ideas is a good model of using the learning cycle in the traditional classroom. It uses the four major parts of cortex that we have been discussing, and it gives us new sensory experience (reading our notes) for another turn of the cycle!

Starting with Action

I have stressed the idea that experiential learning begins with sensory input. We sense what is happening to us as we experience things, and that begins the cycle of learning. This proposal is based on the sense ⇒ integrate ⇒ act model of nervous systems.

However, this is undoubtedly too narrow a view. In fact, we can argue that learning often begins with action rather than with sensing. Sometimes, the sequence of act ⇒ sense ⇒ integrate, makes more sense.

Let's take a look at how newborn babies seem to learn. Neither the sensory nor the motor brain are well developed at the time of birth. Babies move spontaneously and randomly, mostly driven by hard-wired reflexes. This so-called reflex phase of development is a time when the muscle movements of a baby are not directed toward any particular goal but are basically random in nature. The arms move back and forth, the eyes move from side to side, the feet kick, the head twists back and forth.

But these undirected movements still produce learning, because the baby is creating new concrete experience by her own random movements. Her arms and legs bump into things, and she learns the reality of other objects in the world. Her eyes sense different light patterns as they move around the room, and she learns that she can know things about her environment by looking around. She turns her head toward, or away from, the sound of her mother's voice, and she learns that sound is a source of information.

This reflex phase is followed by what is called the *sensorimotor phase* where a baby discovers that specific motions can produce specific results. She finds that she can grasp things if she repeats the motion that puts her hand near an object. She finds movements that always produce the same result—a pattern! She also finds some movements uninteresting because they do not produce any predictable result—no pattern.

Thus, the learning cycle begins to develop. As the baby senses the results of her *actions,* her brain remembers this connection and develops an unconscious theory about it. The theory is, "If I do that action, I will get this result." Of course, she does not put this theory into language but simply acts on it. She acts by trying out the action again.

Even at the level of the unconscious developing brain, it seems that the learning cycle is in operation. Of greatest interest here, it can start not with sensing, but with action!

Action by the learner can initiate her learning. So maybe the teacher should pay more attention to the actions of her students, even when they don't have specific ideas or hypotheses to test, even when they don't seem totally on task.

Sometimes the *search* for ideas may be most important.

Biology and the Search for Ideas

The idea of searching is an interesting one biologically. Searching, of course, is movement, and recently ideas about the biological origins of movement have found their way into philosophy. They have been used by Cotterill to develop a theory of consciousness.[7] He calls his idea a "back to front" theory of consciousness, which "accords primacy to the organism's output, rather than its input." That is, the first and most fundamental part of consciousness is what the organism *does,* not what it senses.

Cotterill's arguments come from the recognition that the machinery for movement and for sensing arose earlier in evolution than the nervous system. Single cell organisms don't have any neurons, but they still move and sense things. They have the molecular machinery for movement and sensing all within one cell.

It can be argued that even simple organisms like this are still capable of "intelligent" behavior. For example, bacteria have a contractile apparatus that allows them to move. And the movement of bacteria brings them into contact with things they can sense, like sugar molecules needed for food. They "swim" around until they accidentally encounter a chemical of interest, such as a sugar, and then they "swim" toward places where there is more sugar. So they learn where food is by moving.

This idea seems similar to what we have been saying about learning. Action produces sensation. Even reading begins with movement. We *scan* the visual world to sense what is in it, we *go* to class to learn chemistry, we *pick up* a book to read it, we *talk* to an expert. These verbs just keep popping up.

Every sentence has a verb. Without action we lose meaning.

Time on Task

It seems obvious that active testing should be designed to keep the learner focused on the task at hand. Just willy nilly rambling is not productive. Student action such as discussion, writing, or doing should always be consistent with learning goals.

But I found myself questioning that assertion as I realized how fundamental action is to the learning process and as I thought about the biological ideas we just discussed. Maybe we should give students time for more random actions. Maybe we should allow them to search around for what is out there rather than insisting that their actions be focused on the task at hand. Maybe our job is to put things in their way and then stand back and let students discover them. After all, this is the biological way. It is only through exploring, through action, that we encounter new information.

Eventually, I began to realize that this idea is not as radical as it may sound. It just opens things up a bit. It is a matter of judgment by the teacher. Allowing a student to explore can be productive for that student as long as the teacher attends to relevance. When we see a student struggling to stay on task but wandering off anyway, it may be worth the wander. If our goal is discovery, and our learners are in the right area, maybe we should just let them look around a bit. If they have no chance of finding something useful because they are too far afield, we can try to move them back toward a better location.

But as long as they stay close, we might resist our instinct to take over and lead them by the hand. We should avoid the old pitfall of making it our learning rather than theirs.

Cognition and Action: A Biological Surprise

A part of the brain we have ignored so far is the cerebellum. This structure resembles the cerebral cortex in some ways, but it is much smaller. It sits right behind and below the cortex.

The cerebellum is important for coordinating, controlling, and remembering complicated actions. It is thought to be evolutionarily a much older structure than the neocortex and has been associated with automated and subconscious processes rather than with cognition.[8]

But one of the more intriguing recent findings using brain imaging techniques suggests that the cerebellum is engaged in some cognitive processes. In this experiment, people were asked to identify a verb they associate with particular nouns, and the parts of the brain that were most active were monitored by imaging techniques. For example, if the person saw a horse, she might think of the verbs "race" or "gallop," and then choose the one that seemed most appropriate. Of importance, the activity in parts of the brain engaged in *saying* the verbs was subtracted (i.e., the motor cortex action needed to produce the speech).

Since this task requires the brain to create language, it is not surprising that Broca's area in the left integrative front cortex (described in chapter 10) was activated. But the big surprise was that the right cerebellum was also strongly activated.

No one claims to know for sure what this means, but the engagement of the cerebellum could be explained by the fact that the thought was about action, about verbs.[9] Also, recently the cerebellum has been implicated in attention and memory retrieval, so there is growing belief that this action-centered part of the brain is important in a range of cognitive functions.

For the teacher, these discoveries reinforce the importance of action, and thinking about action, for the learning process. All verbalized thought centers on action. Asking a learner to describe things in terms of their actions and their anticipated actions brings this additional part of the brain, the cerebellum, into the task.

It just adds more brain power!

Active Learning May Be More than We Think

In this chapter, I have tried to broaden our concept of action. We have become familiar with various *active learning* approaches such as role playing, conversation, and group work over the past decades, but my suggestion is that action extends beyond these. In fact, it includes things that teachers have always asked of their students: asking questions, drawing, writing, taking notes, checking out a reference, taking a test, and even reading. *Anytime* a learner tests out her ideas, she does it through action, and that action generates learning.

The only pathway that seems unproductive for learning is the pathway that excludes testing of ideas. These pathways lead the learner to keep her ideas inside rather than showing them to the world beyond her brain. But it is this encounter with the reality of the world that leads to learning. The magic isn't in the action; it's in the testing.

Our question then becomes, "What makes a learner test her ideas?" The testing will be powerful, if it happens, but what makes it happen? What can a teacher do to encourage it to happen?

As I have suggested repeatedly throughout this book, this is the key question. It is the learner who must engage the learning. At its root, this is a question of emotion. What makes the learner *want* to test her ideas? It is the final, but maybe most important, piece in the *art* of changing the brain.

Notes

1. This discussion of connections between action and learning excludes mention of at least two important areas: (1) procedural learning (or procedural memory) and (2) enhancing learning by movement. Procedural learning is the kind of learning we do when we form habits or subconscious behaviors. People often develop new skills or behaviors (i.e. actions), without realizing it. In fact, procedural memory is thought to be *the* primary component of cognition (the unconscious part). G. Lakoff and M. Johnson, *Philosophy in the Flesh* (New York: Basic Books, 1999), chapter 2. It is also known that action can enhance learning. In her book *Smart Moves* (Arlington, VA: Great Ocean, 1995), Carla Hannaford describes some specific movements designed to enhance learning based on Dennison & Dennison's *Brain Gym* (Ventura, CA: Teacher Ed, 1989).

2. Alfred E Whitehead, *The Aims of Education and Other Essays* (New York: McMillan, 1929).

3. P. MacNeilage and B. Davis, *Science,* 288, (2000) p. 527. Also see perspective on this work by J. Locke on p. 449 of the same issue.

4. L. Petitto and colleagues, *Nature,* 413 (2001) p. 35.

5. D. E. Hunt, *Beginning with Ourselves* (Cambridge, MA: Brookline Books, 1987).

6. M. Gladwell, "Examined Life: What Stanley Kaplan Taught Us About the S.A.T.," *New Yorker* (Dec. 17, 2001), p. 86.

7. R. Cotterill, "Did Consciousness Evolve from Self-Paced Probing of the Environment, and Not from Reflexes?" *Brain and Mind* 1 (1999), p. 283.

8. The cerebellum is structurally remarkable. It is much smaller than the cerebral cortex but probably has even more connections. It is an immensely powerful calculation machine that constantly estimates the times and degrees of muscle contraction needed for continually varying our actions at high speed, so we can carry precise movements such as those needed in ballet, basketball, knitting or writing.

9. Recall Lakoff and Johnson's proposal that "thought" is actually the firing of brain networks associated with physical experience (chapter 1). So if the cerebellum fires when it regulates actions, why shouldn't it fire when we think of action?

12

WE DID THIS OURSELVES

CHANGING THE BRAIN
THROUGH EFFECTIVE USE OF EMOTION

A leader is best when we hardly know
he exists.
When his work is done, his aim ful-
filled, his followers will say,
"We did this ourselves!"
—*Lao Tzu*

Jack was in trouble. Students were complaining about his teaching, and it was serious. "We don't have a clue what he is doing in class," they lamented. "Please get somebody else!"

We were surprised. True, Jack was a new faculty member, and he was very young, but he should have no trouble teaching this class. He was fully qualified and his research was brilliant. He knew his subject!

To find out more, I visited his class. It didn't take long for me to see the problem. Jack started off well, but then he began to go off on tangents. It was amazing, discouraging, and impressive all at the same time. He seemed to know every tangent, and he followed them all!

When I talked to Jack after class, I asked him how he prepared for class. "You seem to have a lot of material," I said. "It must take a long time to get ready."

Jack nodded. "I spend hours on it," he said. "I have never taught such good students before, and I want them to respect me!" And he gave me a worried, but hopeful, look.

Then, having broken the ice, he began to talk more freely. "And I'm really concerned about my reputation in the department. I want to be respected by everybody. I want to be known as a rigorous and demanding teacher. Fair, but demanding!"

I heaved a silent sigh of relief. Jack's heart was in the right place. He just had it backwards. He thought the class was about him. Once he realized that it was about his students, he would be fine!

*   *   *

When people first learn I am a teacher, they generally ask what I teach. And, for many years, I always answered "biochemistry." But recently I overheard another answer to this question, one that was more interesting. So now when people ask what I teach, I use that answer. I say, "I teach students."

Throughout this book I have tried to stress this idea. Teaching is about the students, and a teacher is most successful when his students can say, "We did this ourselves."

This is an emotional claim. It implies elements of both fear and joy. We are proud of what we did, so it must have been a challenge, and we are happy with the result. Success in learning is emotional success, and the effective teacher understands this emotional foundation for learning. No matter how much he appreciates the learning cycle or neuronal networks, a teacher has little hope if his learners don't *feel* engaged.

Emotion and the Brain Cycle of Learning

A lot of our discussion has focused on connections between the major areas of cerebral cortex and their role in the learning cycle. In the diagram that follows I have summarized these connections in a way that shows the centrality of emotion.

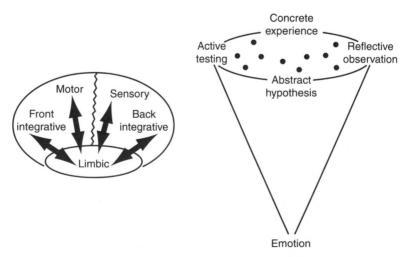

On the left is a diagram of the cortex with its four neocortex sub-divisions, sensory, back integrative, front integrative, and motor, each strongly connected to the central region of limbic cortex. In addition, as we discussed in chapter 5, there are extensive connections between the emotion centers (amygdala and basal structures) and the neocortex. The existence of these connections implies that all parts of the learning cycle are influenced by emotion, which is symbolized in the diagram on the right, in which the four elements of the learning cycle are all sup-ported by a "cone" of emotion.

Importance Influences Learning: A Biological Experiment

Up to now I have inferred the role of emotion in learning. The fact that the limbic brain is connected to the neocortex shows that emotions could affect learning at any stage of the learning cycle. We have so much experience in our own learning, and in watching others, that our belief in this idea is natural and powerful.

However, we can now do better than infer. There are experiments that seem to directly demonstrate the validity of this belief.

The experiment I will show you[1] begins with one of the ideas we discussed in chapter 7, the idea that repeated firing of neuronal net-works can produce growth of new connections. In this case, the audi-tory neurons of rats were stimulated to fire repeatedly by exposing the animals to continuing bursts of high-pitched sound. The idea was that this new experience might produce dendrite branching and new synapse formation in the auditory cortex.

Some change was produced by this new sensory input (the high pitched sounds,) when it continued over weeks. But this change was rel-atively small, even though the sensory neuronal networks were firing repeatedly. It seems that, for the most part, the rat's brain just got used to the sounds. It habituated. This wouldn't be terribly surprising, since the sounds were not associated with anything of particular importance to the rats.

But now we come to the interesting part of the experiment. One of the basal structures I talked about in chapter 5 is called the *nucleus basalis*. This particular structure becomes active when something of basic importance for survival happens—for example, when we satisfy one of our drives, like eating. When the nucleus basalis fires, it seems to mean, "This is important to me. It is something I want."

The experiment, then, was to artificially trigger firing of the nucleus basalis at the same time that the rats were hearing the high-pitched sounds.[2] Since axons from the nucleus basalis extend out into the cortex, including the auditory cortex, the theory was that they might carry signals that would influence the wiring when high-pitched sounds were heard by the rat.

The following figure illustrates the results. This is a diagram of a rat brain, with the nucleus basalis located in the bottom left of the brain. You can see the fibers from this basal structure running up into the cortex and branching at different places, one of which is the auditory cortex, shown as the area enclosed in the small box at the top. The enlarged area shown in the drawing of the brain represents a bigger view of the auditory cortex, which allows us to see which parts are responding to the high-pitched sounds. As you can see, the fraction of the cortex that responds to the stimulus is greatly increased when the nucleus basalis is also active. In fact, considerably more than half of the auditory neurons eventually became responsive to the high pitch.

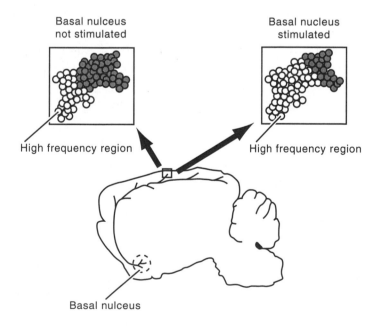

Basal nulceus
not stimulated

Basal nucleus
stimulated

High frequency region

High frequency region

Basal nulceus

Importance Is Physical

Why did this experiment work? What does the nucleus basalis do?

The answer to this question brings us back to something I mentioned in chapter 4. It is a chemical answer. The axons of neurons in the nucleus basalis, which extend out to the auditory cortex, release a chemical on the neurons in this sensory part of the brain. The chemical is called *acetylcholine*. Its function is to trigger chemical changes that increase the responsiveness of existing synapses and alter the expression of genes so that the neurons produce stronger, more numerous synapses.

The bottom line is that when neurons get repeated signals through the sensory system, they will develop stronger and longer lasting responses to those signals, if they also receive the "importance" signal, the signals from the nucleus basalis.

But notice that the high-pitched sound, in fact, was of no biological importance. There was no pleasure or fear associated with it, and it did not have any role in the rat's life. By itself it had little effect on auditory synapses. Nonetheless, when the nucleus basalis was firing, acetylcholine was delivered to the auditory cortex, and biochemistry kicked in. The importance signal had arrived, so the brain changed.

This experiment and others like it are consistent with our life experience. We learn things that are important to us. Plasticity in the brain probably depends more on signals from the emotional centers than it does on new sensory input.

Recognizing Importance Can Take Time

The art of changing the brain includes the art of selling importance. Somehow the learner must "buy in" to importance. We aren't going to wire up the basalis nucleus in a learner's brain, but we may manage things so the learner eventually sees importance.

I stress *eventually*. Buy-in can take time. This is one reason reflection is so important.

What we can understand now is that biochemistry is behind this need for time. As I said above, neurotransmitters like acetylcholine do more than just send a signal. They initiate a complex path of chemical reactions within the neurons.[3] And since there are a number of separate steps in these pathways, each of which takes up some time, those times add up. They can be 100 times slower than the electrical signals, and much slower than that if they go on to change the expressions of genes in the neurons. Their effect is cumulative, and the rearrangement of synapses in billions of neurons may take much longer.

Acetylcholine is not the only slower acting neurotransmitter in the brain. You have heard of some of the others, which include dopamine, serotonin, and a form of adrenaline. These neurotransmitters act in a variety of ways within the neuron and on different parts of the brain, but what they have in common is their use of these chemical cascades that end up affecting the nature and number of synapses. Those changes can increase or decrease synapse number and activity, so the power for changing the brain is great.

The other thing the slower neurotransmitters seem to have in common is their connection with emotion. For example, adrenaline seems to be connected with tension, excitement, and energy, serotonin with peace and tranquility, and as we noted in chapter 5, dopamine with pleasure and action.

The impact of emotion on learning is biochemically complex. We should not lose patience with our learners but continue to give them experiences that help them see the importance of what we want them to learn. When that happens, they will learn!

Having Fun

Teachers will do well if they think seriously about how to engage the emotion centers in the brain. But we should not oversimplify. The real challenge is to find methods that make emotion part of the meaning. Learning is best when it *truly* matters in a person's life, when he believes it is important.

Let me tell you another story to illustrate the point.

*   *   *

I had been trying to improve my teaching for several years before I experimented with games as learning tools. I guess I was a bit afraid of taking that approach with college students. Maybe they would feel that I was treating them like children.

But I finally took the gamble. I invented a version of *Jeopardy* to help my students learn the names of parts of the brain. They really got into it. The competition was fierce, and they were obviously excited and having fun. It seemed to me that they were really learning.

However, I was disappointed later in the week when I asked my students to demonstrate what they had learned. There were two disappointments. First, the parts of their knowledge that were improved seemed very spotty. Different students remembered different isolated things. Second, overall, what they remembered didn't seem that much greater to me. I don't have a controlled experiment to demonstrate this, but it seemed that way.

This was frustrating, and I tried to find out what was happening. First, I inquired about why certain students remembered certain things. One student clarified this for me, when she said, "Well, I remember the things that reinforced what I already believed. It was exciting to discover that I was right about them!"

But the most revealing answer came when I asked why they hadn't learned more. "Dr. Zull," one student exclaimed, "it was just a game, you know!"

*   *   *

You may see other reasons why my experiment seemed to fail, but I saw two primary ones. First, the game was not designed to build on prior knowledge. It was not properly designed for change. And second, the learning didn't really matter in their lives.

We can realize this lack of importance from what the students actually did remember. They remembered, and may never forget, that they played a game in class. And since it was competitive, they remembered who the competition was and how it came out. They remembered what was important to them. But it was not the academic content; it was the game.

Getting Past the Extrinsic: Stories and Ownership

How can we get past this barrier of extrinsic motivation in learning? What is intrinsic?

As I discussed in chapter 4, what is most intrinsic to the brain is living itself. What happens to us, what we did, what we hope to do, what we feared, what we ate, who we met, who we hate, who we love, what we created, what lies we told and were told, our victories, our losses, and all the other things that make up life are the things that we remember and learn. They become the *story* of us. There is a story for everything in our lives.

Roger Schank has explained the importance of stories in learning and in our concepts of intelligence.[4] We judge people by their stories, and we decide they are intelligent when their stories fit with our own stories. Recalling and creating stories are key parts of learning. We remember by connecting things with our stories, we create by connecting our stories together in unique and memorable ways, and we act out our stories in our behaviors

Stories engage all parts of the brain. They come from our experiences, our memories, our ideas, our actions, and our feelings. They allow us to package events and knowledge in complex neuronal nets, any part of which can trigger all the others. And stories are about movement. They are about verbs, the action! They focus on good and bad actions, so they generate fear and pleasure, and all the derivative emotions.

If you believe my claim that learning is deepest when it engages the most parts of the brain, you can see the value of stories for the teacher. We should tell stories, create stories, and repeat stories, and we should ask our students to do the same.

I think of this quite literally. Let me use algebra as an example.

We could tell our students the story of algebra. We could tell them who the characters are and what they do. We could say that the character X is worth half as much as the character Y. We could follow the experience of X and Y as we move them around on a piece of paper and keep track of the movement and progress in the story as we eventually isolate X all by herself (solving for x). And all the time, our story has a moral. Algebra is about fairness. Things must always be equal; if they are not, the story falls apart.

I think this is an example of what cognitive scientists mean when they suggest that teachers should ask their students to "process" things. A learner must use her knowledge to achieve some goal. The story must have a beginning, a middle, and an end. Students become lazy or bored when they can't see a story. When nothing connects in any big overall way to anything else, they lose interest.

Learning is about life. Stories bring things to life and life into things.

How the Brain Remembers Stories

Brain imaging studies show that when we recall stories, the *episodic* kind of remembering, we use our right frontal cortex.[5] This is interesting because it is unique. We use the left front cortex for most other things related to stories—for encoding stories and for recalling the facts of stories. There seems to be something different about recall of stories that requires the right brain.

In earlier chapters I mentioned that the left brain deals with fine detail and structure, while the right brain works with the "big picture." Another interesting difference between the two hemispheres is that the left brain is more creative than the right. In fact it is so creative that it makes things up. It fills in gaps and extrapolates. It needs those details. However, the right brain is more faithful and realistic. It seems to stick to the facts.[6] Let me put these two features about the right brain together into a hypothesis about recall of stories and episodes.

In order to be effective, to be important, there must be a moral to a story. It must have a point. For example, if we just follow Captain Ahab around on the sea as he chases Moby Dick, we get bored. But when we learn the reason for the chase and when we see it coming to a climax, it becomes powerful. It becomes important.

Knowing the big picture of a story is what gives it meaning. Knowing isolated details is essential but meaningless by itself. Our faithful right brain gives us truth but only its skeleton. The left brain then gives us semantic details to fill in the specifics.

This view of the story was new to me. I had just never thought of it. But if it is right, it suggests that teachers should focus on the lynchpins of stories. This is what our learners need for recall. Going back to our algebra story, we might first pay attention to the big idea of equality, to the fact that the characters are of different value, and to the overall goal of isolating one of the characters. Then we know the point.

Being Real

We have been talking about presenting our subject as stories. This is a way to help the learner become emotionally engaged. But there is more to effective teaching than how we present the *subject*. Specifically, there is how we present *ourselves*. And there may be no more important part of teaching than the emotional reaction of a student to a teacher.

A catchy, but now rather tired, phrase that describes one way to present ourselves is "be a guide on the side, not a sage on the stage." The merit of this idea is that it puts the learner at the center of things rather than the teacher. However, as you may have noticed, I have also pointed out places where leadership by the teacher is essential. The student gains security and confidence when the teacher knows, and shows, the path. Being on the side and being on the stage are both important. An effective teacher knows when to lead, and when to step aside.

Teachers differ greatly in their instincts and preferences for guiding or leading. One or the other may seem unnatural to any particular teacher, and if we try to be something we aren't, we become uncomfortable. And that makes the student uncomfortable.

From this perspective, the greatest danger for the teacher is not whether he leads or guides, but whether he is real. Your students cannot be comfortable if you are pretending. Nothing is more powerful than authenticity, and nothing turns the young mind away faster than pretense. As I said in chapter 1, the human animal craves reality. Only real performers can succeed by performing. If it is not our nature to act, we should not even try.

I came to this belief from my experience in my own classes and from watching others teach. But it was only when I thought of the biology that I understood why. This craving for reality and our distrust of pretense comes from our struggle to survive. We need to know if the rustle in the bushes really signals a hungry tiger or whether someone is just fooling us. When it is life or death, we don't like to be fooled.

It isn't life or death, not quite anyway, but remnants of this struggle persist in classrooms. Student tolerance, even acceptance, of teacher behaviors is remarkable as long as they believe they are not seeing an act. But they detest pretense.

I read an extreme example of this in an interview with teacher/scholar George Steiner. Referring to his days of teaching during the Vietnam war, the crusty Steiner said "Students were in an uproar, but I never gave in. I just said to them bluntly, 'Look. I am here to teach you. Now I know an embarrassing lot, and you know next to nothing. So, shut up and learn!' And they did. My experience with them was wonderful."[7]

As shocking as it is, and as contrary to my own approaches, I can't help but be impressed by this. If nothing else, Steiner was authentic. And his students were drawn to the reality of their experience with him.

Beginnings

Biology teaches us that learning is about our real life. People learn when they believe it is about their life—*their* life!

This means we should think about the student *first*. Even before we prepare for our subject, we should prepare for our students. We should ask ourselves questions like, "What are these students like? Why are they in my class? What might worry them?"

If our first encounters are based on questions like these, we are far more likely to convince our students that their learning is the main thing. Then, it is possible that *what* we want them to learn will become part of their life.

Rather than spending time on the rules of the class, the schedule of exams, or even the syllabus,[8] we should start right away with learning. We should begin by showing our students the things we want them to learn. If we stress rules first, the message can be, "This teacher wants order and control." But if we stress learning first, the message is "this teacher wants learning."

And we should do this as soon as we meet our learners. This is the teacher's time of greatest opportunity, when we are part of their life simply because we are the new teacher. We have them in those few minutes. The trick is to keep them.

Polarities in Learning

One approach to stressing the importance of learning and at the same time convincing students that we are interested in them and their unique brains, is to begin by asking individual students, "How do *you* learn? What works for *you*?" And when we ask, we should be prepared for differences, sometimes big differences!

The learning cycle gives us an interesting way to think about differences between learners. As shown in the illustration that follows, the cycle is based on two polarities: concrete-abstract and reflective-active. Most people will lean toward one side or the other of these polarities. Some enjoy the abstract more than the concrete, and vice versa. Some are more active and others more reflective. If we put this in brain terms, we would say that some people prefer using their sensory brain, some prefer using their integrative back cortex, some prefer using their integrative front cortex, and some prefer using their motor brain. A particular student may like new experience, but find that the quiet of reflection makes him nervous. Another student may be happy reflecting and generating ideas but shy away from actually testing them. Different parts of the cycle seem comfortable to different people. These preferences come from our feelings.

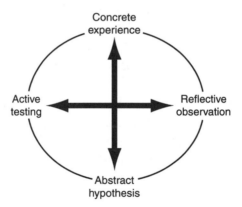

It can help a teacher to find out what his different learners are like, not so he can label or prejudge performance, but so he can see how each student will *start* his learning. If we can find out generally what students prefer, it may help us devise assignments or class exercises that engage the emotional structures in the brain right at the beginning.

Once students are engaged, however, everything we have discussed suggests that we should begin to lead students away from their comfortable style and encourage them to stretch themselves by using parts of the brain.

Intelligences and Styles

The question "How do you learn?" brings up subjects like learning styles and multiple intelligences. If we use these terms as labels, or if we have predetermined recipes for dealing with each "style," there will be trouble. But if we treat them as natural abilities and inclinations, as gifts, they can be put to good use.

A person who has the gift of reflection can make different contributions than one who has the gift of creativity. And the learner with the gift of mathematical intelligence, makes a different contribution from one who has the gift of musical intelligence. The learner with the gift of visual perception offers something different from one with the gift of auditory perception. All learning styles or intelligences are real—and valuable!

Gardner has used the term *multiple intelligences* to describe this diversity in gifts. Others have used the term *learning styles*. Regardless of the terminology, we should expect that these gifts fit into the brain cycle of learning. I have shown this in the following illustration, where each of Gardner's seven intelligences (musical, intrapersonal, spatial, logic/mathematical, linguistic, interpersonal, and kinesthetic), Kolb's four learning dimensions (concrete, reflective, abstract, and active), and Fleming's four learning styles (auditory, visual, read/write, and kinesthetic), are placed at a locus on the brain cycle.[9]

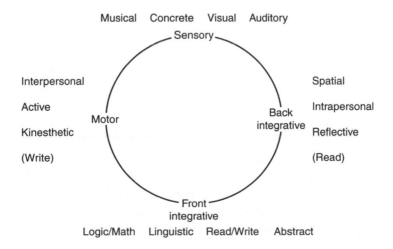

The unification of these various facets of diversity by mapping them onto the brain cycle suggests specific ideas for teaching different types of learners. For example, we might encourage a visual learner to use other parts of the cycle. We might ask him to examine the spatial relationships in images he experienced, organize those relationships into logical patterns, and create his own visualizations of the patterns he has created. This would take him through the brain cycle and deepen his learning. And because it begins with his natural inclinations, the chance that it will engage his emotional brain is increased.

Intelligences, Learning Styles, and Emotion

Different learners enjoy using different parts of their brain. Their gifts come naturally from their brain, and they use the parts they enjoy. But what produces this enjoyment?

I don't say that I have the final answer to this question, but I do have a hypothesis based on our discussion of positive emotion in chapter 5. That chapter placed movement at the center of pleasure. I argued that, to the brain, movement is more than physical movement of parts of the body; it is also *mental* movement, or *imagined* progress.

Perhaps this is easier to understand now. Recall the brain's ability to imagine actions, orchestrated by the executive centers in the front cortex. Those imagined actions give us pleasure when, for example, we read a story. Our body isn't moving, but the story is. And, according to this theory, this is why the brain enjoys a story. It goes somewhere!

Pleasure in learning, then, comes from the perception of progress toward a goal. We find ourselves making the most progress when we use the parts of our brain that have the wiring for our gifts. Success creates enjoyment. As the saying goes, "nothing succeeds like success." We enjoy our progress, and so we seek out those things that produce success.

Learning Is Dynamic

We have been talking about differences between learners, and the discussion would not be complete without mention of Kurt Fischer's concept of "webs" of understanding. The learner is not climbing a ladder of knowledge but rather is progressing along an increasingly complex web of connections that depends on his individual experiences. What could be more biological?

Another concept that Fischer explains may be even more important. That concept is the dynamic nature of learning. Learning does not proceed in a linear way but by stops and starts, reversals and breakthroughs. This is true at any age. Experienced learners have their ups and downs, just like children.[10]

This dynamic image of learning is also obviously consistent with the picture of the brain we have been painting. We can have success, or be blocked, at any part of the cycle. Every time we succeed, positive emotions increase; when we fail, negative emotions get the upper hand. All phases of the learning cycle have the potential for progress or regress; for trial and error, and thus for emotional positives and emotional negatives. The sum of all these fits and starts over time determines learning, but at any moment our progress may be forward, backward, or static. And our feelings may be positive, negative, or in between. Things change moment by moment. Learning is dynamic!

Dynamic Learning and the Teacher

This erratic progress in learning suggests a clear role for the teacher. It takes us back to a proposal I made earlier in this chapter about the art of knowing when to stay on the side and when to take the lead. When learning seems stalled, a teacher can intervene. A learner is likely to be receptive at this stage. But as he begins to progress again, it is time for the teacher to disappear, leaving the learner to face his unique challenges. He is up to it now. He wants to say he did it himself.

This combination of challenge and support seems optimal for learning. The learner may reach high levels of skill with support but will regress when support is withdrawn. Still, ultimately this process of progress and regress produces higher levels of learning than the student can attain on his own. The teacher can make a difference!

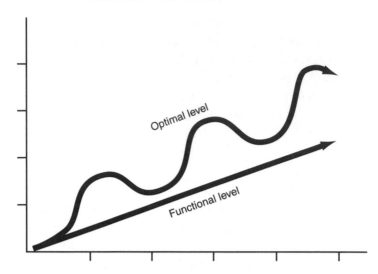

The preceding graph illustrates these ups and downs of learning and the role of the teacher.[11] The ups begin when the teacher gives support, and the downs take over after support is withdrawn. But the overall progress of the learner is upward and, with teacher support (optimal level), is greater than with no support (the "functional" level).

Emotion and Optimal Learning

I have attempted to put some of these ideas together into a model that links the ups and downs in learning with ups and downs in emotion and motivation, while also illustrating the role of the teacher. This model for optimal learning is depicted in the following illustration.

As you can see, the internal circle shows the emotional state of the student, and the outer parallel loop shows the role of the teacher. Their *parallel* paths are an important part of the model. Teacher and student are independent agents. As we have discussed in earlier chapters, there is no direct transfer of information; each has her own neuronal networks to build on.

Let's begin at the left with inertia. The emotional status of the inert learner is probably either frustration or disinterest. Whichever it is, the teacher's first task is to get some emotional movement. To do that, she defines a goal for the student. This goal must do two things: get the student's interest and appear realistic. It must represent a challenge but not

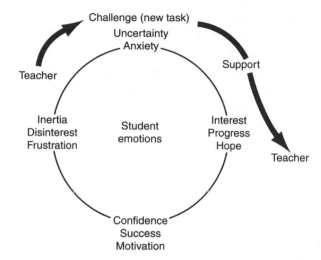

too great a challenge. If it is not a challenge, the learner will have no interest. But if it is impossible, his frustration will just continue.

The student's first reaction to a new challenge could still be somewhat negative. You may have his attention, but you are asking something new. His amygdala may be wary of this new territory, so he may begin to feel anxious or uncertain. But at least he isn't disinterested, and since he hasn't tried the new challenge yet, he can't be frustrated with it either.

Still, the teacher has work to do. She must find a way for her student to begin moving into more positive emotional territory. This is where support comes in. As we have discussed in earlier chapters, at first the teacher can show examples, make suggestions about what to do, and remind the learner of what he already knows. This will be what he can hang his new knowledge on, the "scaffolding" mentioned in chapter 6.

The support given by an effective teacher must allow the student to have some success, no matter how small. He needs to sense movement, as we discussed in chapter 4. If that happens, the student's emotions begin to turn more positive. He feels some hope, and his interest increases. He begins to gain confidence and to develop pride in his progress. He begins to think, "I can do this myself!"

That is the time for the teacher to turn over control. She must allow the learner to take ownership, to create new ideas, and to test his ideas.

This is what the student wants now. He is intrinsically motivated! His progress makes him feel confident and interested. He truly feels joyful, and he wants to keep the joy!

But, cycling is inevitable. Ups must be followed by downs. As our student works away on his ideas and tests them, one of two things will happen. He will either begin to lose interest, because things are no longer new or challenging, or he will become frustrated, because his ideas aren't working out. His active testing indicates that something is wrong, and he cannot fix it. Now it is time for the teacher to step back in.

Motivation Redux

Teachers often complain that their students aren't motivated, as though it were some sort of character flaw. They would learn if they would just get motivated!

But the model we have been discussing suggests something different. It suggests that *motivation comes from learning*. People cannot stay motivated enough to learn unless they experience some success. They may be motivated to try something, but if they are going to keep their motivation, they must sense some progress. And it is the teacher's job to find a way that success can happen. We shouldn't ask "How can I motivate my students?" but rather "How can I support their learning?" They will be motivated if they are learning.

The motivation I am talking about is intrinsic motivation unrelated to any external reward or punishment. It is the most powerful ally of the teacher.

Emotional Support for the Learner

This cycle is easy to discuss, but difficult to achieve. Balancing challenge, support, and disengagement is truly an art!

The way we give support to the learner can be guided by ideas that I have developed about the learning cycle in preceding chapters. I will not repeat them here. But there is another source of support that should be mentioned: *peer support*.

I have said little about the use of groups and other active learning concepts, but the support part of the cycle is where I believe interactions with peers can have a powerful impact. When a learner shares images with his peers, he will not only get new cognitive ideas. He will also gain confidence and begin to recognize the progress he has already made. Without interactions with his peers, the learner may well not realize where he really stands.

And, as we discussed in chapter 6, it is the learner's peers who are most likely to have neuronal networks similar to his. His chances of building on his networks will be improved in a way that will complement the teacher's support if he works with peers.

Judging when to step back is another complex part of this art. When we see that the learner is making progress and is connecting his learning with his real life, we should withdraw. This can be a powerful, private process for the learner, and if learning is to be personal, this is when it will become so. This is the time for the learner to use his front cortex, creating his own ideas and testing them. He may ask for feedback on his ideas, bringing the teacher or peers back in, but that should be up to him. We should wait for him to ask. It is his learning and his choice.

The final part of this art is sensing when the student needs new challenges. The teacher recognizes when the tension and dynamic of learning has cooled, and she knows that it can only be refueled by new challenges.

It may sound confusing to say that a stalled learner needs new challenge. Won't that discourage him even more? But the idea is that the challenge must be changed, not that is must be harder. The artful teacher sees what the hang-up is and reorganizes the challenges or breaks them up into different pieces that the student can address.

Self-Evaluation and Taking Control

In order for a learner to claim ownership, to say "I did this myself," he must examine his own performance and approve it. He must look over his work and say, "This is good." So our final trip into the brain is to visit a region which has been associated with performance evaluation. It seems to be where we oversee what we do and decide if it is satisfactory. It is the brain watching over itself.

An experiment which helps to identify this area of the brain is described in a study carried out by MacDonald and his colleagues.[12] They did brain imaging studies of people who were taking what is called the *Stroop test*. You can take the test yourself, by writing down the word "green" in red ink and then saying the color of the word out loud. As you will see, your instinct is to say the word itself rather than the color, to say "green" rather than "red." If you have a series of such cards in different colors, you will find that it takes great concentration to do this correctly for every card. However, it is much easier to simply read off the words, ignoring their color.

There are two challenges in the Stroop test. One is to say the right word, "green" or "red," and the other is to evaluate your performance, to decide if your response is right and whether you overcame your instinct to say the word.

The results of the PET scanning experiments were fascinating. Speaking the color, of course, engaged the motor and premotor cortex, but evaluating performance strongly engaged the anterior cingulate region of the limbic cortex. You may recall from chapters 4 and 5 that this part of the brain has often been implicated in emotional decision making, but this result seems more specific than general emotion. Judging ourselves is highly personal, and the emotions it produces play a major role in whether or not we take ownership. Once evaluated, we may accept our performance, or we may reject it. Which direction we go makes all the difference.

Self-Evaluation and Ownership

When I read about these experiments with the Stroop test, once again I found myself thinking new thoughts about my teaching. How was I using the anterior cingulate in my teaching? Where did self-evaluation fit?

While I was reflecting on this, I had the following experience in my class.

*   *   *

I had just started teaching my new course, *Human Learning and the Brain*. An important assignment was for my students to write a paper on "motivation in learning."

It was a tough assignment, and I made it even tougher by insisting that they tell me what happens in the brain when people get motivated. To make it interesting, I asked them to write about their own brains. What happens when *they* get motivated?

But I read their papers with growing discomfort. There was a familiar feeling to them, that old feeling of "been there, done that!" These were not inspired. The fact that it was about their own motivation didn't seem to help.

I thought about this for a while, and eventually something occurred to me. Maybe my students still didn't feel that this was their work. Even though the assignment was about their life, I was still controlling the process. I gave the assignment and set the conditions. And now I was going to assess the work—it was still all about me!

So I tried to think of ways that they could reclaim their work. Because I knew about the anterior cingulate and evaluation, I got my new idea. Here was a part of the brain I could ask them to use! I would ask my students to evaluate themselves, to critique their own papers.

Actually, I didn't expect this would lead to much. It was just another thing to try, at the time. But I was surprised when I began to read these critiques. There was a freedom and an assertiveness that I hadn't seen before.

For example, one critique, entitled "My Bad Paper," began: "I thought my paper was good until I began to evaluate it myself. Suddenly I realized it was not very good. But this paper is good. My critique of my bad paper is a good paper!"

And he was right. His critique was insightful, decisive, accurate, and engaged. Every aspect of it said, "This is mine!"

*   *   *

In chapters 10 and 11 I argued that learners must create their own ideas and act on them if they are to take ownership. But now we can see another step in taking ownership. The learner must evaluate his work in order to own it. If it is truly his, it must be formed in a cycle of creating, evaluating, re-creating, and reevaluating.

Stopping Learning by Evaluating Learning

The experience I just described gave me new insights into something that had long puzzled me. I began to realize why my students made so little use of my evaluations when they rewrote their papers. Sometimes I wrote extensive comments and made strong suggestions, followed by exclamation points. But even then, it felt as though my feedback was almost ignored. When these papers were resubmitted, often they still contained the same flaws, or so it seemed. And if I insisted that my students address my concerns, they did, but in half-hearted and unsatisfying ways.

Now I thought I understood this puzzle. They were fighting to keep control. I could not create enthusiasm for my suggestions, exactly because they were *my* suggestions. Their emotional connections are with their own ideas and their own judgments. When I made suggestions, they only knew that they had lost control.

This made me rethink my whole philosophy of assessment and evaluation. In the end we may be forced to be an evaluator. We may have to decide the merits of the work and assign a grade or give a promotion. But, when it comes to learning, self-evaluation is more useful than the teacher's evaluation. The teacher should just stick to her role of challenge and support. When she is dissatisfied with her student, instead of placing value on the work, she should provide more examples and more support. Evaluation can support learning only when the student requests it.

In the final analysis, we still find that we defeat learning when we take it away from the learners, when we make it about us rather than about them. Then learning becomes extrinsic. They cannot say, "I did this myself," and they are lost to us.

Finding the Art

Bringing students to the point where they can say "I did this myself" truly seems to be an art. It cannot be done by formula or coercion. No one can control learning for another person. We cannot give our students our ideas, we cannnot make them learn, and we cannot motivate them. Ultimately, we are left having to give up control, trusting that the student will learn.

But biology also tells us that this trust is justified. The human brain is a learning organ; learning is what it does. The main task for the teacher is to help the learner find connections. Once a student encounters things that connect with her life, her emotions, her experiences, or her understandings, she will learn. She won't be able to help herself. Her brain will change.

When asked "what is art," Count Basie is reported to have replied, "Art is what you have when you remove everything that is not essential." Applying this to what has gone before in this book, it seems that we are left with the following: *the learner is in control, but that is fine. He will learn!*

These are the essentials, the bedrock on which the art of changing the brain must rest.

Notes

1. N. M. Weinberger, *Concepts in Neuroscience* 1 (1990), p. 91, 1990; J. S. Bakin and N. M. Weinberger, *Proceedings of the National Academy of Sciences* 93 (1993), p. 11219. The experiment described here was done by M. P. Kilgard and M. M. Merzenich, *Science* 278 (1998), p. 1714, and reviewed by S. Juliano in the same issue.

2. This was done by surgically implanting a small electrode in the *nucleus basalis* and activating that electrode with radio signals.

3. These more complex pathways commonly include the generation of molecules called *second messengers,* which are responsible for activating a cascade of further reactions both at the cell membrane of the neuron and at the DNA level in the cell nucleus. The best understood of these second messengers is probably cyclic AMP. In addition, calcium is an important regulator of synapse strength, acting through an enzyme (calmodulin dependent kinase), which catalyzes chemical changes in synapse proteins.

4. R. C. Schank, *Tell Me A Story: Narrative and Intelligence* (Evanston, IL: Northwestern University Press, 1990).

5. L. Nyberg and colleagues, *Psychonomic Bulletin and Review* 3 (1996), p. 135.

6. This kind of information comes from the study of "split brain" patients who have been treated for severe epilepsy by severing the connection between the hemispheres. Roger Sperry began this kind of research about fifty years ago, and the work of one of his intellectual descendents, M. Gazzaniga, has greatly advanced our understanding: *Nature's Mind,* (New York: Basic Books, 1992); *The Social Brain* (New York: Basic Books, 1985); *The Bisected Brain* (New York: Appleton, 1970); and *The New Cognitive Neurosciences,* which Gazzaniga edited (Cambridge, MA: MIT Press, 2000).

7. Interview with P. Applebome, *New York Times,* April 13, 1999.

8. Putting a course syllabus on the Web turns out to be a great time saver and makes it easy for the teacher to go directly to content and learning on the first day of class.

9. H. Gardener, *Multiple Intelligences: The Theory in Practice. A Reader.* (New York: Basic Books, 1995); N. Fleming, *Teaching and Learning Styles: VARK Strategies* (Christ Church, New Zealand: N. Fleming, Lincoln University, 2001); D. Kolb, *Experiential Learning: Experience as the*

Source of Learning and Development (Englewood Cliffs, NJ: Prentice Hall, 1984). For more information, see the website: www.vark-learn.com.
10. K. Fischer and T. Rose, Webs of Skill: How Students Learn, *Educational Leadership* 59 (2001), p. 6.
11. Used with permission from ref. 10.
12. A. W. McDonald III and colleagues, *Science* 288 (2000), p. 1385.

SUMMARY
OF PART III

In this section we examined some specific functions of the five major regions of cerebral cortex: sensory cortex, integrative back cortex, integrative front cortex, motor cortex, and limbic cortex. As we proceeded we kept up our habit of asking "what might this mean for teaching?" Now we can look back at the key words that remind us of what we found.

Here are some of the central items: *sense luscious, vision, details, attending, mapping, images, showing, hearing, other senses, unity, what and where, big picture, taking time, search for connections, dreaming, prosody, language comprehension, creating, abstractions, courage, working memory, executive, natural thinking, probabilities, mirror neurons, creating language, test by trial, action, inert ideas, inside and outside, initiation of learning, feedback, verbs, emotion dominates, importance, slow neurotransmitters, play, stories, authenticity, multiple gifts, polarities, dynamic, movement/progress, ups and downs, challenge, support, self-evaluation,* and *ownership.*

This is how we end. Our exploration of the biology of learning has reminded us of many things we already knew but has also given us a deeper respect for the learner and the learning process. Repeatedly we have been reminded that it is our physical body and its interactions with the physical world that produce learning, and that reality leaves us with faith that we will eventually understand this mysterious vocation, and avocation, of teaching.

EPILOGUE
ENRICHMENTS

In the Introduction, I said that our growing understanding of the brain would not necessarily produce a revolution in education—at least not yet. But I also claimed that exploration of the biology of learning would enrich us.

Looking back on the book, I found myself wishing that I had stressed this enrichment aspect more. That is the goal of this brief epilogue.

Enrichment implies adding to our resources or increasing their value. It may or may not lead directly or immediately to improvement or change in our methods. Change, when it comes, may well be subtle rather than revolutionary.

I say this because it seems to me that the most powerful impact of exploring the biology of learning is not on what we do, but on how we feel about what we do. It is a change in attitude. That change in attitude comes because we feel enriched. Our understandings have greater value. In what follows, I have tried to put these enrichments in more concrete form.

First and perhaps most important, biology deepens our understanding of what learning actually is about. It gives us *more light.* As a
teacher who read a draft of this book exclaimed, "It is so enlighten-
ing!" This new light helps us see more clearly why we learn. Biology
shows the essential entanglement of learning with life. This clarifies the
meaning of intrinsic motivation and shows the fundamental inade-
quacy of extrinsic rewards. Learning is seen as a natural outcome of
experience, and this gives us confidence that our students will always
learn. Whatever fits with their life and emotions will be learned.

Second, the biology of learning enriches teaching by making educational theory *more real.* It is one thing to have a theory that learners
construct their own understandings by building on what they already
know and quite another to actually see how this construction happens—
to understand the physical process by which networks of neurons grow
more complex through sensory experience. The latter is a real physical
process that explains the former.

The human mind wants these explanations, wants to know how
things work (and we learned something of why that is true in chapter 4).
We need reasons. So it is better to see the mechanisms and details for ourselves than to be told a theory. Brain science is slowly giving us those reasons. It is giving us the chance to move beyond dependence on authority
and authorities. Understanding the concepts of neuronal networks and
synapse change gives credence to constructivist theories of learning and
of educating. It helps to know why, and we are richer for it!

Third, the biology of learning gives us *better boundaries.* It helps us
recognize the *separateness* of teacher and learner. The diversity of individual brains is infinite. If knowledge is neuronal networks, as I argued
in chapter 6, it cannot be transferred from one brain to another. The
entire issue of how learners take ownership depends on recognizing this
separateness.

It is enriching to see the physical reality of this. We are less inclined
to spend so much time trying to transfer our ideas to our students and
more inclined to find out how they can build their own experiences. We
put more energy into understanding the learner and have deeper respect
for her as an independent creature. That enriches our practice, because
it encourages the learner to trust us when we provide challenges and
support.

Fourth, examining the biology of learning enriches us because it gives us *more ideas*. For example, when we realize that a great deal of the brain is dedicated to physical relationships in space, we may find ourselves searching for spatial analogies for relationships in our subject. No matter what subject we want our students to learn, we can create physical metaphors and analogies that mirror those spatial relationships, and it is worth the effort. Or, in another example, recognizing the ability of the brain to create and remember images may give us ideas about using images to teach our subject.

Finally, exploring the biology of learning can *clarify our values*. This subject deserves another book because it is a profound enrichment. One example, which I mentioned above, is our respect for the individual and our acceptance of diversity. I know of no more profound lesson from biology. Everything that we are learning and have learned about the brain says that we must respect the uniqueness of the individual learner. We may find ourselves generalizing, stereotyping, and judging; it is our nature. But all we have to do is remember the physical difference in the neuronal networks of each brain to remind ourselves that behaviors have physical reasons, and our job is to work with what each learner brings. Neuroscience takes us to this good place!

Ultimately, these enrichments can all be precursors to change in method. Greater resources produce greater confidence and more creativity. A teacher enriched in these ways will be more optimistic and energized. She may begin to try new approaches and create change in her professional practice. She may even begin to see herself as an artist, skilled in the art of changing the brain.

ABOUT THE AUTHOR

JAMES E. ZULL is professor of biochemistry and biology at Case Western Reserve University in Cleveland, Ohio, where he also directs the University Center for Innovation in Teaching and Education (UCITE). Dr. Zull obtained his bachelor's degree at Houghton College in New York State and his doctorate at the University of Wisconsin in Madison. He then conducted biochemical research for over 25 years and published more than 60 papers in peer-reviewed journals. In this time period he received numerous grants and lectured around the world on his research. In 1994 he became the founding director of UCITE, which is now one of the most active centers for teaching and learning in the country. Zull has studied human learning with David Kolb for nearly a decade, and in the last few years has given workshops and lectures on the value of neuroscience for teachers at colleges and universities. Throughout his 36-year career he continued to teach and has been nominated for numerous teaching awards. In 2001 he received a "professor of the year" award from the Greek Life organizations at Case Western Reserve. Zull has five children and two grandchildren. He lives with his wife, Susan, in Cleveland Heights, and spends his spare time working on his small farm in northeastern Ohio.

*　　*　　*

The Art of Changing the Brain brings together this lifetime of experience in biology and education—the first book by a practicing scientist on teaching and the brain.